Ready®
New York CCLS

Language Arts
INSTRUCTION

Acknowledgments

Stephen James O'Meara, "Against All Odds: Earth's Fragile Pioneers" adapted from *Odyssey* issue: Alien Invaders, April 2000. Copyright © 2000 by Carus Publishing Company. Published by Cobblestone Publishing, 30 Grove Street, Suite C, Peterborough, NH 03458. Reprinted with permission. All rights reserved.

National Geographic, "Food Web" from http://education. nationalgeographic.com. Copyright © by National Geographic Stock. Permission pending.

Anthony Mason, "Secrets of the Lost City of Z" adapted from http:// www.cbsnews.com. Copyright © CBS News. Reprinted with permission.

Anna Sewell, excerpt from *Black Beauty* (1911). Public domain.

Sherwood Anderson, excerpt from "Departure" from *Winesburg, Ohio* (1919). Public domain.

Kate DiCamillo, excerpt from *The Magician's Elephant*. Text copyright © 2009 by Kate DiCamillo. Reprinted with permission of the publisher, Candlewick Press, Somerville, MA.

Elena Mannes, adapted from 'The Power Of Music' To Affect The Brain, from NPR, http://www.npr.org/2011/06/01/136859090/the-power-of-music-to-affect-the-brain. Excerpts from *The Power of Music: Pioneering Discoveries in the New Science of Song*. Copyright © 2011 by Elena Mannes. Reprinted with permission of Bloomsbury Publishing Plc

John Roach, "Terra-Cotta Army Protects First Emperor's Tomb" adapted from *National Geographic*. Copyright © Ng News/National Geographic Stock. Reprinted with permission.

"A Thunder–Storm" by Emily Dickinson, from *Poems by Emily Dickinson, Series Two* (1891). Public domain.

Jack London, excerpt from "To Build a Fire" from *Lost Face* (1916). Public domain.

"Those Two Boys" by Franklin P. Adams from *Modern American Poetry* (1919). Public domain.

Philip K. Dick, excerpt from "The Eyes Have It" from *Science Fiction Stories* magazine (1953). Public domain.

Lewis Carroll, excerpt from *Through the Looking-Glass and What Alice Found There* (1899).

"Motto" from *The Collected Poems of Langston Hughes* Edited by Arnold Rampersad, with David Roessel, Associate Editor. Copyright © 1994 by the Estate of Langston Hughes. Used by permission of Alfred A. Knopf, a division of Random House, Inc. and Harold Ober Associates, Inc.

"The Heart of a Woman" by Georgia Douglas Johnson, from *The Book of American Negro Poetry*, James Weldon Johnson, ed. (1922). Public domain.

J. R. R. Tolkien, "I Sit By the Fire and Think" from *The Fellowship of the Lord of the Rings*. Copyright © 1954, 1965 by J. R. R. Tolkien. Copyright © renewed 1982 by Christopher R. Tolkien, Michael H. R. Tolkien, John F. R. Tolkien, and Priscilla M. A. R. Tolkien. Copyright © renewed 1993 by Christopher R. Tolkien, John F. R. Tolkien, and Priscilla M. A. R. Tolkien. Reprinted with permission of Houghton Mifflin Harcourt Publishing Company. All rights reserved.

"Brennan on the Moor," from *The Universal Irish Song Book: A Complete Collection of the Songs and Ballads of Ireland.* New York: P. J. Kenedy, Publisher (1904). Public domain.

Gary Paulsen, excerpt from *Hatchet*. Copyright © 1987 by Gary Paulsen. Reprinted with permission of Atheneum Books for Young Readers, an imprint of Simon & Schuster Children's Publishing Division. Excerpt adapted from *Tracker*. Copyright © 1984 by Gary Paulsen. Reprinted with permission of Atheneum Books for Young Readers, an imprint of Simon & Schuster Children's Publishing Division.

Yoshiko Uchida, excerpt adapted from *A Jar of Dreams*. Copyright © 1981 by Yoshiko Uchida. Reprinted with permission of Margaret K. McElderry Books, an imprint of Simon & Schuster Children's Publishing Division.

"The Migration of the Grey Squirrels" by Mary Howitt, from *Sketches of Natural History* (1834). Public domain.

Bethany Bray, "Longer School Day: Expanded Learning Time Pros and Cons" from *Andover Townsman*, Andover, MA, June 12, 2008. Copyright © 2008 by Bethany Bray. Reprinted with permission of The Eagle Tribune.

Helen Keller, excerpt from *The Story of My Life* (1902). Public domain.

Ji-Li Jiang, excerpt from *The Red Scarf Girl*, HarperCollins, 1998. Permission pending.

"To Fight Aloud Is Very Brave" by Emily Dickinson, from *Poems by Emily Dickinson, Series One* (1886). Public domain.

Julia Alvarez, excerpt adapted from *Before We Were Free*. Copyright © 2002 by Julia Alavrez. Published by Dell Laurel-Leaf in paperback in 2003 and originally in hardcover by Alfred A. Knopf Children's Books, a division of Random House, New York. By permission of Susan Bergholz Literary Services, New York, NY and Lamy, NM. All rights reserved.

Common Core State Standards copyright © 2010 National Governors Association Center for Best Practices and Council of Chief State School Officers. All rights reserved.

All third-party content has been permissioned or is in the process of being permissioned.

Project Manager: John Ham
Cover Designer and Illustrator: Julia Bourque
Book Design: Mark Nodland

ISBN 978-0-7609-8393-5
©2014—Curriculum Associates, LLC
North Billerica, MA 01862

Table of Contents

Unit 1: Key Ideas and Details in Informational Text 1   **CCLS**

Lesson 1: Determining Central Idea and Details 3   RI.6.2

Lesson 2: Summarizing Informational Texts 11   RI.6.2

Lesson 3: Citing Evidence to Make Inferences 19   RI.6.1

Lesson 4: Analyzing Key Ideas in a Text 27   RI.6.3

Unit 1 Interim Assessment **35**

Unit 2: Key Ideas and Details in Literature 43

Lesson 5: Citing Evidence to Make Inferences 45   RL.6.1

Lesson 6: Describing Plot 53   RL.6.3

Lesson 7: Analyzing Character Development. 61   RL.6.3

Lesson 8: Determining Theme or Central Idea 69   RL.6.2

Lesson 9: Summarizing Literary Texts 77   RL.6.2

Unit 2 Interim Assessment **85**

Unit 3: Craft and Structure in Informational Text 93

Lesson 10: Determining Word Meanings:
Figurative, Connotative & Technical 95   RI.6.4

Lesson 11: Analyzing Text Structures 103   RI.6.5

Lesson 12: Determining Point of View 111   RI.6.6

Unit 3 Interim Assessment **119**

Unit 4: Craft and Structure in Literature 127

Lesson 13: Determining Word Meanings:
Figurative and Connotative 129   RL.6.4

Lesson 14: Analyzing Word Choice 137   RL.6.4

Lesson 15: Analyzing the Structure of a Poem 145   RL.6.5

Lesson 16: Analyzing the Structure of Stories 153   RL.6.5

Lesson 17: Explaining Point of View 161   RL.6.6, 6.a

Unit 4 Interim Assessment **169**

Table of Contents

		CCLS
Unit 5: Integration of Knowledge and Ideas in Informational Text 177		
Lesson 18: Evaluating an Argument 179		RI.6.8
Lesson 19: Comparing and Contrasting Texts 187		RI.6.9
Lesson 19W: Writing an Extended-Response Essay 197		RI.6.9, W.6.2, W.6.9
Unit 5 Interim Assessment **207**		
Media Feature 1: Integrating Information 215		RI.6.7
Unit 6: Integration of Knowledge and Ideas in Literature 217		
Lesson 20: Comparing and Contrasting Genres 219		RL.6.9
Unit 6 Interim Assessment 229		
Media Feature 2: Comparing and Contrasting Reading to Viewing . . 237		RL.6.7

Language Handbook

Conventions of Standard English

Lesson 1: Subject and Object Pronouns 241		L.6.1.a
Lesson 2: More About Subject and Object Pronouns. 243		L.6.1.a
Lesson 3: Possessive Pronouns. 245		L.6.1.a
Lesson 4: Reflexive and Intensive Pronouns 247		L.6.1.b
Lesson 5: Shifts in Pronoun Number and Person 249		L.6.1.c
Lesson 6: Correcting Vague Pronouns 251		L.6.1.d
Lesson 7: Recognizing and Correcting Errors 253		L.6.1.e
Lesson 8: Punctuating Parenthetical Elements 255		L.6.2.a

Knowledge of Language

Lesson 9: Varying Sentence Patterns 257		L.6.3.a
Lesson 10: Consistency in Style and Tone 259		L.6.3.b

Table of Contents

Vocabulary Acquisition and Use

CCLS

Lesson 11: Using Context Clues 261   L.6.4.a

Lesson 12: Greek and Latin Word Parts 263   L.6.4.b

Lesson 13: Using a Dictionary or Glossary. 265   L.6.4.c

Lesson 14: Using a Thesaurus 267   L.6.4.c

Lesson 15: Figures of Speech. 269   L.6.5.a

Lesson 16: Relationships Between Words 271   L.6.5.b

Lesson 17: Denotation and Connotation 273   L.6.5.c

Unit 1
Key Ideas and Details in Informational Text

Imagine you are in a scientist's laboratory. You see flasks of bubbling liquids, test tubes, and rubber tubing. The scientist is analyzing a substance by boiling it down to identify its parts. This will help her understand important ideas about the substance and how it can be used.

How is a reader like a scientist? A reader also analyzes a text, breaking it down to identify important **details**. Then, like scientists, readers examine those details to understand the **key ideas** in the text. Sometimes those details provide all the information you need. Other times, readers must use those details to make inferences, or figure out what the author really means.

In this unit, you will learn how to read closely and to use evidence, or details, to support your understanding of an informational text. You will also learn how to use the details to summarize the text. You will read about important people, events, and ideas and show why they are important. Put on your lab coats as you fill your test tubes with unusual plant life, unexplained mysteries, and legendary places. Don't forget your goggles!

✔ **Self Check** **Fill out the Self Check on the next page.** ▶

Before starting this unit, check off the skills you know below. As you complete each lesson, see how many more you can check off!

✓ Self Check

I know how to:	Before this unit	After this unit
find the central idea of a text and the details that help support it.	☐	☐
summarize a text without giving personal opinions.	☐	☐
cite evidence to support inferences about a text.	☐	☐
explain how an individual, event, or idea is introduced and described in a text..	☐	☐

Determining Central Idea and Details

CCLS
RI.6.2: Determine a central idea of a text and how it is conveyed through particular details....

Theme: *Extraordinary Plants*

Think about your favorite story. If you had to tell a friend what it's mostly about, what would you say? A text's **central idea** is the most important point the writer is trying to make. Sometimes the central idea is directly stated, but more often it's not. **Supporting details** are facts, examples, reasons, or descriptions that expand on the central idea.

Look at the picture. What is the central idea? What supporting details do you see?

Complete the chart. First, find and record a third supporting detail. Then figure out what important point the illustrator is trying to make.

Central Idea

Supporting Detail	Supporting Detail	Supporting Detail
A cactus can survive for months without water.	The sign states the cactus should not be touched.	

Readers determine a text's central idea and supporting details so they can better understand the text's meaning. A central idea often needs to be figured out by analyzing the supporting details. Think of yourself as a detective describing a complex situation and finding clues to support your observations.

Read the first paragraph of a scientific account about the Venus flytrap.

Genre: **Scientific Account**

The Unusual Venus Flytrap   *by Amy Baker*

The Venus flytrap is a unique plant with many admirers. This carnivorous plant grows in the bogs of North America. With red-lined lobes that resemble a mouth, the Venus flytrap looks more like a creature than a plant. It uses these lobes to capture and eat insects. It can even digest small frogs! The lobes have small trigger hairs that cause the plant to clamp down in an instant when unsuspecting prey comes too close. Finger-like extensions called *cilia* intertwine to keep the lobes shut tight. It is this trapping action that people find so fascinating.

(continued)

Explore how to answer these questions: *"What is the central idea of the paragraph? What details support this idea?"*

The central idea is the most important point the author makes. The central idea is not always directly stated. You often need to figure it out based on the details and state it in your own words.

Reread the title and the first and last sentences of the paragraph to look for clues about the central idea. Write the central idea in the middle of the web. Then skim the paragraph to find details that support this idea. Two supporting details are shown below.

Central Idea

Supporting Detail	Supporting Detail	Supporting Detail
The Venus flytrap looks like a creature with a mouth.	The Venus flytrap can eat frogs.	

Continue reading about the Venus flytrap. Use the Close Reading and the Hint to help you answer the question.

Close Reading

Find and **underline** the sentence in this paragraph that most closely restates the central idea you found on page 4.

(continued from page 4)

One of the most mysterious things about the Venus flytrap is that scientists still don't understand how the trap closes. The flytrap does not have the muscles, tendons, or nervous system necessary for movement. Scientists guess that the trap might close using some electrical impulses and pressure changes. The longer they study the Venus flytrap, the more likely scientists are to discover how it functions. It should be no mystery, however, why this unusual plant has captured the imaginations of so many people.

Hint

Which choice best represents what the author wants readers to take away from this text?

Circle the correct answer.

Which sentence from the paragraph best shows the text's central idea?

A "One of the most mysterious things about the Venus flytrap is that scientists still don't understand how the trap closes."

B "The flytrap does not have the muscles, tendons, or nervous system necessary for movement."

C "Scientists guess that the trap might close using some electrical impulses and pressure changes."

D "It should be no mystery, however, why this unusual plant has captured the imaginations of so many people."

✎ Show Your Thinking

Explain how the answer you chose conveys the text's central idea.

_____

_____

_____

 Pick one of the answers you did not choose. Tell your partner why that sentence is not the best illustration of the text's central idea.

Read the scientific account. Use the Study Buddy and Close Reading to guide your reading.

The author opens the account by asking why so many people would want to see the corpse flower. I will underline a detail that supports the idea that many people want to see the flower.

Close Reading

Why do people rush to see the corpse flower? **Underline** details that show why people find it so interesting.

Reread the first and last sentences. What similar idea does the author use to open and close the account?

Genre: **Scientific Account**

The Corpse Flower   *by Stacia Alonzo*

1   Why would thousands of men, women, and children wait in line to see a flower that smells like rotting flesh? <u>In May 2003, more than 16,000 visitors did just this when *Titan arum* bloomed in Bonn, Germany.</u> *Titan arum*'s nickname of "corpse flower" emphasizes its unusual smell—like a decomposing body—when in bloom.

2   Scent isn't these flowers' only unique trait. They also grow at an impressive rate. The Bonn corpse flower reached a height of nine feet in full bloom. They bloom for only one to two days at a time, and their leaves open to reveal the dark red color of raw flesh. When a corpse flower blooms, people flock to witness the unforgettable sight of a man-size flower ripe with the color and scent of death.

3   This rare flower was first discovered in Sumatran rainforests in 1878. Although corpse flowers still grow there, they are endangered. To learn about the flowers, biologists raise them in botanical gardens. Some flowers never bloom, and others only bloom once. When a flower opens, biologists have only one or two days to observe the process.

4   Biologists have learned that these plants can grow up to six inches a day and reach nine feet tall. The rotting flesh scent lures in insects for pollination. Biologists analyzed the scent to determine how close it is to that of real rotting meat. Here's one fact they learned: the human nose can't detect a difference in the scents. Given *Titan arum*'s strange traits, who wouldn't jump at the chance to see the world's worst-smelling flower?

Hints

Which choice provides proof that many people want to see the corpse flower?

Which details help explain why someone would want to go all the way to Germany to see the corpse flower?

What does the author most want you to know about the corpse flower? Think about how the account's first and last sentences connect to this idea.

Use the Hints on this page to help you answer the questions.

1 Which of the following details best supports the idea that people are very interested in the corpse flower?

    A   The corpse flower has the smell of rotting flesh.

    B   16,000 people came to see the corpse flower in Bonn, Germany.

    C   The flower was nicknamed "corpse flower" because of its smell.

    D   The inside of the flower looks dark red when it blooms.

2 Which of the following details from the text is not strong support for why people would be so interested in the corpse flower?

    A   It smells like rotting flesh.

    B   It often grows as tall as a man.

    C   It blooms for only a short time.

    D   It lures in insects for pollination.

3 State the central idea of the account. Remember that some central ideas are implied rather than directly stated. Include at least one direct quote from the text to support your explanation.

_____

_____

_____

_____

_____

_____

_____

_____

_____

_____

_____

_____

Read the scientific article. Then answer the questions that follow.

from "Against All Odds: Earth's Fragile Pioneers"

by Stephen James O'Meara, Odyssey Magazine

1   One species every 70,000 years! That's the rate at which plants and animals once colonized the Hawaiian Islands. Countless millions of them had the chance, but only the most rugged pioneers—a salt-resistant seed, an insect clinging to a raft of wood, a strong-winged bird—survived the long voyage across the Pacific from their native continents. Of the hundreds of species that did make it to Hawaii, only a few survived the seclusion and harshness of the burning volcanic islands. It took time, but these barren new "worlds," risen from the sea and born of fire, finally surrendered to the slow but persistent assault of life.

2   Of course, the story of the invasion of life is similar all across the globe. But what makes the Hawaii story special is the incredible distance life had to travel to get there. Remote and alone in the heart of the North Pacific, Hawaii is the most isolated island group on Earth. . . . Yet, life did get to Hawaii, and it did so in three ways: by wind, wings, and water.

3   *Wind.* Many of Hawaii's plants, spiders, and insects have origins in Asia, thanks to a torrent of thin air called the jet stream, which roars across the upper atmosphere with hurricane force. Each January, the eastward-flowing jet stream makes a southerly meander over Asia. As the wind in the jet stream moves away from Asia, it slows to a minimum of about 110 kph just over Hawaii. Are you getting the picture? Quite a transport mechanism here! Now, picture this: A gale-force wind in Asia strips a plant of its seeds and lifts a few spiders and insects off the ground, making them airborne . . . where they are then transported eastward at hurricane force until the winds slow and the seeds, spiders, and insects sprinkle down on the islands. The entire journey can take just four hours!

4   *Wings.* Insects, seeds, and spiders (as well as other life forms) can take alternate means of transport to Hawaii—such as hitching a ride on a migrating or storm-driven bird. With a wingspan of over two meters, the great frigate bird is a soaring wonder. Its powerful wings can carry it effortlessly across the tropical Pacific. Now imagine one of these gets caught in a hurricane. It soars with the wind until it sights land—in this case, Hawaii. After a long journey, it rests. A seed from a favorite berry it has eaten drops into a crevice and, in time, takes root. Years later, another great flier arrives. Preening itself, the bird frees a seed or a sticky land snail from its feathers. One by one, over the millennia, these birds have transported troops of accidental "tourists" to Hawaii.

the great frigate bird in flight

5   *Water.* Partnered with the wind, surface currents waltz around the world's oceans, carrying with them all sorts of debris. Few seafaring seeds have what it takes to survive the long, meandering journey to Hawaii. . . . One plant whose seeds meet these requirements is the Hala—one of the world's oldest known flowering plants, dating back 250 million years. How do its seeds survive the salty ocean? They are snuggled in a blanket of spongy material, which can float in the sea for months or even years. A species of Hawaiian crickets rafted in on pieces of floating wood. They had to struggle to survive on harsh Hawaii, feeding on organic debris tossed to shore by wind and wave. They soon adapted, however, giving rise to an endemic species—one found nowhere else on Earth.

Answer the questions. Mark your answers to questions 1–4 on the Answer Form to the right.

Answer Form

1 Ⓐ Ⓑ Ⓒ Ⓓ
2 Ⓐ Ⓑ Ⓒ Ⓓ
3 Ⓐ Ⓑ Ⓒ Ⓓ   **Number**   ╱4
4 Ⓐ Ⓑ Ⓒ Ⓓ   **Correct**

1   Which of the following is the **best** statement of the central idea of "Against All Odds: Earth's Fragile Pioneers"?

    A   The story of the invasion of life is nearly the same everywhere in the world.

    B   Hawaii's story is unique because of the great distance life traveled to get there.

    C   The jet stream causes the wind to move away from Asia and blow right over Hawaii.

    D   Certain species, such as Hawaiian crickets, struggle and adapt to survive.

2   Which sentence **best** expresses the central idea of the entire article?

    A   "One species every 70,000 years! That's the rate at which plants and animals once colonized the Hawaiian Islands."

    B   "It took time, but these barren new 'worlds,' risen from the sea and born of fire, finally surrendered to the slow but persistent assault of life."

    C   "Remote and alone in the heart of the North Pacific, Hawaii is the most isolated island group on Earth."

    D   "They had to struggle to survive on harsh Hawaii, feeding on organic debris tossed to shore by wind and wave."

3 The central idea of paragraph 3 is that wind helped bring plant and animal life to Hawaii. Which sentence from the paragraph **best** conveys that central idea?

   A "Many of Hawaii's plants, spiders, and insects have origins in Asia, thanks to a torrent of thin air called the jet stream, which roars across the upper atmosphere with hurricane force."

   B "Each January, the eastward-flowing jet stream makes a southerly meander over Asia."

   C "As the wind in the jet stream moves away from Asia, it slows to a minimum of about 110 kph just over Hawaii."

   D "The entire journey can take just four hours!"

4 Which detail **best** conveys the central idea of paragraph 4?

   A Insects and seeds travel on birds that migrate or flee from storms.

   B The great frigate bird has an impressive, two-meter wingspan.

   C Berry seeds often drop into cracks and crevices and start to root.

   D Birds can loosen seeds and snails when they preen their feathers.

5 Paragraph 5 states that Hala seeds "can float in the sea for months or even years." Explain how this detail supports the central idea of the article. Cite at least **one** detail from the text to support your response.

_____

_____

_____

_____

_____

_____

_____

✓ **Self Check**   *Go back and see what you can check off on the Self Check on page 2.*

Lesson 2   Part 1: Introduction 👥
Summarizing Informational Texts

CCLS
RI.6.2: . . . provide a summary of the text distinct from personal opinions or judgments.

Theme: *Links in the Food Chain*

When you give a **summary** of informational text, you briefly restate in your own words the text's central idea and its most important details.

Read the text below. After you read it, locate and underline its central idea.

> The emerald ash borer (EAB) is an invasive pest that is threatening ash trees in the eastern United States. Native to parts of Asia, EABs were likely brought to the United States in the wood of shipping crates or packing material used in international shipping. The insect was identified in 2002 by scientists in Michigan who were investigating the widespread death of native ash trees. EAB larvae live under the bark of ash trees and feed on the trunk, cutting off the flow of water and nutrients that the tree needs to live.

Now complete the chart below. It will help you figure out the most important details to include in a summary of the text.

Important Detail	Important Detail	Important Detail
The emerald ash borer (EAB) is an insect that came to the United States from _____.	When EAB larvae feed on ash trees, they cut off the trees' _____.	The feeding habits of the EAB are causing _____ _____.

Summary
The emerald ash borer is an insect that came to the United States from Asia. When the larvae of this insect feed on ash trees, they cut off the trees' water and nutrients, killing them.

A summary should state only what the text says, not the reader's **opinions** (personal ideas).

Read this draft of a summary about the emerald ash borer. Cross out any opinions.

> The emerald ash borer is an annoying pest that destroys ash trees by feeding on their trunks. The EAB came from Asia, probably in shipping crates, and I wish they would go back there!

When summarizing a text, put its central idea and most important details in your own words. It's a great way to make sure you understand what you're reading!

Read the first two paragraphs of a scientific account about a food chain.

Genre: **Scientific Account**

Snakes' Place in the Food Chain *by Anna Axtell*

Many people consider snakes to be pests, but snakes are a vital part of the food chain, as are all organisms on Earth. A change within a food chain affects all of the organisms in that food chain.

Consider the following food chain, which can be found throughout the United States:

acorn ⟶ mouse ⟶ snake ⟶ hawk

The acorn is the seed of a producer—an organism (an oak tree, in this case) that makes its own food from the sun. The second link is a primary consumer—an organism that eats producers. The snake and the hawk are secondary and tertiary consumers (also called predators) that eat other animals.

(continued)

Explore how to answer this question: *"How can I best summarize this part of the scientific account?"* The author provides a central idea and details. Identifying them and summarizing, or restating in your own words, will help you understand and remember the information.

Reread the account above and do the following:

- Find and underline the central idea
- Circle the three most important details.

Then examine the summary below and cross out the opinion statement.

> Snakes, like all organisms, are a vital link in the food chain even though I think they are pests. In a snake's food chain are acorns (producers), mice (primary consumers), and hawks (tertiary consumers).

Explain to a partner what you crossed out and why. Then take turns summarizing this part of the account without including any opinions or judgments.

Close Reading

Underline the sentence that states the central idea.

Continue reading about connections in a food chain. Use the Close Reading and the Hint to help you answer the question.

(continued from page 12)

If the snake population changes, other changes occur up and down the food chain. If the snake population increases, more snakes eat more mice. Fewer mice are left to eat acorns, so perhaps more acorns grow into oak trees. In addition, more snakes would mean more food for the hawks. Or, consider the alternative. If the snake population decreases, the mouse population would increase. More mice would eat more acorns, so fewer oak trees would grow. And the hawk population, without snakes to hunt, might decrease as well. Changing one link in a food chain affects all of the other links, even if just in small ways.

Hint

Which choice restates the central idea but does not include opinions?

Circle the correct answer.

Which of the following best summarizes the entire scientific account?

A Some people think snakes are pests, but snakes are part of the food chain. They eat mice, which are the real pests.

B Hawks are the fiercest predators in the food chain. They hunt snakes, keeping the snake population from getting too high.

C A changing snake population would affect hawks. They would have less to eat, so there would be fewer hawks.

D Snakes play an important role in a complex food chain. Their population size affects the number of mice, hawks, and oak trees.

✎ Show Your Thinking

Look at one of the answers that you did not choose. Explain why it is not a good summary.

_____

_____

_____

 Find an answer that includes an opinion. Talk with your partner about how you identified it.

Read the scientific article. Use the Study Buddy and the Close Reading to guide your reading.

I'm going to look for "big ideas" that have to do with food webs. I'll underline those big ideas when I find them. That will help me determine the article's central idea.

Close Reading

What forest food chain does paragraph 3 describe? **Underline** the plants and animals in this chain.

Each paragraph gives an example of a food chain in a different ecosystem. **Circle** the name of each ecosystem.

Genre: **Scientific Article**

from "Food Web" *from* National Geographic

1 Food webs connect many different food chains, and many different trophic levels. Food webs can support food chains that are long and complicated, or very short.

2 For example, grass in a forest clearing produces its own food through photosynthesis. A rabbit eats the grass. A fox eats the rabbit. When the fox dies, decomposers such as worms and mushrooms break down its body, returning it to the soil where it provides nutrients for plants like grass.

3 This short food chain is one part of the forest's food web. Another food chain in the same ecosystem might involve completely different organisms. A caterpillar may eat the leaves of a tree in the forest. A bird such as a sparrow may eat the caterpillar. A snake may then prey on the sparrow. An eagle, an apex[1] predator, may prey on the snake. A hawk, another apex predator, may prey on the eagle. Yet another bird, a vulture, consumes the body of the dead hawk. Finally, bacteria in the soil decompose the remains.

4 In a desert ecosystem, an autotroph[2] such as a cactus produces fruit. Herbivorous insects, such as flies, consume the cactus fruit. Birds such as the roadrunner consume these insects. Detritivores[3] such as termites eat the roadrunner after it dies. Bacteria and fungi help decompose the remaining bones of the roadrunner. The carbon in the bones enriches the desert soil, helping plants like cactuses develop.

[1] **apex:** top, highest

[2] **autotroph:** a life-form that makes its own food

[3] **detritivore:** an animal that feeds on dead plants and animals

---

Hints

Which choice tells the central idea of the article?

Use the Hints on this page to help you answer the questions.

1 Which of the following best states the central idea of the article?

   A Both long and short food chains make up food webs.

   B Food webs connect different food chains and trophic levels.

   C Food webs consist of many different food chains, the shortest of which involves grass, rabbits, foxes, and decomposers.

   D The food chains that make up food webs stay in balance naturally as long as humans don't interfere.

Which choice tells the paragraph's central idea without any opinions?

2 Which statement best summarizes the central idea and important details of paragraph 3?

   A A forest food chain that includes leaves, caterpillars, sparrows, snakes, eagles, hawks, vultures, and bacteria is one of the longest in that ecosystem.

   B One forest food chain begins with caterpillars eating leaves. Then birds, snakes, and larger birds eat each other. Finally, bacteria in the soil decompose the remains.

   C A forest food chain starts with trees, leaves, and caterpillars. Birds eat the caterpillars and are eaten by snakes. The chain continues until a vulture eats a disgusting dead thing.

   D One ecosystem may have many different food chains. One example of a food chain in a forest involves leaves, caterpillars, sparrows, snakes, eagles, hawks, vultures, and bacteria.

What is the central idea of the whole article? What important details does each paragraph give?

3 Write a brief summary of the article. Include at least two details from the text in your summary.

_____

_____

_____

_____

_____

_____

_____

Read the scientific article. Then answer the questions that follow.

Spiders: In Pursuit of Prey

by Harry Gardner

1   Have you seen a spider today? If you have, that's not surprising, because spiders live everywhere, indoors and out. They have adapted to living in deserts, caves, high mountain peaks, and even underwater. There are more than 36,000 known species. In the outdoors, there are as many as several million spiders per acre of land. In fact, you are probably six feet from a spider right now!

2   Spiders are predators and eat mainly insects. Because there are so many spiders, they are very important in controlling insect pests. Spiders eat the mosquitoes and yellow flies that can bite us.

3   Many people think that spiders themselves are insects. Actually, they belong to a class of animals called arachnids. Arachnids have two main body parts (insects have three) and eight legs (insects have six). Other arachnids include scorpions, ticks, mites, and daddy longlegs. Both arachnids and insects belong to a larger group called arthropods. All members of this group have a hard outer skeleton that covers the body, called an exoskeleton.

4   Many spiders have a clever tool for catching prey: a web made of silk. The spider produces silk from glands in the abdomen. The spider uses its two hind legs to "reel out" a fine strand of silk, and then it starts to weave its web.

5   Spiders make different kinds of silk. The yellow-and-black garden spider makes a strong, stretchy silk to build the basic framework of its web. Then it adds a sticky variety that makes it hard for a trapped insect to get away. Spider silk, which is made of protein, is very flexible but stronger than steel!

6   The garden spider weaves an elegant snare called an orb web. This web is basically round, with spokes like a bicycle wheel and many strands connecting the spokes. Some orb weavers lie in wait for their prey at the center of the web. Others attach a tripwire to the center of the web. Then they hide nearby, holding onto the line. When the insect struggles, the line vibrates. Then the spider swings into action. A coating of oil on its feet helps it glide across the sticky threads of the web. When it reaches its prey, the spider usually bites it, and the bite is full of venom. As the insect stops struggling, the spider wraps its meal in silk.

7   If the spider is hungry, it starts digesting the prey right away. Because spiders don't have teeth, they must break down their food in another way. They actually do this outside their bodies. They spit digestive juices onto the insect that liquefy it. Then they can suck down part of their meal a little at a time.

8   Other spiders weave different types of webs. Some build triangle webs, which look like a section of an orb web. The spider waits for its prey at one end corner of the web. Others build small sheet webs between tall blades of grass or branches of shrubs. Directly above this sheet, the spider may spin a web of nonsticky threads. The net causes a flying insect to lose its balance and fall onto the sheet, where the spider is waiting. Finally, many indoor spiders build tangle webs, or cobwebs, often in the corner of a room. They may look messy, but they are effective in catching prey.

9   As a spider web continues to catch meals, it becomes damaged and needs repairs. Orb weavers often build a new web every day, and the task can take less than 30 minutes. If the web is not too damaged, the spider repairs it. Often it eats parts of the old web to save silk.

10   About half of all spiders do not build webs to catch prey. Spiders such as the jumping spider and the wolf spider are called wandering spiders. They find hiding places and wait for passing prey. Unlike a web-builder, this hunter has excellent eyesight. It pounces on insects and stuns them with a bite. Then the wanderer settles down for a nice lunch.

11   Although large spiders such as the black widow are often featured in scary movies, most spiders are small and harmless to humans. They are useful animals and amazing food-catchers, and their unusual habits are fascinating to observe.

Answer the questions. Mark your answers to questions 1–3 on the Answer Form to the right.

Answer Form

1 Ⓐ Ⓑ Ⓒ Ⓓ
2 Ⓐ Ⓑ Ⓒ Ⓓ   **Number**   /3
3 Ⓐ Ⓑ Ⓒ Ⓓ   **Correct**

1 Which sentence should **not** be included in a summary of the article?

A It is fun to watch the spiders in the backyard.

B It is common to find spiders in outdoor areas.

C Spiders spin webs that help them catch their prey.

D Spiders are useful because they consume harmful insects.

2 Which is the **best** summary of paragraphs 4 through 6?

A The garden spider weaves an elegant orb web. The web looks like a bicycle wheel. Other species of spiders also create webs with silk spun from their abdomen.

B Spiders spin silk to weave their webs. When an insect encounters the silky thread, it might become the spider's meal. Different sorts of spider spin different types of web.

C The spider uses its rear legs to reel out its silk and then weaves a web. Spider silk is even stronger than steel. The garden spider makes two kinds of silk to trap its insect prey.

D Spider silk is made of protein. The silk creates a strong web that might have a tripwire. Spiders have oily feet. A spider's bite is full of venom.

3 Which of the following **best** summarizes the entire article?

A There are more than 36,000 different kinds of spiders. Some of them catch their food with a web, such as the garden spider with its orb web. Others, like the wolf spider, just jump on their prey, bite it, and then eat it.

B Spiders may resemble insects, but they are actually arachnids, which is a different class of animal. Arachnids have eight legs instead of six, as insects do. Other arachnids include scorpions, ticks, and daddy longlegs.

C From mountain peaks to deserts to caves, the spider is found almost everywhere. Wherever spiders go, they help humans by controlling the insect population through hunting. Since spiders don't have teeth, they dissolve their prey by spitting digestive juices on it.

D Spiders are predators in a group of animals called arachnids. More than half of all spiders catch prey by building webs from silk they spin themselves. Most spiders are harmless to humans, who actually benefit from the pest control provided by these insect-eating creatures.

4 Summarize the two main ways in which different types of spiders catch their prey. Support your answer with at least **two** details from the passage.

_____

_____

_____

_____

_____

_____

_____

_____

_____

_____

_____

✓ **Self Check** *Go back and see what you can check off on the Self Check on page 2.*

Lesson 3   Part 1: Introduction 👥
Citing Evidence to Make Inferences

CCLS
RI.6.1: Cite textual evidence to support analysis of what the text says explicitly as well as inferences drawn from the text.

Theme: *Mysterious Creatures*

Writers don't always tell you exactly what's on their minds. Sometimes you need to make a reasonable guess about what the writer thinks. A reasonable guess, which is based on both evidence and your prior knowledge of a topic, is called an **inference**.

The passage below is about a creature known as the giant squid. You will read it twice.

For many years, both sailors and scientists suspected that a creature they called the giant squid lived in the ocean depths. Over the years, the evidence mounted, and in 2012 came solid proof: They filmed giant squids swimming in the ocean.

Before the 2012 video, nobody had answers to several significant questions about giant squids. How did they act in the wild? Were they hunters? Or did they just float in the water, eating what came their way? What purpose did their huge eyes serve? Thanks to the video, we have some answers. We know that the squid is a hunter that uses its large eyes to spot prey and avoid being eaten. But many fascinating mysteries about the creature still need solving. Will this important research continue?

Read the passage again. This time, underline any evidence suggesting whether the writer feels scientists should keep researching the giant squid.

So, does the writer think that scientists should keep researching the giant squid? You can use evidence from the text to make and support an inference about what she thinks.

Study the chart. It shows how you can support an inference using textual evidence.

What You Know	➕	What the Text Says	➖	Inference
A person with positive feelings about a type of work usually wants that work to continue.		• "Before the 2012 video, nobody had answers to several significant questions about giant squids." • "But many fascinating mysteries about the creature still need solving." • "Will this important research continue?"		The author thinks that scientists should keep researching the giant squid.

By using text evidence and what you already know, you can make and support inferences. In a way, you make the same kinds of educated guesses that scientists do when they study mysterious creatures of the deep!

Read the first part of a scientific account about Bigfoot.

Genre: **Scientific Account**

A Scientist's Search for Bigfoot *by Tetsuo Fujii*

Dr. Jeffrey Meldrum is an Associate Professor of Anatomy and Anthropology at Idaho State University. He specializes in primate foot structure—a category that includes apes, monkeys, and humans. His interests also include evaluating footprints that some claim are left by a mythical North American ape known as Bigfoot.

Meldrum's laboratory houses more than 200 casts and artifacts relating to Bigfoot. Although he believes that some samples are hoaxes, others interest him, such as unidentified hair and unique casts of muscle and foot-bone anatomy.

(continued)

Explore how to answer this question: *"Dr. Meldrum thinks that some samples are hoaxes, but others interest him. Why is he most likely interested in those other samples?"*

Reread the second paragraph. It suggests what Dr. Meldrum thinks, but does not state it directly.

Look for details suggesting why Meldrum is interested in the other samples. One detail is listed in the second column; write another detail there. Then complete the inference statement.

What You Know ➕	What the Text Says ＝	Inference
• If a scientist is interested in something, he or she might think it has scientific value. • A scientist might keep samples that could lead to a discovery.	• "Meldrum's laboratory houses more than 200 casts and artifacts relating to Bigfoot." •	Dr. Meldrum is most likely interested in those other samples because . . .

On the lines below, explain how the details you presented in the chart support your inference.

_____

_____

_____

Continue reading the account about Meldrum's research. Use the Close Reading and the Hint to help you answer the question.

Close Reading

What do most other scientists think about Meldrum's work? **Underline** the sentence that tells how they feel about it.

(continued from page 20)

　　Many anthropologists criticize Meldrum's work. They feel he is trying to find an imaginary creature that exists only in folklore. Meldrum tells critics he is not saying that Bigfoot exists. He just believes there is enough evidence to justify scientific investigation.

　　Unsurprisingly, most anthropologists reject Meldrum's evidence. Dr. David J. Daegling, a University of Florida anthropologist who thinks Meldrum's methods of analyzing data are unscientific, sums up this feeling: "Meldrum's evidence doesn't look better on deeper analysis; it looks worse."

Hint

Which choice gives evidence of what most scientists think of Bigfoot research?

Circle the correct answer.

Which sentence from the account best supports the idea that most scientists do not find value in investigating Bigfoot artifacts?

A　"Many anthropologists criticize Meldrum's work."

B　"They feel he is trying to find an imaginary creature that exists only in folklore."

C　"Meldrum tells critics he is not saying that Bigfoot exists."

D　"He just believes there is enough evidence to justify scientific investigation."

✎ **Show Your Thinking**

Look at the answer you chose above. Explain how the evidence in your answer helped show that most scientists do not find value in investigating Bigfoot artifacts.

_____

_____

_____

Read the scientific account. Use the Study Buddy and Close Reading to guide your reading.

As I read, I'm going to underline clues that help me infer the author's viewpoint about chupacabras.

Close Reading

According to the author, why do people hope that chupacabras are real? **Underline** a sentence that shows the author's explanation.

What examples of new discoveries does the author give? **Underline** the evidence that new creatures have been discovered.

Genre: **Scientific Account**

Tales of Chupacabras   *by Cynthia Burnham*

1   Legend tells of the chupacabra, a monster that sucks the blood of livestock. *Chupacabra* means "goat sucker" in Spanish. For many in the southwestern United States and Mexico, these tales are more than just stories; they have been accepted as fact. In Puerto Rico in 1995, hundreds of livestock fatalities were blamed on the chupacabra.

2   Some describe chupacabras as two-legged, lizard-like creatures with claws, spikes, and piercing red eyes. Others insist they are hairless, four-legged creatures that are part kangaroo, part dog, and part rat. Many similar beasts have been brought to labs for DNA testing, but most have been coyotes with mange, a disease that strips animals of fur.

3   <u>Why do we want these mythical beasts to be real?</u> Surely not because we want livestock to fall prey to vampires! Perhaps it is because of our natural desire to shed light on the unknown. Scientists constantly identify new life-forms. According to the World Wildlife Federation, more than 1,200 species of plants and vertebrates were discovered in the Amazon rain forest between 1999 and 2009. Given this fact, the idea that undiscovered species could exist empowers our imaginations and gives us hope.

4   Although we have explored much of this planet, there are still creatures that lurk in the underbrush, evading recognition. That is a thrilling concept. So even as evidence mounts against the existence of chupacabras, a part of us hopes that one will creep from the shadows and boggle our minds.

Hints

Think about the word choice in each sentence. Which choice helps you infer what the author actually thinks about chupacabras?

Use the Hints on this page to help you answer the questions.

1 A student makes the following claim about the author of "Tales of Chupacabras."

> The author believes that chupacabras are imaginary even though she would like to think they exist.

Which sentence from the text best supports this claim?

  A "*Chupacabra* means 'goat sucker' in Spanish."

  B "Some describe chupacabras as two-legged, lizard-like creatures with claws, spikes, and piercing red eyes."

  C "Why do we want these mythical beasts to be real?"

  D "Scientists constantly identify new life-forms."

Which sentence offers support for why people hope chupacabras are real?

2 Which sentence from the text explains why the author thinks people want to believe in chupacabras?

  A "For many in the southwestern United States and Mexico, these tales are more than just stories: they have been accepted as fact."

  B "Legend tells of the chupacabra, a monster that sucks the blood of livestock."

  C "Others insist they are hairless four-legged creatures that are part kangaroo, part dog, and part rat."

  D "Perhaps it is because of our natural desire to shed light on the unknown."

What kinds of life-forms were discovered between 1999 and 2009? What is the author's purpose for including this evidence?

3 Explain how the examples of recent scientific discoveries support the idea that chupacabras may one day be found. Use details from the text in your explanation.

_____

_____

_____

_____

_____

_____

_____

Read the scientific account. Then answer the questions that follow.

Looking for the Loch Ness Monster

by Stuart Clyburn

1   The word *loch* is a Scottish Gaelic word for *lake*. And there are a whole lot of lochs in Scotland—more than 500 of them! But one loch, Loch Ness in the Scottish Highlands, is known around the world. The reason for its fame is not its great size or beauty. People know the name *Loch Ness* because it is said to be the home of a mysterious, giant creature known as "the Loch Ness monster." Whether the creature really exists or not has been a matter of great debate for decades.

2   What does "Nessie," the popular nickname for the monster, supposedly look like? By most accounts, she has a small head on a very long neck. Her body is broad and rounded, with four flippers and a long tail. If you know your prehistoric creatures, you might be thinking: Nessie sounds like a *plesiosaur*, a giant sea reptile that lived hundreds of millions of years ago. One common theory about Nessie is that she actually *is* a plesiosaur. Other explanations for Nessie are far less dramatic. Some people think that the "mysterious" creature people have mistaken for a monster may have been nothing more than a walrus, seal, or eel.

an artist's depiction of a plesiosaur

3   How could a creature as big as a plesiosaur hide in a lake? Well, Loch Ness is a huge body of water. It's the second largest loch in Scotland, based on the surface area of its water. Loch Ness covers more than 21 square miles, and only Loch Lomond is bigger. But if you look at the volume of water, Loch Ness is the biggest. And that's because it's deep—about 755 feet at its deepest point. This single loch contains more water than all the freshwater lakes in England. In other words, it's one big place to hide.

4   Some people who believe in Nessie say that she's made her home in the region for more than a thousand years. A book written in the seventh century tells about an Irish monk who saw a giant "water beast" in the River Ness in 565 c.e. No one thought much about that story until 1933. A couple was driving home along the loch late one night. They said they were forced to stop when a giant, dragon-like creature crossed the road and slid into the water. Their story appeared in newspapers. Soon, many more people claimed to have seen the monster. The following year, in 1934, a doctor from England took a photo that became famous worldwide. The poorly lit, grainy photo shows what looks like the head and long neck of a plesiosaur-like creature rising from the water. The photo served as "proof" of the monster until 60 years later—when it was revealed to be a fake.

5   Since the 1930s, dozens of serious, scientific searches have been undertaken to find the Loch Ness monster. One early effort involved placing scouts with cameras and binoculars around the loch for five weeks. Later searches relied on the use of sonar. This method involves bouncing sound waves through the deep

waters of the loch to detect moving objects. In 2003, the famous British Broadcasting Corporation (BBC) sponsored one of the most thorough searches ever. Scientists used 600 sonar beams and satellite tracking. What did they find? Nothing of note, really. They concluded that Nessie was a myth.

6   After so many attempts, you have to wonder why people keep looking for the Loch Ness monster. It may just be that there's something exciting about the idea of mysterious creatures living so close to us, always just out of view. There's a word for such creatures: *cryptids*. It comes from a Greek word meaning "to hide." The Loch Ness monster is one of many cryptids that have captured the public imagination. Others include Bigfoot in North America, the Yeti in the Himalaya Mountains, and the chupacabra in the southwestern United States and Mexico.

7   Many animals whose existence we take for granted today might once have been considered cryptids. Komodo dragons and giant squids were once thought to be tall tales. Until 1902, people regarded stories of "giant ape-men" living in Africa as just a myth. Today, we know them as mountain gorillas. The odds of "Nessie" turning out to be real may not be quite as good. But if it were true, we'd all love it, wouldn't we? It's exciting to think that a real live monster lives deep in a loch in Scotland.

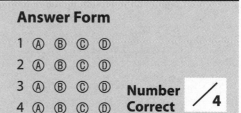

Answer Form

1 Ⓐ Ⓑ Ⓒ Ⓓ
2 Ⓐ Ⓑ Ⓒ Ⓓ
3 Ⓐ Ⓑ Ⓒ Ⓓ   **Number** ╱4
4 Ⓐ Ⓑ Ⓒ Ⓓ   **Correct**

1   According to the account, what is one reason many people believe the Loch Ness monster does not exist?

A   The earliest sighting of the Loch Ness monster occurred in 565 C.E.

B   The photo taken in 1934 has been proven to be a fake.

C   Plesiosaurs, like the dinosaurs, lived hundreds of millions of years ago.

D   Sonar beams and satellite tracking found no evidence in the loch.

2   Which detail provides evidence that a creature as huge as a plesiosaur could really hide in Loch Ness?

A   Loch Ness has a surface area of 21 square miles and is 755 feet deep.

B   The Loch Ness monster might actually be an ordinary walrus, seal, or eel.

C   Dozens of scientific searches of Loch Ness have been conducted.

D   The Loch Ness monster is known as a cryptid, a word whose root word means "to hide."

3   Which statement is **best** supported by the account?

A   It is illogical to think that a plesiosaur could still be living in Loch Ness today.

B   Someday, scientists will prove that no giant creatures live in Loch Ness.

C   Some people want to believe in the Loch Ness monster and ignore scientific evidence showing it does not exist.

D   People have always been fascinated by the idea of strange creatures such as Bigfoot and the Loch Ness monster.

4   Despite the great interest in the Loch Ness monster, it is highly unlikely that such an animal actually exists. Which sentence from the passage **best** supports this conclusion?

A   "Whether the creature really exists or not has been a matter of great debate for decades."

B   "Some people who believe in Nessie say that she's made her home in the region for more than a thousand years."

C   "Since the 1930s, dozens of serious, scientific searches have been undertaken to find the Loch Ness monster."

D   "Many animals whose existence we take for granted today might once have been considered cryptids."

5   Some people firmly believe that the Loch Ness monster is actually a plesiosaur. Use at least **three** details from the account to explain why some people believe this.

_____

_____

_____

_____

_____

_____

 **Self Check**   *Go back and see what you can check off on the Self Check on page 2.*

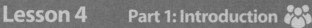
CCLS

RI.6.3: Analyze in detail how a key individual, event, or idea is introduced, illustrated, and elaborated in a text (e.g., through examples or anecdotes).

Theme: *Legendary Places*

How do you keep your friends interested when you're talking to them? You might tell them a story. An **anecdote** is a brief story about an interesting, funny, or strange event, told to entertain or to make a point. An author might use examples and anecdotes to introduce unfamiliar ideas or events in a way that helps readers better understand them.

Read the passage below. Consider the types of information it provides about lost cities.

Lost Cities

Lost cities are places that were once well populated but whose locations were later forgotten. In a few cases, there is physical proof that a city once existed. Other lost cities live only in stories.

Did the lost city of El Dorado, ruled by a king covered in gold, really exist? In 1594, the Englishman Sir Walter Raleigh led an expedition to South America to find the mythical golden kingdom. He did not find the city, but upon his return he claimed to have done so. Stories such as Raleigh's help keep the idea of finding lost cities alive.

Now read the passage again. This time, circle the name of the person mentioned in the text, and underline the anecdote about that person.

Who was the person? What anecdote did the passage tell about them? Read the table below to see one fact, one example, and one anecdote from the passage above.

Fact	Example	Anecdote
Lost cities are places that were once well populated, but whose locations were later forgotten.	El Dorado is one example of a lost city.	Sir Walter Raleigh led an expedition to South America to find El Dorado and told people he succeeded even though he failed.

In a text, the purpose of anecdotes and examples is to help readers better understand individuals, events, or ideas. Anecdotes and examples introduce, illustrate, and elaborate on important information. They turn dry facts into lively discussions of the real world around us.

27

Read the historical account about the lost city of Atlantis.

Genre: **Historical Account**

Atlantis: Lost City?   *by Julio Gonzales*

Archaeologists and writers have long speculated about the legendary city of Atlantis and its location. According to one theory, Atlantis was an island empire located off Europe in the Atlantic Ocean. It was home to an advanced civilization that existed thousands of years ago. The people of Atlantis tried to dominate the Mediterranean region of the world. Their plans for ruling the area were cut short when the Athenians defeated their army. Soon afterward, a massive earthquake devastated the island, causing it to sink beneath the ocean.

A second theory suggests that Atlantis may have existed on the island of Thera in the Aegean Sea. The island sank into the sea after a major volcanic eruption. There is no evidence, however, to support either theory.

Explore how to answer this question: *"What information does the author include to elaborate on the history of Atlantis?"*

Think about the theories the author gives about Atlantis's location and what happened to the city.

Look for examples that explain what may have happened to Atlantis. The chart gives an example relating to the first theory. Underline an example relating to the second one. Write it in the box.

Fact	Example
One theory is that Atlantis was located off Europe in the Atlantic Ocean.	A massive earthquake devastated the island, causing it to sink beneath the ocean.
Another theory is that Atlantis may have existed on the island of Thera, in the Aegean Sea.	

Explain the purpose of each fact and example listed in the chart above. What does this information help you understand about Atlantis?

_____

_____

_____

Read the account about the Seven Cities of Gold. Use the Close Reading and the Hint to help you answer the question.

Genre: **Historical Account**

Seven Cities of Gold   *by Claudia Vandango*

Five centuries ago, a monk named Marcos de Niza explored the land that would one day be called New Mexico. Niza told fantastic stories about Cibola, a place also called the Seven Cities of Gold. He claimed that he saw cities full of gold.

Spanish explorer Francisco Vásquez de Coronado and his soldiers set out for Cibola with Niza as their guide. When they arrived, however, Coronado was greatly disappointed to find a settlement of small pueblos instead of a golden city. One account tells that Niza admitted he had not actually seen Cibola himself.

Close Reading

In the second paragraph, the author says that Coronado left for Cibola with Niza as a guide. **Underline** the sentence that provides key information about how Coronado felt once he reached Cibola.

Hint

Which choice gives key information about what happens to Coronado as a result of Niza's stories?

Circle the correct answer.

Which sentence from the text best illustrates how Coronado was affected by Niza's stories?

A "Niza told fantastic stories about Cibola, a place also called the Seven Cities of Gold."

B "When they arrived, however, Coronado was greatly disappointed to find a settlement of small pueblos instead of a golden city."

C "He claimed that he saw cities full of gold."

D "Spanish explorer Francisco Vásquez de Coronado and his soldiers set out for Cibola with Niza as their guide."

✎ Show Your Thinking

Look at the answer you chose above. Explain how the anecdote about Niza and his stories helped you understand how Coronado felt when he reached Cibola.

_____

_____

 Tell a partner why the other choices do not illustrate how Niza's stories affected Coronado.

Read the historical account. Use the Study Buddy and the Close Reading to guide your reading.

The author includes an anecdote about Pizarro's quest to find El Dorado. I am going to underline the sentence in this anecdote that ties it to the idea that many people have searched for this city.

Close Reading

What happened when a new Muisca chief came into power? **Underline** the sentence that discusses the actual event that occurred.

What examples of riches were present in El Dorado and the Muisca region? **Underline** the sentences in paragraphs 2 and 4 that give information about these areas' wealth.

Genre: **Historical Account**

The Search for El Dorado   *by Lauren Octavio*

1   Where did the story of the lost city of gold, known as El Dorado, come from? During the 16th and 17th centuries, explorers searched for this legendary land. The lure of gold led to much disappointment, wasted years, and even death.

2   Gonzalo Pizarro, a Spanish explorer in South America, first heard the tales of the golden land from the natives. They told about a place in the Andes Mountains where people worshipped a chieftain covered in gold who tossed golden treasures into a lake. Stories claimed that the chief's followers adorned themselves with gold and jewels that were plentiful in this rich land. The chieftain was known as El Dorado— one who is gilded, or covered in gold.

3   <u>When the story of the golden city reached Pizarro, he was determined to find this place for himself and claim the gold.</u> In 1541, he led an expedition to find El Dorado. The party suffered hunger, sickness, and attacks by hostile natives. After much hardship, Pizarro was forced to return home.

4   Where did the stories of El Dorado come from if such a city never existed? They might be based on an actual place near Bogota, Colombia. The Muisca people living there were governed by a chief. When a new chief came into power, he was covered in oil or clay and sprinkled with gold dust. In a ritual to ensure a good harvest, the chief would float out to the middle of a lake on a raft and leap in. Later, it was found that the area contained some gold mines, but the riches were nowhere as abundant as in the stories about El Dorado.

Hints

Which sentence does the author use to support the idea that many have struggled to find El Dorado?

Use the Hints on this page to help you answer the questions.

1 Which sentence from the text develops the idea that many explorers have searched for the legendary land of El Dorado?

   A "When the story of the golden city reached Pizarro, he was determined to find this place for himself and claim the gold."

   B "Stories claimed that the chief's followers adorned themselves with gold and jewels that were plentiful in this rich land."

   C "The lure of gold led to much disappointment, wasted years, and even death."

   D "In a ritual to ensure a good harvest, the chief would float out to the middle of a lake on a raft and leap in."

Which choice helps the reader understand the origin of the myth of the golden chieftain?

2 Which sentence describes an actual event that may have led people to believe that the chieftain of El Dorado was covered in gold?

   A "They told about a place in the Andes Mountains where people worshipped a chieftain covered in gold...."

   B "When a new chief came into power, he was covered in oil or clay and sprinkled with gold dust."

   C "In 1541, he led an expedition to find El Dorado."

   D "The chieftain was known as El Dorado—one who is gilded, or covered in gold."

How did the stories about the city being filled with riches differ from the reality of the Muisca region?

3 Describe how the mythical El Dorado was different from the actual place where the Muisca people and their chief lived. Include at least one quote and specific examples from the account to support your answer.

_____

_____

_____

_____

_____

_____

_____

Read the article. Then answer the questions that follow.

from "Secrets of the Lost City of Z"

by Anthony Mason, CBS News Sunday Morning

1   Since the dawn of the modern age, the notion of a pre-historic world, hidden deep in the jungle and untouched by the passage of time, has captivated our imaginations.

2   Before "Jurassic Park," before "King Kong," there was "The Lost World." Written in 1912 by Sherlock Holmes' creator, Sir Arthur Conan Doyle, "The Lost World" was in turn largely inspired by the real-life adventures of one remarkable man: Col. Percy Harrison Fawcett.

3   David Grann, a staff writer for *The New Yorker* magazine, says in his time Fawcett was a larger-than-life figure: "Oh, he really was. I mean, he was the last of these kind of great territorial explorers who would plunge into the blank spots on the map, carrying a machete, essentially, and an almost divine sense of purpose."

4   Grann was researching an article on Conan Doyle when he came across a reference to Fawcett.

5   "I had typed Fawcett's name into one of these newspaper databases, and up came all these kind of crazy headlines: *Fawcett disappears into the unknown. A movie star kidnapped trying to save Fawcett.*

6   "I had never heard of this man, and I quickly discovered there was this legendary figure," Grann said. "And this enormous mystery that had been eclipsed by history. And it really intrigued me."

7   So Grann started digging. Fawcett, he learned, was an honored member of Britain's renowned Royal Geographical Society.

8   "He would live in the jungle for years at a time without contact with the world," Grann said. He discovered stories about "how he'd battle anacondas and electric eels, and how he'd emerge with maps of regions that no one had ever came back from."

9   In April 1925, Fawcett set out with just two others—his 21-year-old son Jack, and Jack's best friend, Raleigh Rimmel—on what was to be his crowning adventure . . . finding the remains of a lost world he believed existed deep in the Amazon jungle of South America.

10   Fawcett called his mythical city, simply, "Z."

11   After 30 years as an explorer, Fawcett's survival skills were unrivaled. But this time, he went in . . . and never came out.

12   "Well, we know he got as far as a place called Dead Horse Camp, where he would send these dispatches back for five months," said Grann. "And then after the fifth month, the dispatches ceased. And they were never heard from again."

13   . . . setting off one of the greatest manhunts of the 20th century.

14   George Dyott was the first, taking a film crew with him into the Amazon in 1928 and radioing back regular progress reports.

15   But he never found Fawcett.

16   In 1996 Brazilian financier James Lynch launched a multi-million dollar expedition to finally solve the mystery. But he and his party were kidnapped by tribesmen.

17   They were released only after surrendering $30,000 worth of gear.

18   Now, finally, after 85 years, the mystery that has tantalized so many may finally have been solved by perhaps Fawcett's least likely pursuer.

19   Grann turned his jungle adventure into a best-seller, "The Lost City of Z," in which he recounts Fawcett's final days.

20   "We stayed with many of the same tribes that Fawcett stayed with," said Grann. "And to my astonishment, they had an oral history about Fawcett and his expedition.

21   "It describes how Fawcett had insisted on moving eastward, towards the 'River of Death.' And the tribe tried to persuade them not to go in that direction. In that direction were what they referred to as 'the fierce Indians.' And off he marched.

22   "And they could see the fire for five days, rising above the treetops. And then on the fifth day, it went out as if it was snuffed out. And they had no doubt that they had been killed by the Indians."

23   No physical trace of Fawcett has ever been found. But Grann's efforts did bring one revelation to light: Fawcett may have been right about the "lost civilization" after all.

24   "In the last few years, archaeologists are now going into this region using high-tech gadgetry that Fawcett could never imagine—satellite imagery, ground penetrating radars to pinpoint various artifacts," said Grann. "And they are discovering ancient ruins scattered throughout the Amazon.

25   "One archaeologist has found, in the very area where Fawcett believed he would find Z, 20 pre-Columbian settlements that had roads built at right angles, bridges, causeways, and that a cluster of these settlements that were interconnected had populations of between 2,500 to 5,000 people, which would have made them the size of many medieval European cities at the time."

Answer the questions. Mark your answers to questions 1–3 on the Answer Form to the right.

Answer Form

1 Ⓐ Ⓑ Ⓒ Ⓓ

2 Ⓐ Ⓑ Ⓒ Ⓓ   **Number**   /3

3 Ⓐ Ⓑ Ⓒ Ⓓ   **Correct**

1   How does the author introduce the idea of a hidden, prehistoric city in the jungle?

   A   He provides details about the precise time in which the city existed.

   B   He describes what a prehistoric jungle city would have been like.

   C   He lists novels and movies that feature examples of such cities.

   D   He explains why Percy Fawcett was interested in looking for such a city.

2 How does the author support the claim that the search for Fawcett was "one of the greatest manhunts of the 20th century"?

A by discussing the time, money, and effort put into finding Fawcett

B by describing the mystery surrounding Fawcett's disappearance

C by telling how researcher David Grann went looking for Fawcett

D by describing the high-tech gadgetry used to find Fawcett

3 Why does the author include the anecdote about James Lynch's search for Fawcett?

A It illustrates the idea that many people tried unsuccessfully to find Fawcett.

B It proves that David Grann is a more capable explorer than James Lynch.

C It shows that the tribesmen who kidnapped Lynch also killed Fawcett.

D It suggests that Fawcett's theories about a "lost civilization" were correct.

4 The author of the passage thinks that Percy Fawcett was "a remarkable man." Write a short paragraph explaining how the text supports the idea that Fawcett was a remarkable man. Use at least **two** details from the text in your response.

_____

_____

_____

_____

_____

_____

_____

_____

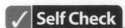 **Self Check** *Go back and see what you can check off on the Self Check on page 2.*

Read this account of important moments in the history of science. Then answer the questions that follow.

Luck Favors the Prepared

by Maria Malzone

1   Making a great discovery generally requires hard work, years of study, and experiment after experiment. However, people sometimes accidentally stumble upon amazing discoveries. Some of the things we use in everyday life—such as sticky notes, microwaves, and artificial sweeteners—were all chance discoveries that changed the way we live. The inventor of the sticky note just happened to stumble on a type of glue that could be reused. The scientist who discovered microwaves wasn't looking for them. He was doing experiments with a new type of vacuum tube. Then one day the chocolate bar in his pocket began to melt, and he realized the machine in front of him could change the way people cooked. A scientist who was trying to find new uses for coal tar happened by chance to notice that it tasted sweet, thus discovering the first artificial sweetener.

2   It is exciting to think that anyone could discover something important, such as sticky notes or microwave ovens. However, most of the accidental discoveries you hear about required more than just luck. While the discoverers may have been lucky, they were also prepared. Some of the most famous "accidental" discoveries were made by scientists who had been working to solve problems for a long time.

3   The discovery of penicillin, which is a medicine used to kill bacteria, is one of the most famous stories of accidental discovery. In the early 1900s, a scientist named Alexander Fleming was trying to find ways to cure diseases and infections. While doing his research, Fleming grew bacteria on special plates called petri dishes.

4   One day he noticed a type of mold, called penicillin, growing on the plate. To Fleming's amazement, the mold killed the bacteria. He discovered that the mold could be used as an antibiotic, which is a medicine that fights bacterial infections. The penicillin antibiotic was used to treat cuts, infections, and diseases that made many people seriously ill. Because of this, it was called a "miracle drug." It is still used today to help save lives.

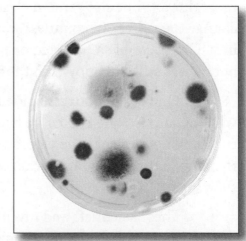

Mold growing in a petri dish. Alexander Fleming's chance observation of how a type of mold killed bacteria led to the development of modern antibiotics.

5   X-rays were another accidental discovery. A scientist named Wilhelm Röntgen, who had studied physics and engineering, was working as a professor in the late 1800s. At that time, Röntgen was performing experiments by passing an electric current through gas. His experiments sometimes produced sparks in the gas. Röntgen noticed that every time the gas sparked, a plate treated with a special chemical lit up. Röntgen thought that perhaps the sparks were producing some sort of rays. These rays were not like anything known at the time, however. For this reason, Röntgen called them X-rays.

6   After making this discovery, Röntgen decided to investigate the rays further. For example, he placed different objects in front of the rays. He tested whether the X-rays would pass through the objects or be blocked by them. Röntgen's most famous image is the X-ray shadow of his wife Bertha's hand. This image shows that the rays do not pass through bone. Doctors quickly realized that they could use X-ray images to look at broken bones.

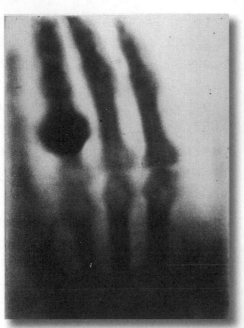

the first X-ray photograph, showing Bertha Röntgen's hand

7   Another scientist who made an accidental discovery was Charles Goodyear. Goodyear was experimenting with natural rubber because he hoped to find a way to make it more useful. Natural rubber, which comes from the sap of rubber trees, is too soft and sticky to be used in many products. Goodyear was determined to find a way to change the rubber so that it would be more durable but also remain elastic, or stretchy. He tried to change the rubber in countless ways, but each attempt disappointed him. Goodyear even patented one method of changing the rubber, but he was still unhappy with the results.

8   One day, Goodyear spilled a mixture containing natural rubber onto a hot stove. The result was the hard, strong rubber he had been seeking. The process resulted in what we now call vulcanized rubber. Goodyear patented a process for making vulcanized rubber in 1844 and then sold his product to manufacturers. Today vulcanized rubber is used in everything from bowling balls to car tires to shoe soles.

9   These scientists and inventors are all known for their accidental discoveries. Could these discoveries have been made by anyone else? Perhaps. But Fleming, Röntgen, and Goodyear all studied and worked hard for many years. When their lucky accidents happened, they had learned enough to understand what they saw. They then worked hard to make their observations useful. Lucky accidents can happen to anybody, but great discoveries are almost always the result of hard work.

Answer Form

1 Ⓐ Ⓑ Ⓒ Ⓓ
2A Ⓐ Ⓑ Ⓒ Ⓓ
3 Ⓐ Ⓑ Ⓒ Ⓓ
4 Ⓐ Ⓑ Ⓒ Ⓓ
5 Ⓐ Ⓑ Ⓒ Ⓓ   **Number** /6
6 Ⓐ Ⓑ Ⓒ Ⓓ   **Correct**

1 Which sentence from the article **best** supports the idea that the discovery of X-rays helped to improve people's health?

A "After making this discovery, Röntgen decided to investigate the rays further."

B "He tested whether the X-rays would pass through the objects or would be blocked by them."

C "Röntgen's most famous image is the X-ray shadow of his wife Bertha's hand."

D "Doctors quickly realized that they could use X-ray images to look at broken bones."

2 Answer Parts A and B below.

Part A

Which statement is true about Alexander Fleming's initial understanding of penicillin?

A He hoped that penicillin would cure certain diseases.

B He was unaware that penicillin would have any effect.

C He was sure penicillin would be a helpful medicine.

D He knew penicillin was deadly to some bacteria.

Part B

Select **two** pieces of evidence from "Luck Favors the Prepared" that support the answer to Part A.

☐ "one of the most famous stories of accidental discovery"

☐ "a medicine used to kill bacteria"

☐ "trying to find ways to cure diseases and infections"

☐ "To Fleming's amazement"

☐ "the mold could be used as an antibiotic"

☐ "it was called a 'miracle drug'"

3 The author believes that Charles Goodyear was a dedicated scientist who kept improving on his work. Which sentence from the article **best** supports this statement?

   A "Another scientist who made an accidental discovery was Charles Goodyear."

   B "He tried to change the rubber in countless ways, but each attempt disappointed him."

   C "One day, Goodyear spilled a mixture containing natural rubber onto a hot stove."

   D "Goodyear patented a process for making vulcanized rubber in 1844 and then sold his product to manufacturers."

4 Which of the following **best** matches a central idea from the text with a detail that supports it?

   A Central idea: Many important discoveries are made during experiments.
      Supporting detail: Doctors began using X-rays to examine injured patients.

   B Central idea: Some important discoveries are not well understood at first.
      Supporting detail: Artificial sweetener was based on a kind of coal tar.

   C Central idea: Some scientists make accidental discoveries that help people.
      Supporting detail: Penicillin is still used in modern times to save lives.

   D Central idea: Dedicated scientists may accidentally become great inventors.
      Supporting detail: Fleming used plates called petri dishes to grow bacteria.

5 Vulcanized rubber continues to be an important part of modern products. How does the author illustrate this idea in the passage?

   A She lists examples of different uses for vulcanized rubber.

   B She tells the story of the invention of vulcanized rubber.

   C She compares vulcanized rubber with natural rubber.

   D She notes the year in which vulcanized rubber was patented.

6 Which of the following **best** summarizes the article?

A Sticky notes, microwaves, and artificial sweeteners all have something in common. Each of these useful things was discovered by accident. The same is true of a number of other discoveries, including penicillin, X-rays, and vulcanized rubber.

B Many important scientific discoveries have been made by accident. These include the discoveries of penicillin, X-rays, and vulcanized rubber. In each case, the scientist making the discovery had the experience to see the usefulness in what others might have considered a mere "accident."

C Alexander Fleming may be the person who made the most important accidental discovery of all time. He was working in his lab when he noticed a type of bread mold that killed bacteria. This led to the invention of penicillin, an antibiotic that has saved countless lives.

D When a good scientist discovers something by accident, the discovery involves more than just luck. Microwaves, penicillin, and X-rays are all examples of useful things discovered by scientists who knew how to turn a mistake into something good. Their "lucky accidents" had more to do with hard work than good luck.

7 Explain how the author uses anecdotes, or stories, to illustrate key ideas of the passage. Use details from the passage to support your answer.

_____

_____

_____

_____

_____

_____

_____

8 Below is information from paragraphs 5 and 6 of the passage "Luck Favors the Prepared." Organize the information by writing each phrase from the passage into the proper section of the table: <u>central idea</u>, <u>supporting detail</u>, and <u>example used to make a point</u>.

Röntgen was performing experiments by passing an electric current through gas.

Röngten's image of his wife's hand showed that X-rays do not pass through bone.

X-rays were another accidental discovery.

Every time the gas sparked, a plate treated with a special chemical lit up.

Central idea	
Supporting detail	
Supporting detail	
Example used to make a point	

Performance Task—Extended Response

9

How does the author introduce and illustrate the differences between truly "accidental" discoveries and those made by hard-working scientists? How does the author feel about the two kinds of discoveries? Write an essay of two to three paragraphs explaining your answer. Be sure to include examples from the passage in your answer.

In your answer, be sure to
- explain how the author presents the differences between these discoveries
- explain how the author feels about these types of discoveries
- use examples from the passage in your answer

Check your writing for correct spelling, grammar, capitalization, and punctuation.

_____

_____

_____

_____

_____

_____

_____

_____

_____

_____

Unit 2
Key Ideas and Details in Literature

You are sitting in a darkened theater, waiting for a play to begin. Finally, the lights come on, the curtain rises, and the actors begin speaking their lines. As you watch, the story unfolds. From the **details** in the action and dialogue, you learn **key ideas** about the plot. When you read a story, play, or poem, you are that text's audience. You understand key ideas by paying close attention to the author's descriptions and the characters' dialogue. Sometimes, you have to "read between the lines" and use the details in the text to figure out information that the author doesn't tell you directly.

In this unit, you will learn how to understand a literary work by reading closely and using evidence, or details, to make inferences. You will learn to describe how a story's or play's plot unfolds and how characters change over time. Finally, you will learn how to use all that information to summarize the text. Let the curtain rise and the show begin!

 **Self Check** **Fill out the Self Check on the next page.** ▶

Before starting this unit, check off the skills you know below. As you complete each lesson, see how many more you can check off!

✓ Self Check

I know how to:	Before this unit	After this unit
cite evidence to support inferences about a text.	☐	☐
describe how a story's or drama's plot unfolds.	☐	☐
explain how characters respond to changes in the plot.	☐	☐
find the theme or central idea of a text.	☐	☐
summarize the text without including personal opinions.	☐	☐

Citing Evidence to Make Inferences

CCLS

RL.6.1: Cite textual evidence to support analysis of what the text says explicitly as well as inferences drawn from the text.

Theme: *Passing Wisdom Down Through the Ages*

Have you heard the story of Pinocchio, the wooden boy who came to life? Each time he lies, his nose grows. Later in the story, Pinocchio says he has been to school, and—*zoink!*—his nose grows. Now, the author doesn't say at this particular point in the story that Pinocchio lied. But you can make an **inference**—a conclusion based on what you already know and text evidence—that he did.

Good inferences are supported with textual evidence. You can practice this right now.

Read the paragraph below. Then use the chart to support an inference about the narrator.

Abraham Lincoln once said, "Whatever you are, be a good one." Easy for him to say—he was good at *everything*. It's nice advice, I guess. Still . . . you can say that you're going to be good at playing the piano. You can even say that you'll perform beautifully at the big recital. You can say that all you want, and you can still forget the notes to your song halfway through and run off the stage in tears. I wonder what Lincoln would have said about that! He probably wouldn't have felt as miserable as I do right now, at the very least.

The chart below states an inference about the narrator. Complete the chart by writing one more phrase from the paragraph that directly supports the inference.

What You Know	➕	What the Narrator Says	＝	Inference
People sometimes feel bad when embarrassed.		• "Still . . . you can say that you're going to be good at playing the piano." •		The narrator has just had a bad experience performing in a piano recital.

When reading, always support your inferences with textual evidence. An unsupported inference won't make your nose grow an inch, but you won't be on your way to a better understanding of the story, either!

Read the first two paragraphs of an ancient Greek myth.

Genre: **Myth**

Athena, Arachne, and the Weaving Contest

by Sofia Lillios

Athena, the goddess of wisdom, was an exceptional weaver. She shared her knowledge with humans, as long as they consistently showed her their deepest gratitude. Athena's most talented student was a young woman named Arachne.

Each day, Athena and Arachne sold their creations at a country market, and everyone said Arachne's cloth was incredible. Athena overheard Arachne tell customers she taught herself to weave. Athena cringed as she listened to Arachne's lies. Then, on one fateful day, Arachne kept bragging to customers that she was the greatest weaver in the world, and that her creations were more beautiful than all the others at the market.

(continued)

Explore how to answer this question: *"How does Athena feel about Arachne's bragging? Make an inference about how Athena feels. Support your inference with two details from the text."*

Look for details from the text that hint at how Athena feels about Arachne. One detail is shown in the chart below. Write a second detail next to the second bullet point. Then write down your inference.

What You Know	+	Details from the Text	=	Your Inference
Someone who expects gratitude would likely be upset if she did not receive it.		• She shared her knowledge with humans, as long as they consistently showed her their deepest gratitude." •		

Use details from the chart to support the inference that Athena is upset about Arachne's bragging.

_____

_____

_____

Continue reading "Athena, Arachne, and the Weaving Contest." Use the Close Reading and the Hint to help you answer the question.

Close Reading

On page 46, the author says that Athena shares her skills with humans on one condition. **Circle** the phrase stating this condition.

(continued from page 46)

An old woman in a cloak smiled and challenged Arachne to a weaving contest, which Arachne gladly accepted. The rules were simple: each would weave one complete tapestry by nightfall, and customers would judge the winner.

Throughout the day, the two sat at looms, weaving furiously. Just before sunset, they finished. Both tapestries were marvelous to behold, but the crowd chose the old woman, for her creation was flawless. "Spin and weave forever without my help, fool," the old woman suddenly said, and pointing one finger at Arachne, turned her into a spider.

Hint

The question asks *why* Arachne was turned into a spider, not *how*.

Circle the correct answer.

Which sentence best explains why Arachne was turned into a spider?

A The old woman had special powers.

B Arachne did not show her thanks to Athena.

C Athena was disguised as the old woman.

D Like Arachne, spiders are good at weaving.

✎ **Show Your Thinking**

Look at the answer you chose above. Explain how the details in the story helped you infer why Arachne was turned into a spider.

_____

_____

_____

_____

Read the Native American story. Use the Study Buddy and the Close Reading to guide your reading.

Based on the first paragraph, I think Young Man is a patient and determined person. I'll underline the phrase that tells me about Young Man's character.

Close Reading

What does Young Man learn on his journey? **Underline** the sentences that explain the lesson of his journey.

The willow tree is kind and wise. **Circle** words and phrases that describe the tree.

Genre: **Native American Legend/Myth**

The Wisdom of the Willow Tree

by Wilson Mekashone

1   Young Man often felt lost and pondered questions about the purpose of his life. He decided to journey far away, seeking wisdom. He <u>hiked tirelessly</u> for several days.

2   One day, the sun blazed down and he was hot, thirsty, and desperate for shade. In the distance, he saw a willow tree and crawled to it. Exhausted, he lay between its roots and had a vivid dream. In the dream, the tree had a wise old face that smiled at him and looked strangely familiar.

3   Young Man said to the tree, "I have failed on my journey. I still don't understand how to live my life. I'm thirsty and weary, and I cannot summon the strength to return home."

4   The tree then reached down its oldest branch, stroked Young Man gently on the cheek, and said, "Sleep in my shade. I am old and know the value of rest. When you wake up, follow my roots. They are wrinkled but know the way."

5   Young Man awoke and followed the tree's enormous roots to a burbling stream. As he drank, he saw his reflection and was shocked when he realized that the face he had seen in the willow's trunk had been his own, only much older.

6   He smiled as he now understood that he must age like the wise tree and help others find their way when they feel lost and defeated. Over time, he would gradually become Wise Man, whom people would seek out for help, shelter, and advice. This, he knew, would take much strength and patience.

Hints

Which choice describes what it takes for Young Man to become Wise Man?

Read each answer choice carefully. Which answer contains a word that describes something people do when they are happy?

How does Young Man feel when he approaches the willow tree? How does the willow tree encounter change Young Man's feelings?

Use the Hints on this page to help you answer the questions.

1 A student makes the following claim about Young Man in "The Wisdom of the Willow Tree."

Young Man has to develop skills if he wants to become Wise Man.

Which sentence from the text best supports this claim?

A "He decided to journey far away, seeking wisdom."

B "This, he knew, would take much strength and patience."

C "I am old and know the value of rest."

D "In the distance, he saw a willow tree and crawled to it."

2 Which sentence from the text best shows that Young Man is happy about his encounter with the willow tree?

A "Young Man awoke and followed the tree's enormous roots to a burbling stream."

B "As he drank, he saw his reflection and was shocked when he realized that the face he had seen in the willow's trunk had been his own, only much older."

C "I'm thirsty and weary, and I cannot summon the strength to return home."

D "He smiled as he now understood that he must age like the wise tree and help others find their way when they feel lost and defeated."

3 Explain how the willow tree's kindness and wisdom help Young Man. Include at least one detail from the story to support your explanation.

_____

_____

_____

_____

_____

_____

_____

Read the story. Then answer the questions that follow.

A Sewing Sensation

by William Rivera

1   Juan sat on the floor of Mom's sewing room with one eye on his soccer magazine and one eye on his mother. His mother was making a wedding dress for their neighbor's daughter, and Juan could see that the dress was going to be beautiful. Juan's mother had designed and sewn dresses for many of the girls in his town, and Juan felt proud that people wanted to wear his mother's creations on their special days.

2   Juan glanced up again from his magazine and asked, "Is your machine running okay, Mom? I think it's making a weird noise."

3   Mom hardly looked up and said, "I think it's working just fine. It's whirring and humming away, just as always."

4   Juan looked disappointed, but he went back to pretending to read his magazine. A few minutes later, he asked, "Do you want me to sew the hem of the dress so that you can rest your fingers? I've watched you do it millions of times, so I could do it if you are really tired." This time, Juan's mother studied Juan's face carefully.

5   "You know, I could use a break," she said, "and we need some new pillowcases. I've got the pattern cut out, and all you'd have to do is stitch up the sides." Juan dropped his magazine and was sitting in Mom's sewing chair in no time. Juan's mom carefully removed the dress she was working on, showed Juan how to thread the sewing machine, and brought him some pillowcases to sew.

6   In his enthusiasm, Juan stomped on the foot pedal and almost sewed over his finger. Then he remembered the patience that his mother always showed, and he slowed down. His seams were straight and even. Juan had a huge smile on his face when he looked over his shoulder at his mom.

7   "I can't believe you sewed that so perfectly on your first try," Mom said, patting Juan on the back. "It took me years of practice to perfect my technique, and you're already a sensation. Why don't you try making a pillow for your room? You can design it, and I'll show you how to make the pattern and cut it out."

8   Juan's face lit up, but then a dark shadow seemed to pass over it. "I think I should probably just go outside and kick the ball with my friends." To himself, he muttered, "What would Anthony think if he saw me at a sewing machine?" as he headed outdoors.

9   Mom didn't say anything as she watched Juan's reaction, but that night at dinner, she and Juan's dad began talking about a local fashion designer who had moved to Dallas and become a very successful clothing designer. Juan pretended he wasn't listening, but the scowl slowly vanished from his face. "Many of the best fashion designers are men," Juan's dad continued. "They can make a lot of money for their designs."

10   After dinner, Juan got out his notebook and began sketching. Then he showed his notebook to his mother, and she nodded approvingly. Together, they headed to the sewing room for pattern tracing paper and scissors.

11   Juan cut out two large round pieces of cloth and began stitching them together, leaving one section open. He turned the cloth inside out, stuffed the opening with cotton batting, and then sewed up the open section. Finally, he used fabric markers to add details. He placed his finished creation on his bed.

12   The next day, Anthony came over to kick the ball with Juan, but it started to rain. The two headed to Juan's room to watch soccer videos instead. When Anthony saw the new oversized soccer ball on Juan's bed, he asked Juan where he got it. Juan grinned at his friend and said, "Mine is one-of-a-kind, but I think I know how to get you one that's almost like it."

Answer the questions. Mark your answers to questions 1–4 on the Answer Form to the right.

Answer Form

1 Ⓐ Ⓑ Ⓒ Ⓓ
2 Ⓐ Ⓑ Ⓒ Ⓓ
3 Ⓐ Ⓑ Ⓒ Ⓓ   **Number**   /4
4 Ⓐ Ⓑ Ⓒ Ⓓ   **Correct**

1 Juan does not have a lot of experience with sewing. Which sentence from the passage is the **best** evidence of this claim?

   A "Juan glanced up again from his magazine and asked, 'Is your machine running okay, Mom? I think it's making a weird noise.'"

   B "'I can't believe you sewed that so perfectly on your first try,' Mom said, patting Juan on the back."

   C "To himself, he muttered, 'What would Anthony think if he saw me at a sewing machine?' as he headed outdoors."

   D "'Many of the best fashion designers are men,' Juan's dad continued."

2 Juan is very excited about learning to sew. Which of the following sentences from the passage **best** supports this statement?

   A "Juan felt proud that people wanted to wear his mother's creations on their special days."

   B "Juan sat on the floor of Mom's sewing room with one eye on his soccer magazine and one eye on his mother."

   C "Juan had a huge smile on his face when he looked over his shoulder at his mom."

   D "Then he remembered the patience that his mother always showed, and he slowed down."

3 Which detail **best** supports the idea that Juan's mother encourages her son's interests?

   A She tells him that her sewing machine doesn't require fixing.

   B She gives him some pillowcases to sew on his own.

   C She sends him outside to play ball instead of sewing.

   D She gives him a notebook for sketching and drawing.

4 What is one reason Juan chooses to play soccer with his friends instead of continuing to sew?

   A He knew that he needed to practice if he wanted to improve his soccer skills.

   B He did not want his friends to think he was rude for keeping them waiting.

   C He thought that his father would not approve of his interest in sewing.

   D He was concerned that his friends might make fun of his sewing talent.

5 Juan seems somewhat embarrassed about his strong interest in sewing. Write a paragraph in which you agree or disagree with that statement. Use at least **two** details from the story to support your answer.

_____

_____

_____

_____

_____

_____

_____

_____

✓ **Self Check** *Go back and see what you can check off on the Self Check on page 44.*

Lesson 6   Part 1: Introduction
Describing Plot

CCLS
RL.6.3 Describe how a particular story's or drama's plot unfolds in a series of episodes . . . as the plot moves toward a resolution.

Theme: *Adventure and Conflict*

In a story or play, the **plot** is the series of episodes, or events, that make up the story. These episodes are moments in the story that are driven by a **conflict**, or struggle, that the main character tries to overcome. Like a trail of footprints, the episodes in a plot lead to the **resolution**, or the end of the conflict.

Look at the images below. What series of episodes led up to the last image?

Read the following diagram to see one idea for how the plot may have unfolded.

3. Climax   Supplies are running out. As their last resort, the survivors send a message in a bottle.

2. Rising Action   Search planes miss the island despite the survivors' efforts to signal for help.

4. Falling Action   A fisherman from a nearby island finds the bottle.

1. Exposition   A storm at sea causes a boat to crash on the rocks of a tiny island.

5. Resolution   The fisherman rescues the survivors.

In most stories and plays, one event leads to another, unfolding in a way that increases tension and builds up to a turning point, called the **climax**—the moment of greatest suspense, surprise, or excitement. Think of plot as a roller coaster ride: The events move you up until you reach the very top, and then send you zooming down to the story's end!

Read the first two paragraphs of the short story.

Genre: **Historical Fiction**

Alma's First Cattle Drive *by Nancy Seago*

Blinding lightning flashed across the sky, followed by deafening thunder and driving rain. Alma had grown up listening to her father's astounding stories of cattle drives. She had always wanted to join in, but her father told her she wasn't ready. Now, he was finally giving her the chance to prove to him that she would be more help than trouble on the trail. This was her first cattle drive, and the weather was Alma's first challenge.

When they reached the river, Alma instantly noticed that the water was dangerously high. When the cattle began to cross at a shallow spot, Alma was the only one to notice a calf getting swept up in the current. Alma charged into the water and stopped her horse downstream from the calf to keep it from losing its footing.

(continued)

Explore how to answer this question: *"How does the story's plot build to a climax?"*
One plot episode leads to the next until Alma must act. This critical moment is the climax.

Read the following plot diagram. Fill in the rest of the diagram to finish mapping out the plot.

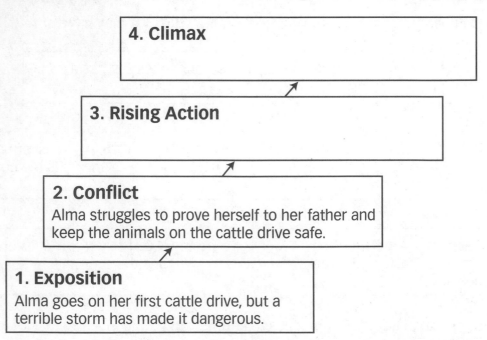

4. Climax

3. Rising Action

2. Conflict
Alma struggles to prove herself to her father and keep the animals on the cattle drive safe.

1. Exposition
Alma goes on her first cattle drive, but a terrible storm has made it dangerous.

As you read the story's ending, think about its resolution, or how Alma's conflict is solved.

Continue reading "Alma's First Cattle Drive." Use the Close Reading and the Hint to help you answer the question.

Close Reading

On page 54, Alma's quest to prove herself is challenged when the weather creates a dangerous situation for the cattle. Find and **underline** the sentence here that shows the end result of Alma's efforts.

(continued from page 54)

Alma stayed there in the stinging rain, her horse breathing hard beneath her. She was cold and hungry, but she kept her horse on the edge of the shallow riverbank until each animal had safely passed.

When she finally rode ashore, her father waved to get Alma's attention. He paused for just a moment to tip his hat to her before they continued. Alma knew then that she had proven herself to be a valuable member of the team.

Hint

The final part of the story includes the resolution. Remember that the main character's problems are usually solved at this point.

Circle the correct answer.

Which sentence best shows the resolution of the story?

A "She was cold and hungry, but she kept her horse on the edge of the shallow riverbank until each animal had safely passed."

B "Alma stayed there in the stinging rain, her horse breathing hard beneath her."

C "When she finally rode ashore, her father waved to get Alma's attention."

D "Alma knew then that she had proven herself to be a valuable member of the team."

✎ **Show Your Thinking**

Explain how you could tell which choice was the resolution of the story.

_____

_____

_____

 With a partner, discuss the episodes that took place in this story. Decide whether the resolution is a satisfying conclusion to the story's events.

Read the drama. Use the Study Buddy and the Close Reading to guide your reading.

To help me understand the plot of this drama, I'm going to identify its episodes.

Close Reading

How is James and Jamaal's problem solved? **Circle** the episode at the end of the play that resolves their conflict.

Underline sentences that illustrate the play's rising action, climax, and falling action. How do these events work together to lead to the story's resolution?

Genre: **Drama**

Lost in Time   *by Marcus Factor*

1   [*Curtain rises on an elaborate museum exhibit featuring a gigantic T-Rex skeleton. Two boys gaze up at it with awe.*]

2   JAMAAL: Look at the enormous size of that thing's teeth!

3   JAMES: That *thing* is the tyrant king of the dinosaur world—the ferocious and infamous *Tyrannosaurus rex.*

4   JAMAAL: Cool! Mr. Flin will have a field day with this guy!

5   [*As they glance around, the boys discover they're alone.*]

6   JAMES: We've lost our class! They must've kept going!

7   JAMAAL: Well, we'll just have to find the mummies, right?

8   JAMES: Yeah, but we have a ton of territory to cover.

9   [*The boys begin walking. As they pass the T-Rex, a tremendous roar booms out and they jump back, terrified.*]

10   JAMAAL: Is it just me, or did that skeleton make noise?

11   JAMES [*breathing heavily*]: Yes. Sound effects, I suppose. We have to find our class—we're four hours from home.

12   JAMAAL: Feels like we're in the jungle a billion years ago.

13   [*A vast variety of dinosaur sounds resonate as the boys continue trekking through the museum. Suddenly, a distressed teacher hurriedly runs onto the stage.*]

14   MR. FLIN: James! Jamaal! I've been searching everywhere! What were you . . . [*extremely distracted*] . . . This is a remarkable new exhibit. We have just enough time to get the class and take in the dinosaur display before lunch!

Hints

Which choice illustrates the main problem that drives the rest of the story's events?

Which choice shows how the play's problem is solved without focusing on the events leading up to the resolution?

What is the conflict in this plot? Would an alternative resolution solve the problem? Why or why not?

Use the Hints on this page to help you answer the questions.

1 What is the conflict in the play?

  A The dinosaur exhibit distracts people too much.

  B The boys have gotten separated from their class.

  C The boys don't know their way around the museum.

  D The teacher is angry at the boys for not paying attention.

2 Which episode from the plot serves as the resolution?

  A James and Jamaal get distracted by the *T-Rex* and end up lost.

  B James and Jamaal make a plan to search for their class.

  C James and Jamaal hear noises coming from the dinosaur display.

  D James and Jamaal are found by Mr. Flin and go get their class.

3 Explain another way that the author could have resolved the conflict in this play. Describe whether or not it would be a good resolution based on the play's plot events. Use at least two specific examples to support your response.

_____

_____

_____

_____

_____

_____

_____

_____

_____

_____

_____

Read the excerpt from a novel. Then answer the questions that follow.

This excerpt is from a novel told from the point of view of a horse named Black Beauty.

from *Black Beauty*

by Anna Sewell

1   One day late in the autumn, my master had a long journey to go on business. I was put into the dog-cart, and John went with his master. . . . There had been a great deal of rain, and now the wind was very high and blew the dry leaves across the road in a shower. We went along merrily till we came to the toll-bar and the low wooden bridge. The river banks were rather high, and the bridge, instead of rising, went across just level, so that in the middle, if the river was full, the water would be nearly up to the woodwork and planks; but as there were good substantial rails on each side, people did not mind it.

2   The man at the gate said the river was rising fast, and he feared it would be a bad night. Many of the meadows were under water, and in one low part of the road the water was halfway up to my knees; the bottom was good, and master drove gently, so it was no matter.

3   When we got to the town of course I had a good bait, but as the master's business engaged him a long time we did not start for home till rather late in the afternoon. The wind was then much higher, and I heard the master say to John that he had never been out in such a storm; and so I thought, as we went along the skirts of a wood, where the great branches were swaying about like twigs, and the rushing sound was terrible.

4   "I wish we were well out of this wood," said my master.

5   "Yes, sir," said John, "it would be rather awkward if one of these branches came down upon us."

6   The words were scarcely out of his mouth when there was a groan, and a crack, and a splitting sound, and tearing, crashing down among the other trees came an oak, torn up by the roots, and it fell right across the road just before us. . . .

7   "That was a very near touch," said my master. "What's to be done now?"

8   "Well, sir, we can't drive over that tree, nor yet get round it; there will be nothing for it, but to go back to the four crossways, and that will be a good six miles before we get round to the wooden bridge again. . . ."

9   So back we went and round by the crossroads, but by the time we got to the bridge it was very nearly dark; we could just see that the water was over the middle of it; but as that happened sometimes when the floods were out, master did not stop. We were going along at a good pace, but the moment my feet touched the first part of the bridge I felt sure there was something wrong. I dare not go forward, and I made a dead stop. "Go on, Beauty," said my master, and he gave me a touch with the whip, but I dare not stir; he gave me a sharp cut; I jumped, but I dare not go forward.

10   "There's something wrong, sir," said John, and he sprang out of the dog-cart and came to my head and looked all about. He tried to lead me forward. "Come on, Beauty, what's the matter?" Of course I could not tell him, but I knew very well that the bridge was not safe.

11   Just then the man at the toll-gate on the other side ran out of the house, tossing a torch about like one mad. . . .

12   "What's the matter?" shouted my master.

13   "The bridge is broken in the middle, and part of it is carried away; if you come on you'll be into the river."

14   "Thank God!" said my master. "You Beauty!" said John, and took the bridle and gently turned me round to the right-hand road by the river side. The sun had set some time; the wind seemed to have lulled off after that furious blast which tore up the tree. It grew darker and darker, stiller and stiller. I trotted quietly along, the wheels hardly making a sound on the soft road. . . .

15   We saw a light at the hall-door and at the upper windows, and as we came up mistress ran out, saying, "Are you really safe, my dear? Oh! I have been so anxious, fancying all sorts of things. Have you had no accident?"

16   "No, my dear; but if your Black Beauty had not been wiser than we were we should all have been carried down the river at the wooden bridge." I heard no more, as they went into the house, and John took me to the stable. Oh, what a good supper he gave me that night, a good bran mash and some crushed beans with my oats, and such a thick bed of straw! and I was glad of it, for I was tired.

Answer the questions. Mark your answers to questions 1–3 on the Answer Form to the right.

Answer Form

1 Ⓐ Ⓑ Ⓒ Ⓓ
2 Ⓐ Ⓑ Ⓒ Ⓓ   **Number**
3 Ⓐ Ⓑ Ⓒ Ⓓ   **Correct**   /3

1   Read this sentence from paragraph 3.

> The wind was then much higher, and I heard the master say to John that he had never been out in such a storm; and so I thought, as we went along the skirts of a wood, where the great branches were swaying about like twigs, and the rushing sound was terrible.

Which part of the story's plot structure does this sentence illustrate?

A exposition

B climax

C rising action

D falling action

2   Which of these sentences shows how the plot is resolved?

   A   "We were going along at a good pace, but the moment my feet touched the first part of the bridge I felt sure there was something wrong."

   B   "Of course I could not tell him, but I knew very well that the bridge was not safe."

   C   "'The bridge is broken in the middle, and part of it is carried away; if you come on you'll be into the river.'"

   D   "'No, my dear; but if your Black Beauty had not been wiser than we were we should all have been carried down the river at the wooden bridge.'"

3   What is the main conflict in the story?

   A   The storm causes a large branch to fall and nearly hit Black Beauty and the men.

   B   The men want Black Beauty to cross the bridge, but he knows it is out.

   C   The bridge breaks and is washed away by the rising water.

   D   The master must go into town for business during a terrible storm.

4   Explain how Black Beauty's decision not to cross the bridge changes the story. Use at least **two** details from the story in your answer.

_____

_____

_____

_____

_____

_____

_____

_____

 **Self Check**   *Go back and see what you can check off on the Self Check on page 44.*

Analyzing Character Development

CCLS

RL.6.3: Describe … how the characters respond or change as the plot moves toward a resolution.

Theme: *Recognizing Potential*

What makes the characters in a story seem real? It's all in the details. Authors can describe the characters' **attitudes**, or how they think, act, and feel. They can also describe the characters' **motivations**, or the reasons for their actions.

Often, a character's attitude and motivation change during a story. As the story unfolds, readers learn more about a character based on how that person responds to events.

Study the cartoon. For each panel, think about what the boy does and why he does it.

Complete the chart below, based on details you can see in the cartoon above.

What the Boy Does	Why He Does It	What This Shows About Him
He takes an ice-cream cone from a little girl.	He might think it is funny.	He is not always kind; he likes to play jokes.
He hesitates when the girl becomes very upset.	He wonders if his joke was such a good idea.	
He gives the ice-cream cone back to the girl.		

Describe how the boy seems to change over time. _____

_____

Characters in stories often change in response to events. If this sounds familiar, it should. It's one of the ways in which authors make their stories similar to real life.

Read the first part of a story about a girl named Rosalyn.

Genre: **Realistic Fiction**

Lost! *by Janelle Aaker*

"Peanut!!" Rosalyn yelled hoarsely for the fiftieth time as panic surged through her veins. How often had Gram said, "Ros, without you and Peanut, I'd be lost"? Well, now yappy, pampered little Peanut *was* lost.

"I was so distracted by my texting that I dropped his leash," Rosalyn groaned. "How can I face Gram?"

"Peanut!!" Rosalyn hollered into the woods. "I have to be careful or I'll get lost, too," she worried. "I need . . . a *map*." Rosalyn darted back to Gram's house, returning moments later with a pencil and paper.

10 steps—tree, she scribbled and illustrated. "Peanut!" Then, *12 left—bush*. "Pea—!"

"*Yap*," Peanut barked as Rosalyn finally saw him, his leash tangled in branches and his paws flailing. Rosalyn nearly shed tears of joy.

(continued)

Explore how to answer this question: *"Based on her responses to events, what kind of person is Rosalyn? Support your response with details from the story."*

To answer this question, pay attention to what Rosalyn's responses to story events say about her.

Complete the chart to show how Rosalyn responds to events. Consider what character trait each response reveals.

What Happens	How Rosalyn Responds
Peanut gets lost.	Rosalyn is upset because Gram loves Peanut.
Rosalyn worries about getting lost, too.	
Rosalyn sees Peanut.	

Describe Rosalyn's character. Use details from the story and the chart to support your answer.

_____

_____

_____

Continue reading about Rosalyn and Peanut. Use the Close Reading and the Hint to help you answer the question.

Close Reading

At first, Rosalyn thinks of the dog as "yappy, pampered little Peanut." **Underline** the sentence on this page that shows how her attitude toward Peanut has changed.

(continued from page 62)

　"Oh! Peanut!" Relief flooded over Rosalyn as she rushed toward the distressed dog. "I've never been so happy to see anyone!" She untangled the leash and embraced the disgruntled animal. Then, referring to her map, Rosalyn retraced her steps and escorted Peanut home.

　Later, when Gram returned home, Rosalyn confessed everything. "I'm sorry," she concluded, "I'd be lost without you—and Peanut."

Hint

What conclusion does Rosalyn reach at the end of the story?

Circle the correct answer.

Why does Rosalyn's attitude toward Peanut change?

A Losing Peanut makes Rosalyn realize how important the dog is to both her and Gram.

B Rosalyn is sure she'll get into trouble for texting instead of watching Peanut.

C Rosalyn's fear of getting lost in the woods makes her understand how Peanut feels.

D Rosalyn is grateful to Peanut for giving her the chance to become a better person.

✎ **Show Your Thinking**

Look at the answer that you chose above. Write down at least two details from the story that helped you identify your answer.

_____

_____

_____

 With a partner, compare and contrast Rosalyn's character at the beginning and end of the story.

Read the drama. Use the Study Buddy and the Close Reading to guide your reading.

Yu does not stay the same throughout the play. To help me analyze his growth, I'm going to underline clues from the play that show how his character develops.

Close Reading

What a character says reveals details about him or her. **Circle** particular words Yu says that show what he thinks about hiking at the play's start.

At what point in the play does Yu's attitude about hiking change? **Draw a box** around the line that shows the shift in his feelings.

Genre: **Drama**

Reaching the Top   *by Ken Ruble*

1   Yu [*breathlessly*]: Just how much farther is it, Lian?

2   Lian: The top is just around the bend—won't be long now!

3   Yu: That's what you said an eternity ago! Are you sure?

4   Lian: Dad and I hiked this trail three times last month.

5   Yu: Seeing the same old rocks sounds as fascinating as watching a turnip grow. Where exactly are we going again?

6   Lian: You're beyond hopeless, Yu. We're on the Kinsman Ridge Trail now, heading to the summit of Cannon Mountain, about 4,080 feet above sea level.

7   Yu: More like 4,080 blisters above sea level. Would it really have been so horrible to have taken the aerial tramway?

8   Lian: That would be so—anti-climactic! It'll be worth it, I swear—there's nothing quite like that magnificent view.

9   Yu [*muttering*]: Tramways are an excellent form of transportation—nice comfy seats, no shooting foot pain . . .

10   Lian [*exclaiming from out of sight*]: Oh, Yu! Come see!

11   [Yu *glumly trudges up the trail to join* Lian *at the summit, which affords a miles-long view of the White Mountains.*]

12   Yu [*breathless with awe, not exhaustion*]: Woooow! This is so not what I expected—we're on top of the world! Look at that giant one over there—can we climb that, too?

13   Lian: Climb a mountain? Oh, that would be too *difficult*.

14   Yu [*earnestly*]: No, we could do it. It would be *worth* it.

Hints

Why does Yu mention the tram more than once?

Use the Hints on this page to help you answer the questions.

1 How does Yu feel about climbing up Cannon Mountain before he reaches the top?

   A He is fascinated by the beauty of the rocks.

   B He is happy to be hiking the trail again.

   C He is troubled by the difficulty of the hike.

   D He is frustrated by how slowly Lian walks.

Which choice suggests that Yu would like the hike to be over?

2 Which sentence from the passage best supports the answer to question 1?

   A "Just how much farther is it, Lian?"

   B "Where exactly are we going again?"

   C "This is so not what I expected—we're on top of the world!"

   D "It would be *worth* it."

What experience causes Yu to change his mind about hiking? What does the hike teach him?

3 How and why does Yu change during the play? Include your ideas about how Yu responds to events as they unfold.

_____

_____

_____

_____

_____

_____

_____

_____

_____

_____

_____

Read the story. Then answer the questions that follow.

from "Departure"

by Sherwood Anderson

1   All through his boyhood and young manhood George Willard had been in the habit of walking on Trunion Pike. He had been in the midst of the great open place on winter nights when it was covered with snow and only the moon looked down at him; he had been there in the fall when bleak winds blew and on summer evenings when the air vibrated with the song of insects. On the April morning he wanted to go there again, to walk again in the silence. He did walk to where the road dipped down by a little stream two miles from town and then turned and walked silently back again. When he got to Main Street clerks were sweeping the sidewalks before the stores. "Hey, you George. How does it feel to be going away?" they asked.

2   The westbound train leaves Winesburg at seven forty-five in the morning. Tom Little is conductor. His train runs from Cleveland to where it connects with a great trunk line railroad with terminals in Chicago and New York. Tom has what in railroad circles is called an "easy run." Every evening he returns to his family. In the fall and spring he spends his Sundays fishing in Lake Erie. He has a round red face and small blue eyes. He knows the people in the towns along his railroad better than a city man knows the people who live in his apartment building.

3   George came down the little incline from the New Willard House at seven o'clock. Tom Willard carried his bag. The son had become taller than the father.

4   On the station platform everyone shook the young man's hand. More than a dozen people waited about. Then they talked of their own affairs. Even Will Henderson, who was lazy and often slept until nine, had got out of bed. George was embarrassed. Gertrude Wilmot, a tall thin woman of fifty who worked in the Winesburg post office, came along the station platform. She had never before paid any attention to George. Now she stopped and put out her hand. In two words she voiced what everyone felt. "Good luck," she said sharply and then turning went on her way.

5   George glanced up and down the car to be sure no one was looking, then took out his pocketbook and counted his money. His mind was occupied with a desire not to appear green. Almost the last words his father had said to him concerned the matter of his behavior when he got to the city. "Be a sharp one," Tom Willard had said. "Keep your eyes on your money. Be awake. That's the ticket. Don't let anyone think you're a greenhorn."

6   After George counted his money he looked out of the window and was surprised to see that the train was still in Winesburg.

7   The young man, going out of his town to meet the adventure of life, began to think but he did not think of anything very big or dramatic. Things like his mother's death, his departure from Winesburg, the uncertainty of his future life in the city, the serious and larger aspects of his life did not come into his mind.

8   He thought of little things—Turk Smollet wheeling boards through the main street of his town in the morning, a tall woman, beautifully gowned, who had once stayed overnight at his father's hotel, Butch

Wheeler the lamp lighter of Winesburg hurrying through the streets on a summer evening and holding a torch in his hand, Helen White standing by a window in the Winesburg post office and putting a stamp on an envelope.

9　　　The young man's mind was carried away by his growing passion for dreams. One looking at him would not have thought him particularly sharp. With the recollection of little things occupying his mind he closed his eyes and leaned back in the car seat. He stayed that way for a long time and when he aroused himself and again looked out of the car window the town of Winesburg had disappeared and his life there had become but a background on which to paint the dreams of his manhood.

Answer the questions. Mark your answers to questions 1 and 2 on the Answer Form to the right.

Answer Form

1　Ⓐ　Ⓑ　Ⓒ　Ⓓ
2　Ⓐ　Ⓑ　Ⓒ　Ⓓ

Number Correct ／2

1　How does George's attitude toward his hometown change as events unfold?

　A　He begins to miss scenes of his childhood.

　B　He feels the town now belongs to his past.

　C　He thinks that the townspeople are critical of him.

　D　He begins to enjoy speaking with the people of the town.

2　George Willard thinks more about his past than his future as he is leaving Winesburg. Which of the following sentences from the passage **best** supports this statement?

　A　"The young man, going out of his town to meet the adventure of life, began to think but he did not think of anything very big or dramatic."

　B　"He thought of little things—Turk Smollet wheeling boards through the main street of his town in the morning. . . ."

　C　"The young man's mind was carried away by his growing passion for dreams."

　D　"One looking at him would not have thought him particularly sharp."

3   Answer Parts A, B, and C below.

Part A

Circle **one** word that describes George based on evidence from the text. There is more than one correct choice listed below.

dreamy	friendly	ambitious
bold	angry	inexperienced

Part B

Find a sentence in the passage with details that support your response to Part A. Write the sentence on the lines below.

_____

_____

Part C

Find a second sentence in the passage with details that support your response to Part A. Write the sentence on the lines below.

_____

_____

4   George has a hard time leaving Winesburg because he realizes how much the people and place have meant to him. Write a paragraph in which you agree or disagree with this claim. Cite information from the text that supports your answer.

_____

_____

_____

_____

_____

_____

✓ **Self Check**   *Go back and see what you can check off on the Self Check on page 44.*

Determining Theme or Central Idea

CCLS

RL.6.2: Determine a theme or central idea of a text and how it is conveyed through particular details....

Theme: *A Time to Change*

Do you know the story of Spider-Man? After Peter Parker is bitten by a mutant spider, he mostly goofs around with his new powers. He doesn't capture criminals; in fact, he lets one go. But this bad decision teaches Peter an important lesson: With great power comes great responsibility. In other words, if you're Spider-Man, you owe it to the world to use your powers to help others. This is a major **theme**, or lesson, of the Spider-Man comics.

Look at the picture below. What lesson, or theme, does the picture seem to convey?

Before you can describe the theme of a picture or story, you must first understand its central idea. The **central idea** is what a picture or story is mainly about.

In the chart below, write two details from the picture that support its central idea.

Central Idea
The boy practiced soccer every day and became the "Most Improved Player."

Detail	Detail	Detail
Used to be worst on the team		

Based on the chart, describe a general lesson the reader might learn from the picture.

_____

While reading, ask yourself: What lesson is the author trying to tell the reader? What details does the author use to tell it? If you can ask and answer such questions, you'll succeed in the "great responsibility" of better understanding what you read.

Read the first four paragraphs of the following story.

Genre: **Realistic Fiction**

Tiana's Scar   *by Maria Kane*

When she was five years old, Tiana was bitten by Rex, her uncle's dog. The bite left a small scar on Tiana's finger.

Now 11, Tiana still avoids dogs wherever she goes. Every morning, Tiana walks an extra block to school to avoid walking by her neighbor's dog, Millie. Millie lies quietly behind a locked gate and doesn't bark much, but Tiana insists on avoiding the dog at all costs.

When her best friend, Kim, laughed at Tiana's extra hike one morning, Tiana exclaimed, "I don't care what you think! Passing a ferocious beast is not how I want to start my day."

"OK, calm down, Tiana," Kim responded as Tiana rushed away angrily.

(continued)

Explore how to answer this question: *"What is the central idea of this part of the story?"*

To find the central idea of this part of the story, underline the most important details.

In the chart below, write down the important details you find. One has been done for you. Then, use these details to find the central idea.

Central Idea

Detail	Detail	Detail
"When she was five years old, Tiana was bitten by Rex, her uncle's dog."		

Continue reading Tiana's story. Use the Close Reading and the Hint to help you answer the question.

Close Reading

Underline important details. Find the sentence that shows Tiana is changing.

(continued from page 70)

One day, Tiana's class took a field trip to an animal shelter. The tour guide explained different types of dogs and their behaviors. Tiana asked the guide many questions and described her fear of dogs. "You should never act scared of a dog," the guide explained. "If you walk calmly and with confidence, dogs are less likely to bark at you." The guide demonstrated this for Tiana and her class.

Walking home from school that day, Tiana decided to be brave and give it a try. She walked confidently past Millie. At first, the dog stood up and stared, but when it saw Tiana holding her head high, it sat down quietly. Tiana felt proud—and not scared at all.

Hint

Which choice best sums up the main message of the story?

Circle the correct answer.

What sentence below best expresses a theme of this story?

A Knowledge can help a person overcome fears.

B Friends stand by you even when times are tough.

C Dogs only bark at people who act scared.

D Confidence does not help people solve problems.

✎ Show Your Thinking

Look at the answer you chose above. Explain which details from the story helped to convey this theme.

_____

_____

_____

 Choose an incorrect answer. Explain to a partner why it is not a theme of the story.

Read the text. Use the Study Buddy and the Close Reading to guide your reading.

Maybe the author is giving clues about the theme by showing how the main character changes. I'm going to underline sentences that show the main character's feelings change.

Close Reading

Why does the narrator think the family trip will be boring? **Underline** the sentence that explains why the narrator is not looking forward to the trip.

What is the narrator's final opinion of Mount Rushmore as a place to see and visit? **Circle** words or phrases that describe the narrator's opinion at the end of the story.

Genre: **Realistic Fiction**

Rushmore   *by Mark Santiago*

1   This summer, my parents planned a trip for us to visit Mount Rushmore. Our sixth-grade class had studied Mount Rushmore, and a visit there sounded really boring. Last summer, we went to a theme park, and I went on about fifty rides. Now I was supposed to enjoy staring at a huge carved rock?

2   As we drove to the airport, I prepared myself for the boredom that I would have to endure over the next week. A few hours later, we landed in Rapid City, and we spent the afternoon driving through a wildlife park, where we saw all kinds of amazing creatures. <u>I was starting to think this trip might not be a huge waste of time after all.</u>

3   Seeing the animals was fascinating, but nothing could prepare me for what we saw the next day. We drove about 30 miles to Mount Rushmore. I knew that Mount Rushmore was a mountain with the faces of the presidents George Washington, Thomas Jefferson, Theodore Roosevelt, and Abraham Lincoln carved into its side. I've seen statues of famous people before. <u>I didn't know why these would be any different, but boy did I find out!</u>

4   When I saw the monument for the first time, I felt frozen in my tracks. Mount Rushmore is simply majestic. The size of the carvings is astonishing—each head is about 60 feet high! I never thought anything could top the theme park adventure I had last year, but now I know that sometimes a big rock can actually take my breath away.

Hints

Which sentence describes how the narrator initially feels about the trip to Mount Rushmore?

Use the Hints on this page to help you answer the questions.

1 In this story, the narrator's feelings are clues about the story's central idea. Which sentence from the story shares an important detail about the author's feelings?

   A "Last summer, we went to a theme park and I went on about fifty rides."

   B "Our sixth-grade class had studied Mount Rushmore, and a visit there sounded really boring."

   C "This summer, my parents planned a trip for us to visit Mount Rushmore."

   D "I've seen statues of famous people before."

Think about why the narrator's feelings about the summer vacation have changed.

2 Which of the following sentences best states a theme about human behavior as described in "Rushmore"?

   A People often dread situations that turn out to be fine or even fun.

   B What is pleasing to one person may be disappointing to another.

   C We should always do what we can to make the best of a difficult situation.

   D Memories of great times in the past can help us through boring times in the present.

What aspects of the trip surprise the narrator? What can readers learn from the narrator's feelings about the trip?

3 Select **two** pieces of evidence from "Rushmore" that support your answer to question 2. Check the boxes of your two choices.

   ☐ "planned a trip for us to visit Mt. Rushmore"

   ☐ "and a visit there sounded really boring"

   ☐ "As we drove to the airport"

   ☐ "the size of the carvings is astonishing"

   ☐ "We drove about 30 miles"

   ☐ "I knew that Mt. Rushmore was a mountain with the faces of presidents"

   ☐ "I've seen statues of famous people before."

Read the story. Then answer the questions that follow.

Vivian's Move

by Miguel Pereira

1   On a gray, rainy morning, Vivian waved goodbye to the red door she had walked through for the last time. She waved goodbye to her bus stop, which looked lonely in the rain. She waved goodbye to her favorite bakery, the grocery store, and the neighborhood softball field, which was a swirl of cold, brown mud. She waved goodbye to the frozen Charles River, and a tear fell down her face as she watched Boston vanish in the rearview mirror of the truck they had rented to move their lives across the country.

2   Vivian had known for over six months that she was going to move to San Francisco, but she didn't want to believe it. Boston had been her home since she was born; it was all she knew, and she loved it. After all, Boston had the best Italian food, beautiful buildings, subways, and—most importantly—her friends. What would she do in a new city without her friends?

3   For the past couple of months, Vivian and her dad had been reading about San Francisco and California. He wanted her to be excited, but she didn't care that San Francisco was on a beautiful bay with scenic hills. She didn't care that the city was known for having some of the best food in the world. She didn't care about the spectacular Golden Gate Bridge and the warmer winters. Boston was beautiful and had wonderful restaurants, and she adored the fall leaves and the snowy winters.

4   Vivian and her dad took two and a half weeks to drive to San Francisco. By the time they crossed the California state line, they had driven through twelve states, four mountain ranges, three national parks, and countless cities and towns. Vivian felt exhausted from the long trip, and now she had to face the reality of why she was on the trip in the first place: California was her new home.

5   The book that said San Francisco is hilly was right. Vivian thought that "hilly" was an understatement. She felt like she was on a roller coaster as they drove through the steep hills of the city. She thought it was too bad that San Francisco didn't get snow like Boston does. These hills would be amazing for sledding! On the other hand, she thought about how much more fun the double-seated bike that she and her dad rode around Boston would be on these hills—at least going down!

6   After driving around for a while, Vivian's dad stopped the truck at the top of a hill in front of a house with a pink door. Her dad wasn't particularly excited about the bubble-gum-colored entrance, but Vivian was thrilled. The red door on their house in Boston suddenly didn't feel so far away. She ran through the door, up the stairs, and into the second room on the right, just like her dad had explained. This was her room, and it was perfect. It had blue walls, a slanted ceiling, and a circle window that looked out on the street. The movers already had set up her bed in the room. San Francisco was starting to feel more like home every minute.

7   Vivian and her dad left their new house after several hours of unpacking to find somewhere to eat dinner. They found themselves in a part of town called North Beach. Vivian smiled when she saw restaurants with names like Mama Mia and Mangia Bene, and red, white, and green flags hanging in the windows. She was delighted to smell the delicious aromas floating in the air. She recognized that this was the Italian section of town and couldn't believe how similar it was to the North End in Boston.

8   Before going home, Vivian and her dad decided to take a trolley car to a nearby beach. They wanted to watch the sun set on their first day in San Francisco. When Vivian stepped off the trolley, she saw the waves lapping onto the beach in front of the silhouette of the Golden Gate Bridge. She wondered if it were possible for San Francisco to be as wonderful as Boston. So far, San Francisco was pretty great. She let out a sigh as she watched the sun turn colors and fade away. She thought about how her friends in Boston were probably asleep, and she wondered what new friends she would meet in San Francisco.

Answer the questions. Mark your answers to questions 1–3 on the Answer Form to the right.

Answer Form

1 Ⓐ Ⓑ Ⓒ Ⓓ
2 Ⓐ Ⓑ Ⓒ Ⓓ   **Number**
3 Ⓐ Ⓑ Ⓒ Ⓓ   **Correct** /3

1 Which sentence helps convey the central idea that Vivian is changing her mind about the move?

A "On a gray, rainy morning, Vivian waved goodbye to the red door she had walked through for the last time."

B "San Francisco was starting to feel more like home every minute."

C "For the past couple of months, Vivian and her dad had been reading about San Francisco and California."

D "Boston was beautiful and had wonderful restaurants, and she adored the fall leaves and the snowy winters."

2 What is the central idea of paragraph 3?

A Vivian's dad thinks San Francisco is better than Boston.

B San Francisco doesn't get snow like Boston does.

C Vivian doesn't want to leave Boston for San Francisco.

D Only Vivian loves the fall and the winter seasons.

3   Vivian starts to like San Francisco better when she sees ways in which it is like Boston. A reader could agree or disagree with this statement. Choose the sentence from the story that could be used to support **agreement** with the statement.

   A   "She thought it was too bad that San Francisco didn't get snow like Boston does."

   B   "On the other hand, she thought about how much more fun the double-seated bike that she and her dad rode around Boston would be on these hills—at least going down!"

   C   "Vivian smiled when she saw restaurants with names like Mama Mia and Mangia Bene, and red, white, and green flags hanging in the windows."

   D   "She wondered if it were possible for San Francisco to be as wonderful as Boston."

4   The story "Vivian's Move" explores the theme that change can be both sad and exciting. Write a short paragraph in which you describe how Vivian is feeling about her move by the end of the story. Use details from the text to support your answer.

_____

_____

_____

_____

_____

_____

_____

_____

_____

_____

_____

_____

_____

 **Self Check**   *Go back and see what you can check off on the Self Check on page 44.*

Summarizing Literary Texts

CCLS
RL.6.2 . . . [P]rovide a summary of the text distinct from personal opinions or judgments.

Theme: *Puzzles and Mysteries*

When you tell someone about your day, you include the important people, places, and events but leave out the little details. Similarly, a **summary** of a story is a brief retelling. It includes only the main characters, setting, conflict, and important events.

When reading a story, you might have **personal opinions**, or feelings, about it. You might also make **judgments** about the story—whether it's believable, well-written, and so on. Although it's fine to have opinions and make judgments, don't include them in a summary. A summary is supposed to be objective, or tell only the facts.

These pictures tell a story. What details would you include in a summary of the pictures?

Now read the summary below. Cross out phrases that seem like opinions or judgments.

In an unrealistic story, a boy and girl enter a living room and see drips coming from the ceiling. Although confused at first, they at least have the sense to check the bathroom above the living room. There, they discover the water is from an overflowing bathtub.

So, what did you cross out? A version of this summary without judgments and opinions would read like this: "A boy and girl enter a living room and see drips coming from the ceiling. Although confused at first, they check the bathroom above the living room. There, they discover the water is from an overflowing bathtub."

Remember that a summary of a literary text includes only its most important aspects. It's perfectly fine to have opinions and make judgments about what you read. When summarizing a story, though, just stick to the facts.

Read the first part of a mystery story about a boy and his brother.

Genre: **Mystery**

Where Is Lady Fish Pants? *by Anita Benton*

"I want to see the lady with the fish pants!" cried Ted. The day was scorching hot, and my four-year-old brother was driving me crazy. We had seen every exhibit in Oceanside Aquarium. Each time, Ted would look around and then yell, "Sam, where's the lady with the fish pants!"

I tried to convince him that there was NO lady with fish pants there, but he just shook his head and said, "She is too here!"

"Let's go back and look at the jellyfish exhibit," I told him. "Maybe she'll be there."

(continued)

Explore how to answer these questions: *"What would be a good summary of this story? What would it include and not include?"*

Remember: A summary is a brief retelling. It does not include your opinions or judgments.

Below is a student's draft of a summary. Read the draft carefully. There are three statements that do not belong. Cross out those statements in the draft that do not belong in the final summary.

> In this well-written part of the story, Sam and his brother Ted visit Oceanside Aquarium. Ted says he wants to see the lady with the fish pants and acts like a spoiled brat. Sam says that there is no lady with fish pants, but Ted insists she's there. Ted should listen to his brother.

In the chart, list what you crossed out. Then explain why they don't belong in the summary.

Statements That Don't Belong	Why They Don't Belong
"In this well-written part of the story"	It gives a judgment about how the story was written.

Continue reading the mystery "Where Is Lady Fish Pants?" Use the Close Reading and the Hint to help you answer the question.

Close Reading

Underline the names of the characters and any clues that help you understand the story's setting and events.

(continued from page 78)

    At the jellyfish exhibit, Ted screamed, "Sam! There's no lady with fish pants here!" Everybody looked at me, and I quickly rushed him out the door.

    "Look," I told him, "Mom's picking us up soon. Let's hang out in the gift shop until she gets here."

    "Will the lady with the fish pants be there?"

    "Sure, maybe," I said. We walked in, and I expected to hear Ted scream—but instead he was smiling. He held up a stuffed mermaid for me to see. "See! Lady with the fish pants!"

Hint

A good summary describes characters, setting, and important events.

Circle the correct answer.

Which sentence best summarizes this part of the story?

A Sam should have realized that Ted was telling the truth about the lady with the fish pants.

B The mystery of the lady with the fish pants is solved when Sam and Ted visit the gift shop and Ted sees the stuffed mermaid.

C Sam and Ted's mother is supposed to pick them up soon.

D Sam got tired of listening to Ted whine so he took him into the gift shop.

✎ **Show Your Thinking**

Explain why the other answer choices are not good summaries of the text.

_____

_____

_____

_____

 With a partner, take turns summarizing the end of the story in your own words. Include characters, setting, and important events, and avoid giving any opinions or judgments.

©Curriculum Associates, LLC   Copying is not permitted.

Read the text. Use the Study Buddy and Close Reading to guide your reading.

Because this is a mystery, I know there will be a question and clues that lead to the answer.

Close Reading

How did Harrison's camera get to the top of the control tower? **Circle** a sentence that offers an explanation.

What are some key events in the story? **Underline** evidence in the text that tells what led up to the mystery being solved.

Genre: **Mystery**

Mystery on "The Blue Ghost"   *by Saj Mobi*

1   "Let's pack up," Mr. Sanchez told the twenty students in the gigantic aircraft carrier, the U.S.S. *Lexington*. To become acquainted with life aboard a Navy ship during World War II, they had slept in the floating museum's narrow bunks.

2   Suddenly, Harrison cried out, "My camera—it's gone!" He emptied his duffel bag and pawed through his possessions.

3   "When did you last see it?" said Mr. Sanchez.

4   "On the flight deck, when we were watching pelicans."

5   Mr. Sanchez sighed. The carrier's flight deck could hold three football fields, but at least it narrowed things down.

6   "Maybe the blue ghost took it," teased Victoria.

7   "Forget about the ghost stories you heard. Why is the aircraft carrier really called 'The Blue Ghost'?" Mr. Sanchez asked. One student answered that during World War II, the U.S.S. *Lexington* was reported to have sunk four times, so the Japanese gave it its ghostly nickname.

8   "Right. Now, to the flight deck, class!" The students trudged up the stairs. "There it is!" shouted Harrison. He pointed to the control tower, which rose 150 feet high. Dangling from a tall antenna was a silver rectangle.

9   "Nobody could have gotten way up there!" said Victoria.

10   "Perhaps not, but look!" exclaimed Mr. Sanchez. Near the dangling camera, a pelican flapped lazily toward the outer bay, scanning the water for the silver flash of a tasty fish.

Hints

Remember, summaries should not contain judgments. Which choice does not contain a fact about the story?

Use the Hints on this page to help you answer the questions.

1 A student wrote the following summary of the story.

> Mr. Sanchez's class visits the aircraft carrier *Lexington*. When it's time to leave, Harrison can't find his camera. He should have kept the camera in his bag. The class looks for the camera on the flight deck. They find it dangling from a tall antenna near a pelican.

Which sentence should not have been included?

A "Mr. Sanchez's class visits the aircraft carrier *Lexington*."

B "When it's time to leave, Harrison can't find his camera."

C "He should have kept the camera in his bag."

D "The class looks for the camera on the flight deck."

Which sentence explains what actually happened to the camera?

2 Which sentence best summarizes how the mystery was solved?

A The carrier is called "The Blue Ghost" because it was reported to have sunk four times during World War II.

B The class figured out that the pelican had mistaken the silver camera for a fish.

C Harrison brilliantly realized that the camera was on an antenna.

D Harrison should not have brought his camera with him because it created a big problem.

Where does this story take place? Who are the main characters? What events lead to the mystery being solved?

3 Write a brief summary of the story "Mystery on 'The Blue Ghost.'" Include information about the characters, setting, and events.

_____

_____

_____

_____

_____

_____

_____

_____

_____

Read the story. Then answer the questions that follow.

from *The Magician's Elephant*

by Kate DiCamillo

1   At the end of the century before last, in the market square of the city of Baltese, there stood a boy with a hat on his head and a coin in his hand. The boy's name was Peter Augustus Duchene, and the coin that he held did not belong to him but was instead the property of his guardian, an old soldier named Vilna Lutz, who had sent the boy to the market for fish and bread.

2   That day in the market square, in the midst of the entirely unremarkable and absolutely ordinary stalls of the fishmongers and cloth merchants and bakers and silversmiths, there had appeared, without warning or fanfare, the red tent of a fortuneteller. Attached to the fortuneteller's tent was a piece of paper, and penned upon the paper in a cramped but unapologetic hand were these words: *The most profound and difficult questions that could possibly be posed by the human mind or heart will be answered within for the price of one florit.*

3   Peter read the small sign once, and then again. The audacity of the words, their dizzying promise, made it difficult, suddenly, for him to breathe. He looked down at the coin, the single florit, in his hand.

4   "But I cannot do it," he said to himself. "Truly, I cannot, for if I do, Vilna Lutz will ask where the money has gone and I will have to lie, and it is a very dishonorable thing to lie."

5   He put the coin in his pocket. He took the soldier's hat off his head and then put it back on. He stepped away from the sign and came back to it and stood considering, again, the outrageous and wonderful words.

6   "But I must know," he said at last. He took the florit from his pocket. "I want to know the truth. And so I will do it. But I will not lie about it, and in that way, I will remain at least partly honorable." With these words, Peter stepped into the tent and handed the fortuneteller the coin.

7   And she, without even looking at him, said, "One florit will buy you one answer and only one. Do you understand?"

8   "Yes," said Peter.

9   He stood in the small patch of light making its sullen way through the open flap of the tent. He let the fortuneteller take his hand. She examined it slowly, moving her eyes back and forth and back and forth, as if there were a whole host of very small words inscribed there, an entire book about Peter Augustus Duchene composed atop his palm.

10   "Huh," she said at last. She dropped his hand and squinted up at his face. "But, of course, you are just a boy."

11   "I am ten years old," said Peter. He took the hat from his head and stood as straight and tall as he was able. "And I am training to become a soldier, brave and true. But it does not matter how old I am. You took the florit, so now you must give me my answer."

12   "A soldier brave and true?" said the fortuneteller. She laughed and spat on the ground. "Very well, soldier brave and true, if you say it is so, then it is so. Ask me your question."

13   Peter felt a small stab of fear. What if, after all this time, he could not bear the truth? What if he did not really want to know?

14   "Speak," said the fortuneteller. "Ask."

15   "My parents," said Peter.

16   "That is your question?" said the fortuneteller. "They are dead."

17   Peter's hands trembled. "That is not my question," he said. "I know that already. You must tell me something that I do not know. You must tell me of another—you must tell me . . ."

18   The fortuneteller narrowed her eyes. "Ah," she said. "Her? Your sister? That is your question? Very well, she lives."

19   Peter's heart seized upon the words. He closed his eyes. He concentrated. "If she lives, then I must find her, so my question is, how do I make my way there, to where she is?"

20   He kept his eyes closed; he waited.

21   "The elephant," said the fortuneteller.

22   "What?" Peter said. He opened his eyes, certain that he had misunderstood.

23   "You must follow the elephant," said the fortuneteller. "She will lead you there."

Answer the questions. Mark your answers to questions 1–3 on the Answer Form to the right.

Answer Form

1 Ⓐ Ⓑ Ⓒ Ⓓ

2 Ⓐ Ⓑ Ⓒ Ⓓ **Number** /3

3 Ⓐ Ⓑ Ⓒ Ⓓ **Correct**

1   Which event belongs in a summary of the story?

    A   Peter looks down at the coin in his hand.

    B   Peter takes off the soldier's hat, then puts it back on.

    C   The fortuneteller calls Peter a brave soldier.

    D   The fortuneteller tells Peter to follow the elephant.

2 Which sentence expresses an opinion?

A Peter has a coin that belongs to his guardian.

B Peter sees a fortuneteller's sign pinned to a tent.

C Peter learns that his sister is still alive.

D Peter makes a good decision in giving up his coin.

3 Which sentence **best** summarizes paragraphs 4 through 6?

A Peter walks around the fortuneteller's red tent.

B Peter worries about telling a lie to his guardian, Vilna Lutz.

C Peter has trouble deciding whether to visit the fortuneteller.

D Peter tells himself that the truth is definitely worth knowing.

4 Write a brief summary of the excerpt. Include at least **three** details from the story.

_____

_____

_____

_____

_____

_____

_____

_____

_____

_____

 **Self Check** *Go back and see what you can check off on the Self Check on page 44.*

Read the story. Then answer the questions that follow.

In the 1930s, the United States was stuck in a deep economic depression that left millions of people without jobs. In part of the Great Plains, an environmental disaster known as the Dust Bowl added to the hard times. A long drought combined with years of poor farming practices made the land vulnerable to extreme wind erosion. Farmers watched helplessly as the topsoil that had once nourished their crops blew away. In this fictional selection, a boy and his family struggle with the hardships of the Dust Bowl.

Dust

by Charles Grayson

1   As Edwin rested his cheek against the side of his cow, Nelly, he could hear the wind whistling through the barn walls and see the air begin to darken with dust. Annie and Jewel were giggling as they played in the hayloft above him when one of the girls began to wheeze. Edwin quickly finished milking the cow and called to his sisters. "Hurry up, girls," he said, "another black blizzard is coming."

2   The wind suddenly picked up strength, and before Edwin's eyes, the farmhouse—only 50 feet away—became nearly invisible. Without hesitation, Edwin grabbed two pieces of heavy twine, tied one around each girl's waist, and then tied the two girls together. He took Annie's hand and instructed her to hold tightly to Jewel. Leaning into the blinding wind, Edwin slowly navigated them back to the house.

3   Inside, Ma was relieved to see the children. With a sigh, she took the milk from Edwin, eyeing the familiar dust that she would try to skim off before serving the milk to her family. Although it was early morning, the dust storm outside made the small farmhouse dark and dismal. Edwin slapped the dirt from his jacket with his hands. He was weary of the dust, too, but he was smiling inside because tomorrow his father was coming home.

4   The next morning dawned clear and calm. Edwin swept the house while his mother worked in the yard, rescuing her daffodils from the dust that had drifted against the foundation of the house like gritty snow. The clatter of a rundown automobile heralded the arrival of Edwin's father, and the boy raced outside.

5   The family gathered around Pa, who hugged each one of them tightly. He had been in Arizona for three weeks picking cotton. This spring the ground was hard and barren, and the constant dust storms made it impossible to cultivate crops. Pa had to find some way to earn money—his children were wearing tattered hand-me-downs, and his small herd of cattle was slowly starving.

6   When Ma asked about the work, Pa said that the wages he earned were far less than what had been promised. Still, he'd brought home enough money to see them through another month. Eventually, the joy of being reunited with his family faded, and the careworn expression returned to Pa's face.

7   After Pa had been home a few days, Edwin overheard his parents having a serious discussion. "I just don't know if I can leave our home," Ma said, a note of grief in her voice. Pa had heard there was work on commercial farms in California, where cotton, oranges, and other crops grew nearly year round.

8   "I know it's not like owning our own farm, but what choice do we have?" Pa pleaded. Afterward, Ma went into the yard and stood for a long time by her beloved lilac bush, staring out at the desolate fields.

9   Later, Pa asked Edwin to ride the horse into town to purchase provisions. Edwin rode at a slow pace, thinking. He didn't like it when his parents argued, and he didn't like it when his father had to leave home to work. Most of all, Edwin wished there was something he could do to assist his family. At the store, he walked past the half-empty shelves to the back counter and asked Mr. Harburger for beans and flour.

10   As Edwin waited, something bright and orange caught his eye. It was an old advertisement on the shelf in front of him—a photograph of a glistening orange grove with the words "Sunny California" splashed across the top. Edwin had never seen an orange grove before. Studying the picture, Edwin's face brightened. "Take it," Mr. Harburger said with a wink. At home, Edwin tacked the picture up next to his bed. One day, Edwin even caught his mother examining the photograph of the orange grove, smiling for the first time in a long time.

11   When autumn arrived, Edwin's parents learned the government was offering to buy starving livestock for slaughter. Most farmers knew their animals could not survive another winter, so they accepted the offer in exchange for some much-needed cash. After a long discussion, Edwin's parents did the same. Edwin sensed a change was coming.

12   The cow Nelly remained, but Edwin could see that she was becoming desperately thin. The next day, Edwin sold Nelly at the Baileys' farm. The Baileys were doing better than most folks, though Edwin couldn't say why. He returned home with 16 dollars in his pocket and a little relief knowing that Nelly would be cared for.

13   Later that evening, Edwin's parents made an important announcement: they would be packing whatever would fit into their old automobile and moving to California. Then Edwin made his own announcement. "Here," he said, handing his father the 16 dollars. "We can buy fuel with this!"

1　Read this sentence.

Edwin wants to help his family during this difficult time.

Which of the following sentences from the story **best** supports this statement?

A "After Pa had been home a few days, Edwin overheard his parents having a serious discussion."

B "Later, Pa asked Edwin to ride the horse into town to purchase provisions."

C "At home, Edwin tacked the picture up next to his bed."

D "The next day, Edwin sold Nelly at the Baileys' farm."

2　Which statement **best** supports the idea that the Dust Bowl made it difficult for families to survive?

A "With a sigh, she took the milk from Edwin, eyeing the familiar dust that she would try to skim off before serving the milk to her family."

B "Although it was early morning, the dust storm outside made the small farmhouse dark and dismal."

C "He was weary of the dust, too, but he was smiling inside because tomorrow his father was coming home."

D "Edwin swept the house while his mother worked in the yard, rescuing her daffodils from the dust that had drifted against the foundation of the house like gritty snow."

3　Which statement **best** expresses the theme of this story?

A Don't rely on others for help.

B You can't make a person change.

C Try to find the good in every situation.

D Be content with what you have.

4 The family in the story demonstrates the idea that people are adaptable, or willing to change when needed. Which sentence from the passage **best** shows this idea?

   A "Annie and Jewel were giggling as they played in the hayloft above him when one of the girls began to wheeze."

   B "Although it was early morning, the dust storm outside made the small farmhouse dark and dismal."

   C "Most farmers knew their animals could not survive another winter, so they accepted the offer in exchange for some much-needed cash."

   D "He returned home with 16 dollars in his pocket and a little relief knowing that Nelly would be cared for."

5 Answer Parts A and B below.

Part A

Based on the passage, how do Ma's feelings about moving change over time?

   A She becomes more and more resistant to the idea of moving.

   B She grows more comfortable with the idea of moving.

   C She likes the idea of moving initially, then comes to dislike it.

   D She becomes more confident that the family should not move.

Part B

Which sentence from the passage **best** shows Ma's changing feelings about moving?

   A "With a sigh, she took the milk from Edwin, eyeing the familiar dust that she would try to skim off before serving the milk to her family."

   B "'I just don't know if I can leave our home,' Ma said, a note of grief in her voice."

   C "Afterward, Ma went into the yard and stood for a long time by her beloved lilac bush, staring out at the desolate fields."

   D "One day, Edwin even caught his mother examining the photograph of the orange grove, smiling for the first time in a long time."

6   What evidence in the story helped you to know that the family would move to California, even before Edwin's parents made their announcement? Describe how the events in the story support this inference.

_____

_____

_____

_____

_____

7   Write a summary that includes the conflict in the story and how it is resolved. Use details from the story to support your answer.

_____

_____

_____

_____

_____

_____

8 Answer Parts A, B, and C below.

Part A

Circle only **one** word that describes Edwin based on evidence from the text. There is more than one correct choice listed below.

thoughtless	resourceful	timid
observant	optimistic	stubborn

Part B

Find **one** sentence in the passage with details that support your response to Part A. Write that sentence on the lines below.

_____

_____

_____

_____

Part C

Find a **second** sentence in the passage with details that support your response to Part A. Write that sentence on the lines below.

_____

_____

_____

_____

Performance Task—Extended Response

9 What inferences can you make about Edwin's character based on his actions in the story? What events and details from the text helped you make those inferences? Write an essay of two to three paragraphs explaining your answer.

In your answer, be sure to
- explain what inferences you made about Edwin while reading the story
- explain what events and details from the text support your inferences
- cite evidence from the story in your answer

Check your writing for correct spelling, grammar, capitalization, and punctuation.

_____

_____

_____

_____

_____

_____

_____

_____

_____

_____

_____

_____

_____

_____

_____

_____

_____

_____

_____

_____

_____

_____

_____

_____

Unit 3
Craft and Structure in Informational Text

Have you ever thought about the work that goes into taking a photograph? A photographer carefully adjusts the lighting and camera angles to capture exactly what he wants to appear in the photo. The photographer has a purpose in mind and carefully **crafts** the photo to achieve that purpose and to express his thoughts, or point of view, about the subject. An author of informational text also has a purpose in mind. The author chooses words, phrases, and sentences in the same way as the photographer chooses light and camera angles. These elements are carefully selected to fit into the overall structure, or framework, that the author has chosen for the text.

In this unit, you will learn to pay attention to the choices an author makes in crafting a text. You will figure out the meanings of words, including words that the author has used in unusual or very specific ways. You will also learn how the author chooses a structure and expresses a definite point of view to achieve his or her purpose. Look through your camera lens, focus carefully, and prepare to capture some fascinating information!

✓ **Self Check**   **Fill out the Self Check on the next page.** ▶

Before starting this unit, check off the skills you know below. As you complete each lesson, see how many more you can check off!

✓ Self Check

I know how to:	Before this unit	After this unit
explain the meanings of words and phrases in a text.	☐	☐
determine figurative, connotative, and technical meanings of words in a text.	☐	☐
describe how each part of an informational text fits into the overall structure.	☐	☐
explain an author's point of view and how it is expressed in a text.	☐	☐

Lesson 10 Part 1: Introduction

Determining Word Meanings:
Figurative, Connotative & Technical

CCLS

RI.6.4: Determine the meaning of words and phrases as they are used in a text, including figurative, connotative, and technical meanings.

Theme: *The Power of Music*

Think about the lyrics to your favorite song. What pictures or images do they bring to mind? How do the words make you feel?

Writers use words in different ways, depending on their purpose. They might use words with a **figurative meaning** that is different from their literal, or usual, meaning. They might use words with a **technical meaning** when writing about a specific subject area, like music. Sometimes writers choose words with a positive or negative **connotative meaning** to show how they feel about the topic. You can figure out an author's intended meaning by thinking about the word's **context**, or the text that comes before and after it.

Look at the picture below and read how the boy and girl describe the music. Circle words and clues in the picture that tell you how each person feels about the music.

The words *intense* and *earsplitting* are both ways of saying that something is loud. But *intense* suggests positive feelings, while *earsplitting* suggests negative ones. Although they have similar meanings, the words have different connotations.

Look again at how the girl describes the music. Are her ears literally splitting? _____

What does she really mean? _____

Why do you think she uses that word? _____

The word *earsplitting* is a figurative expression. It is an exaggeration used to describe something unpleasantly loud.

Knowing the literal meaning of a word or phrase is not always enough. It's also a good idea to pay attention to the context in which that word or phrase appears. Context will help you figure out if the author is using a word for its technical, connotative, or figurative meaning.

Read the first two paragraphs of an account about the famous musician Chuck Berry.

Genre: **Historical Account**

The Father of Rock and Roll   *by LaTisha Hammond*

Rock musicians can trace their roots back to one individual: Chuck Berry. He rose to stardom in the 1950s with music featuring driving beats and catchy guitar riffs—short series of notes that repeat throughout a song. Berry's groundbreaking sound combined rhythm and blues with country music. As a guitarist, he was known for his phrasing. Aerosmith guitarist Joe Perry describes the way Berry grouped notes into quick bursts as "that double-note stop, where you get the two notes bending against each other and they make that rock & roll sound."

Berry's clever lyrics about high school and dancing also won over teenage audiences. The words to his songs told the stories of their generation. "Everything I wrote about wasn't about me, but about the people listening," said Berry.

(continued)

Explore how to answer this question: *"What does the author mean when she says that Chuck Berry 'was known for his phrasing'?"*

The sentence says that, as a guitarist, Berry was known for his phrasing. The usual meaning of *phrasing* is "putting a group of words together." What does this term mean in music?

The author is using a word's technical meaning here. In order to understand that meaning, look for clues in the sentences that come before and after it. Fill in the context chart.

Example	Context Clues
"As a guitarist, he was known for his phrasing."	

On the lines below, state the technical meaning of the word *phrasing*. Then explain how the context helped you figure it out.

_____

_____

Meanings: Figurative, Connotative & Technical

Continue reading about Chuck Berry. Use the Close Reading and the Hint to help you answer the question.

Close Reading

The author says Berry "shined a light on many rock stars' paths." How can the context help you understand this figurative expression?

(continued from page 96)

Berry also revolutionized guitar showmanship with his signature "duck walk." It involved playing guitar while squatting and moving forward. One leg would swing back and forth in the air while he hopped on the other.

Chuck Berry has shined a light on many rock stars' paths. Even the Beatles' John Lennon credited Berry's sound and style. He said, "If you tried to give rock and roll another name, you might call it 'Chuck Berry.'"

Hint

Substitute each choice for the phrase in the text to see which meaning makes sense.

Circle the correct answer.

Based on the text, which of the following is closest to the figurative meaning of the phrase "shined a light on many rock stars' paths"?

A made it possible for musicians to play rock and roll for a living

B drew attention to the talents of other rock musicians, making them famous

C helped musicians learn their craft by studying his songwriting and performing

D exposed the secrets of rock musicians and the music business

✎ **Show Your Thinking**

Look at the answer that you chose above. Explain how the context in the paragraph helped you understand the meaning of "shined a light on many rock stars' paths."

_____

_____

 With a partner, discuss other words from both parts of the account that have figurative, technical, or connotative meanings.

Read the text. Use the Study Buddy and the Close Reading to guide your reading.

Authors use words with connotative meaning to show how they feel about a topic. As I read, I'll look for words that suggest the author's feelings about guitars.

Close Reading

What does the context suggest about the meaning of the phrase "drowned out" as it is used in paragraph 3?

What does a magnetic pickup do to the sound of a guitar? **Circle** sentences that explain this technical term.

Genre: **Historical Account**

The Evolution of the Guitar   *by Pat Frisell*

1   Guitars are dynamic, evolving instruments. Today, guitars are flat-bodied wonders with fretted necks and six strings. Frets are metal pieces cut into the neck at specific intervals. By pressing a string down onto a fret, guitarists change the string's length. This changes its tone when it vibrates.

2   The guitar has a rich history that dates back to ancient times, but the first instruments that modern audiences would recognize as guitars developed in the 15th century. They arrived in Spain from Northern Africa. Initially, some had only four strings and were much smaller than guitars today. Guitars were all acoustic—that is, their melodic sound was made from string vibrations in their hollow bodies. People used them to accompany songs and poetry.

3   Acoustic guitars delight the ears but are not very loud. By the 20th century, they were often drowned out by trumpets, pianos, and even singers. Few could actually hear them.

4   This changed in the 1920s when Lloyd Loar designed the first magnetic pickup, which could capture the acoustic guitar's string vibrations and amplify them electronically through speakers. A guitar could now hold its own with louder instruments. This was the birth of the electric guitar.

5   Now, guitarists can either amplify their acoustic hollow-body guitars with pickups or play solid-body electric guitars. The ways guitars sound, and even how they are built, continue to develop in fascinating ways.

Hints

Which choice contains words that show the author's personal feelings about guitars?

Look for clues before and after this phrase in the text that help you understand its figurative meaning.

Amplify is used twice by the author. Find both instances and think about their context.

Use the Hints on this page to help you answer the questions.

1 Which words from the account have positive connotations?

    A *fretted, acoustic, vibrations, amplify*

    B *evolving, specific, modern, solid*

    C *wonders, rich, delight, fascinating*

    D *ancient, smaller, hollow, louder*

2 What does the author mean when he writes that guitars were often "drowned out" by singers and other instruments?

    A There was a chance that guitars would be replaced by other instruments.

    B The moisture in a hollow-body guitar kept it from being loud enough.

    C It was difficult to hear acoustic guitars over other instruments and voices.

    D Other instruments were becoming more popular than the acoustic guitar.

3 Describe the technical meaning of the word *amplify*. Include two context clues from the account that help you provide its definition.

_____

_____

_____

_____

_____

_____

_____

_____

_____

_____

Read this excerpt from a book. Then answer the questions that follow.

from *The Power of Music*

by Elena Mannes

1   Many musicians have an instinctive understanding of how musical sound interacts with our bodies. They know—they feel—that sound impacts our bodies in a way no other art does. Opera singer Irene Gubrud says, "As a very young child, I experienced who I was through sound. I felt whole."

2   Daniel Bernard Roumain, a young cross-genre violinist who is known as DBR, thinks one reason music is so powerful is that sound actually penetrates our bodies: "You know when someone says that a piece of music 'touched me' or 'moved me,' it's very literal. The sound of my voice enters your ear canal and it's moving your eardrum. That's a very intimate act. I am very literally touching you, and when you speak to me, you are literally touching me. And then we extend that principle to the sound of a violin."

3   The conductor and pianist Daniel Barenboim believes that our early connection to sound is another reason for its power—one that in today's world we sometimes forget. He thinks that because we live in a very visual society we're more aware of what we see than what we hear. But he reminds us that the latest scientific evidence reveals that the ear, which we now know is active even in the womb, has an advantage over the eye. He also says: "The ear has a head start over the eye, which doesn't see anything until it comes out. The eye is also something that one can control more fully. If you don't like the way I look, and you don't want to see me, you close your eyes and I disappear. But if you don't like my voice and you're in the same room, then you cannot shut your ears in a natural way. Sound literally penetrates the human body."

4   This human relationship to sound starts early. The fetus begins to develop an auditory system between seventeen and nineteen weeks. Already we are in a world of sound, of breath and heartbeat, of rhythm and vibration. But how do we know what the fetus actually hears? Until recently, there were different theories. Some doctors thought that the fetus could hear only some frequencies, probably high ones. It certainly wasn't known whether we could hear and respond to music before birth until the groundbreaking research of Sheila Woodward, a South African, who wanted to know more about musical sound in the womb. She was a young scientist in the early 1990s—and pregnant; she wondered what music her own child was being exposed to before birth. In her studies at the University of Capetown, she worked with the Institute for Maritime Technology to adapt an underwater microphone so it could be placed in the uterus. . . .

5   As we listen to the recordings that Woodward conducted with several mothers in early stages of labor, we first hear the rhythmic sound of blood coursing through the uterine artery. Says Woodward, "Nature allows us to evolve with rhythm all around us." And her recordings reveal that a landscape of musical sound does indeed surround the fetus. Along with the natural womb sounds, we can hear the strains of a Bach Brandenburg Concerto being played, or the melody of "Mary Had a Little Lamb" as Woodward sings in a normal tone of voice. The recordings show that the very high frequencies, like the sharp attack of an instrument, are attenuated and sound a bit muffled. The overall effect is like listening to music underwater. But when listening to the human voice, one can still detect whether it's a woman or a man. And the tonal quality of the voice comes through.

6   Just because the sound of music exists in the womb doesn't necessarily mean that the fetus hears it. Yet, the "startle response" of the fetus was measured as well, and Woodward's team found that when music was played, the fetal heart rate became slightly elevated. Woodward says it was clear that the fetus reacted, as if to say, "Something's happened and now there's music!" Other studies show that even if only the mother hears music—if she has headphones on, and it is music that she finds soothing—the baby's heart rate lowers while the mother is listening. If the mother finds a certain piece of music stressful, the baby's heart rate goes up. So the fetus is echoing the mother's response to the quality of the music.

7   Woodward is convinced that we begin learning about music even before birth. She points out that even when music that can penetrate the womb is absent, the fetus is surrounded by those natural rhythms of the body—heartbeat and pulse and breath.

Answer the questions. Mark your answers to questions 1–4 on the Answer Form to the right.

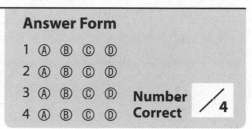

Answer Form

1. Ⓐ Ⓑ Ⓒ Ⓓ
2. Ⓐ Ⓑ Ⓒ Ⓓ
3. Ⓐ Ⓑ Ⓒ Ⓓ   **Number**
4. Ⓐ Ⓑ Ⓒ Ⓓ   **Correct**   /4

1   In paragraph 1, when opera singer Irene Gubrud says "I felt whole," what does she mean?

  A   She always knew she would grow up to sing opera.

  B   She realized that nothing was missing from her life.

  C   She understood that sound affected her body.

  D   She believed that opera was the best type of music.

2   Read this sentence from paragraph 5.

    The overall effect is like listening to music underwater.

  What does this sentence tell the reader about how the music sounded?

  A   The music sounded like waves.

  B   The music sounded loud and thunderous.

  C   The music sounded muted and distant.

  D   The music sounded mysterious.

3 Which sentence from the book excerpt shows the author's positive feeling about music?

  A "They know—they feel—that sound impacts our bodies in a way no other art does."

  B "He thinks that because we live in a very visual society we're more aware of what we see than what we hear."

  C "This human relationship to sound starts early."

  D "Woodward is convinced that we begin learning about music even before birth."

4 Which phrase from the book excerpt **best** helps a reader understand the meaning of the term "startle response"?

  A "the fetal heart rate became slightly elevated"

  B "the baby's heart rate lowers while the mother is listening"

  C "the mother finds a certain piece of music stressful"

  D "the fetus is echoing the mother's response"

5 The author uses the phrase "tonal quality" in paragraph 5. Review the context surrounding the phrase. Then explain the meaning of this technical term in your own words.

_____

_____

_____

_____

_____

_____

_____

 **Self Check** *Go back and see what you can check off on the Self Check on page 94.*

Lesson 11   Part 1: Introduction 👥

Analyzing Text Structures

CCLS
RI.6.5: Analyze how a particular sentence, paragraph, chapter, or section fits into the overall structure of a text and contributes to the development of the ideas.

Theme: *Ancient Civilizations*

Suppose you put together a jigsaw puzzle. You'd fit the pieces together to form a picture. But what if one piece were missing? You wouldn't be able to see the image as a whole.

Authors have to fit ideas together just as carefully. The way they organize information is called **text structure**. Depending on their purpose, authors might choose to organize their ideas in different ways. They may present a **problem and solution**; order events from earliest to latest (**chronologically**); **compare and contrast** people, things, or ideas; or explain **causes and effects**. Whichever method they choose, the sentences, paragraphs, and sections must work together to present information clearly and logically.

Look at the image below. Circle each reference to Greece. Underline each reference to Rome. Think about how the parts fit together to form a whole.

| Ancient Rome and Greece both began as city-states. | Greece had no central authority, but Rome was the capital of its empire. | The Greeks were known for science, philosophy, and art. | The Romans, on the other hand, were known for their military might and their civil engineering. |

Read the chart below to see how the sentences in the puzzle work together. Notice how each part develops the main idea. Fill in the function of Sentence 4 on your own.

Part	Function
Sentence 1	introduces the topic of the paragraph, ancient Rome and Greece
Sentence 2	contrasts the way the two city-states were organized
Sentence 3	adds information about what the Greeks were known for
Sentence 4	

Like the pieces in a puzzle, the parts of a text work together to make something bigger. As a reader, think about how the sentences, paragraphs, and sections work together to convey information and develop ideas. Remember that the parts are in order for a reason—just as a puzzle piece fits only where it belongs.

Read the first part of a history article about an important discovery.

Genre: **History Article**

from "Terra-Cotta Army Protects First Emperor's Tomb" *by John Roach,* National Geographic

Workers digging a well outside the city of Xi'an, China, in 1974 struck upon one of the greatest archaeological discoveries in the world: a life-size clay soldier poised for battle.

The diggers notified Chinese authorities, who dispatched government archaeologists to the site.

They found not one, but thousands of clay soldiers, each with unique facial expressions and positioned according to rank. And though largely gray today, patches of paint hint at once brightly colored clothes. Further excavations have revealed swords, arrow tips, and other weapons, many in pristine condition.

(continued)

Explore how to answer this question: *"How does paragraph 3 build on the information presented in paragraphs 1 and 2?"*

This part of the article tells how the clay soldiers were discovered. It follows a chronological structure. Each paragraph adds important events or details to the story of the discovery.

Read the paragraphs again. What was the first event in the discovery? Put a number 1 beside it. Continue to number the other events in the text. One of the sentences should not be numbered.

Fill in the chart below to tell what each paragraph adds to your understanding of the terra-cotta army and its discovery.

Part	Function
Paragraph 1	
Paragraph 2	continues the account of the discovery process by explaining how archaeologists got involved

Think about the purpose of paragraph 3. Explain how the sentences in paragraph 3 develop the information provided in paragraphs 1 and 2.

_____

_____

Continue reading about the terra-cotta army. Use the Close Reading and the Hint to help you answer the question.

Close Reading

These paragraphs tell more about what the archaeologists found. How does each sentence and paragraph develop key ideas of the text?

(continued from page 104)

The soldiers are in trenchlike, underground corridors. In some of the corridors, clay horses are aligned four abreast; behind them are wooden chariots.

The terra-cotta army, as it is known, is part of an elaborate [tomb] created to accompany the first emperor of China into the afterlife, according to archaeologists. . . .

Archaeologists estimate the pits may contain as many as 8,000 figures, but the total may never be known.

Hint

Reread the first paragraph on page 104. What phrase is used to describe the discovery?

Circle the correct answer.

How does the final sentence build on a key idea mentioned in the first paragraph?

A It suggests there is no point in trying to learn more about the terra-cotta army because it is too big.

B It explains how extensive the site is and suggests that the story of the discovery is not yet complete.

C It reveals how little the government's archaeologists actually know about the terra-cotta army.

D It implies that archaeologists do not plan any further exploration and must rely on existing findings.

✎ **Show Your Thinking**

Look at the answer that you chose above. Explain why your choice is correct.

_____

_____

 Discuss with a partner how the two parts of the article work together to present important ideas about the terra-cotta army. How does the second half build on the first?

Read the historical account. Use the Study Buddy and the Close Reading to guide your reading.

I can use the subheads to help me understand how ideas will be presented. I see that there is a question and two possible answers. That's probably how the text is organized.

Close Reading

According to the author, what have visitors to Stonehenge wondered about? **Draw boxes** around details that provide possible answers.

How do paragraphs 3 and 4 fit into the overall structure? **Underline** one sentence from each paragraph that helps you understand their purpose.

Genre: **Historical Account**

Secrets in the Stones   *by Michael Burgan*

1   Huge stone slabs dot a grassy field on a plain located in southern England. Some stones lie scattered; others stand upright and form part of a large circle. For centuries, visitors have wondered how and why this giant structure was built.

What Are the Secrets of Stonehenge?

2   These slabs are part of Stonehenge, an ancient stone construction that dates back 5,000 years. In their quest to unlock the structure's mysteries, archaeologists have found many artifacts at the site including animal bones, stone tools, and bone skewers. But even though some questions about the site's purpose have been answered, many remain.

Two Possible Answers

3   At first, the site included just a circular ditch surrounding two barrows, or burial mounds, and a smaller circle of 56 pits. Archaeologists have found ashes in these pits and in the circular ditch, and they believe the ashes are from the cremation, or ritual burning, of dead bodies. One theory is that Stonehenge was initially a place where people held religious ceremonies and buried the dead.

4   Some scientists believe that Stonehenge is much more than a burial ground. On the summer solstice, the rising sun's rays align perfectly with a huge outlying stone and the center of the stone circle. This suggests that Stonehenge may have been used to track the seasons. Whatever its true purpose, however, Stonehenge remains a majestic sight.

Hints

Which choice best develops the ideas of the account?

Use the Hints on this page to help you answer the questions.

1 The account states that "even though some questions about the site's purpose have been answered, many remain." Why does the author include this statement?

   A It suggests that we can never know the purpose of Stonehenge.

   B It shows that archaeologists are not able to explain the past.

   C It explains why people are losing interest in the site.

   D It begins the discussion of different ideas about Stonehenge.

Think about how the last paragraph relates to the subheads.

2 What does the final paragraph contribute to the account's overall structure?

   A It is the second of two possible answers to the question of why Stonehenge was built.

   B It summarizes what the secrets of Stonehenge are.

   C It raises more questions for readers to consider about the secrets in the stones.

   D It explains why some scientists disagree about the origins of Stonehenge.

Think about how each of the first two paragraphs ends. How do they lead into the second half of the account?

3 Explain how the first two paragraphs fit into the account's overall structure. Cite at least two details from the text to support your explanation.

_____

_____

_____

_____

_____

_____

_____

_____

_____

Read the account. Then answer the questions that follow.

The Dead Sea Scrolls

by Christa Smith

1   One day, a young Bedouin shepherd tossed a rock into a desert cave on the northwest shore of the Dead Sea. He was looking for a stray goat and thought it might have wandered into the cave. The boy heard a cracking sound and became curious. What the shepherd discovered in that cave were old jars filled with seven ancient scrolls. The boy may not have realized the full importance of his find on that day in 1947, but luckily, others did. The young shepherd brought the scrolls to an antiques dealer, who sold four of them to an archbishop of the Syrian Orthodox Church. Two archaeologists at Hebrew University bought the other scrolls and donated them to Israel. A museum was founded to house these precious documents, which became known as the Dead Sea Scrolls.

2   Over the next decade, ten other caves containing manuscripts were found in the Judean Desert. Archaeologists also excavated the ruins of Qumran, not far from the caves. They turned up more documents written in Hebrew, Greek, and Aramaic. There were hundreds of documents, either complete or in fragments. Some of the scrolls were written on dried animal skins, while others were written on papyrus, the largest measuring thirty feet long. These were very old manuscripts, of course, around 2,000 years old. Scientists used a special technique called carbon dating to determine how old they were; ancient coins found near the scrolls also indicated their age.

Some of the caves near Qumran, in the Judean Desert.

3   Why are the Dead Sea Scrolls so important to historians? Some of them are copies of fragments from the Hebrew Bible. In fact, the scrolls are the earliest known copies of the Bible. Other parchments contain commentary on biblical texts, and still others are copies of the prayer books of the Jewish people, showing their views on religion and society. Scholars say these papers reveal important information about the Second Temple Period. This period spanned the third century B.C.E. to 68 C.E., a time of political conflict. During this period, the Jews lived uneasily under Roman rule.

4   Through the examination of the scrolls, historians have gained insight into Jewish life and thought in ancient Palestine. Who actually did the work of copying out documents in the scrolls? There are several theories. One suggests that the Essenes may have performed all or much of this task. The Essenes were a very strict group of Jews who left Jerusalem to live in the desert. The Essenes believed that people had become too worldly, and so they went to live apart from society.

5   The discovery of the Dead Sea Scrolls sparked a half-century of study and debate. It is difficult to prove that they were left behind by just one group of people. We know that they were created over a period of 300 years. It is quite possible that different groups of people created or copied these manuscripts and fragments. It is not clear who hid them or why. Some say that the Essenes or other sects wanted to conceal them from the Romans. There is no way to be sure, though. What we do know is that the Dead Sea Scrolls are one of the most important discoveries of our time.

Answer the questions. Mark your answers to
questions 1–4 on the Answer Form to the right.

1   How does paragraph 1 prepare readers for the rest of the account?

   A   It describes how the scrolls were discovered.

   B   It introduces the scrolls and suggests their importance.

   C   It explains that the scrolls are really documents.

   D   It describes what scholars learned from the scrolls.

2   Read these sentences from paragraph 2.

> Over the next decade, ten other caves containing manuscripts were found in the Judean
> Desert. Archaeologists also excavated the ruins of Qumran, not far from the caves.

   How does this information fit into the overall structure of the account?

   A   It continues the chronology of events from Paragraph 1.

   B   It answers the question of the manuscripts' origins.

   C   It compares the desert caves to the ruins of Qumran.

   D   It shows what caused archaeologists to excavate the ruins.

3   How do paragraphs 3 and 4 support a key idea of the account?

   A   They explain why the scrolls are so important.

   B   They show just how old the scrolls really are.

   C   They demonstrate how the scrolls are used by scholars.

   D   They prove that the scrolls are as important as the Bible.

4   Which graphic **best** represents the structure of the informational text "The Dead Sea Scrolls"?

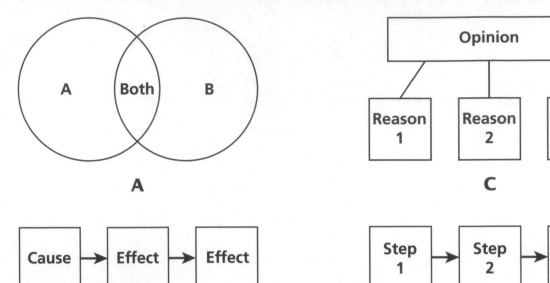

5   Explain why the author includes paragraph 5 in the account. Use at least **three** details from the text to show how this paragraph fits into the overall structure of the account.

_____

_____

_____

_____

_____

_____

_____

_____

_____

_____

✓ **Self Check**   *Go back and see what you can check off on the Self Check on page 94.*

Lesson 12 Part 1: Introduction 👥

Determining Point of View

CCLS

RI.6.6: Determine an author's point of view or purpose in a text and explain how it is conveyed in the text.

Theme: *Extreme Sports*

Did you ever read an article that tried to convince you to agree with the writer's ideas? If so, you may have noted that certain words were chosen to appeal to your emotions. The writer may have made different choices if the text were meant to inform or entertain, for example. After all, content is shaped by the **author's purpose**, or main reason for writing. Content is also shaped by the **author's point of view**, or feelings about a topic. The words and ideas used in a text provide important clues about an author's perspective.

In the picture below, what is each judge's point of view about an athlete's performance?

Circle clues that helped you figure out each judge's point of view.

Read the chart below to analyze evidence that helped you determine points of view.

Topic	Evidence	Positive (+) or Negative (−)	Point of View
Athlete's performance	Judge 1: gives a score of 10, smiles, uses the word "perfect"	+	Judge 1 thought the performance was wonderful.
Athlete's performance	Judge 2: gives a score of 2, frowns, uses the word "awful"	−	Judge 2 thought the performance was terrible.

Recognizing an author's reason for writing and feelings about a topic can help you decide what to do with the information. Should you treat it as a simple set of facts? Will you agree with the author, or will you develop your own opinion? To determine an author's point of view, think about the words chosen, the opinions expressed, and the details given (or left out). All are valuable clues to an author's purpose and point of view.

Read the essay about the extreme sport of ice climbing.

Genre: **Essay**

Climbing Ice!   *by Melissa Thompson*

Imagine facing an enormous frozen waterfall. You are at the bottom of this huge ice formation, staring up and thinking through the steps you'll take to climb it. Yes, it's dangerous—and that's part of the fun!

For adventure-seekers, ice climbing offers a physical challenge and a unique thrill. The surface of ice varies greatly from one location to another, so an ice climber must be ready for any situation that could arise during a climb. One wrong step could lead to a deadly fall. Yet to enthusiasts, the risks seem small when compared to the reward of finally reaching the top!

Speed competitions are for ice climbers who need more adventure than simply scaling a steep ice wall. These events offer the rush of danger coupled with the excitement of speed and competition.

Explore how to answer these questions: *"What is the author's point of view about ice climbing? What words, phrases, or sentences reveal this viewpoint?"*

The author does not directly state her opinion or attitude about ice climbing. Complete the chart below to determine her point of view based on text details and word choice.

Topic	Words, Phrases, or Sentences	Positive (+) or Negative (−)	Point of View
Ice climbing	"dangerous," "unique thrill," "deadly fall"	+ and −	
Ice climbing speed competitions	"rush of danger coupled with the excitement of speed and competition"		

Based on details in the chart above, describe the author's purpose for writing this essay.

_____

_____

_____

Read the editorial about ice climbing. Use the Close Reading and the Hint to help you answer the question.

Close Reading

Consider the title and the words the author uses in the editorial's first paragraph. **Circle** words and phrases that help you understand the author's point of view.

Genre: **Editorial**

Worth the Risk?   *by Chris Lau*

Ice climbing is a dangerous sport in which people attempt to climb frozen waterfalls and icy mountainsides. Training and proper equipment, along with protective clothing, are essential, but they are not enough to guarantee safety. Even experienced climbers continue to be injured and killed while participating in this high-risk sport.

Do the thrills outweigh the risks? When an ice climber is buried under an avalanche, emergency responders are dispatched at great expense to the community. If by luck the climber survives, it may take months or even years for him or her to recover. Are such costs worth a few hours of excitement?

Hint

How would you describe the author's feelings about ice climbing? Is he simply providing information, or does he have another purpose?

Circle the correct answer.

What is Chris Lau's point of view about ice climbing?

A   He admires the bravery of people who participate in the sport.

B   He strongly encourages people to get the proper equipment and training before trying ice climbing.

C   He questions the wisdom of people who think the thrill of ice climbing is worth the dangers.

D   He downplays the high costs and serious risks of the sport.

✎ **Show Your Thinking**

Look at the answer you chose above. Explain which words and phrases in the editorial helped you identify the author's point of view.

_____

_____

 With a partner, discuss the differences between the two authors' purposes and points of view.

Read another essay about extreme sports. Use the Study Buddy and the Close Reading to help guide your reading.

To help me understand the author's point of view, I am going to pause at the end of each paragraph and restate it in my own words.

Close Reading

How does the author feel about whitewater rafting? **Underline** a sentence that gives his opinion of this sport.

Reread the last paragraph to figure out why the author believes people like extreme sports. **Circle** phrases that explain the author's own point of view.

Genre: **Essay**

Just for the Thrill of It   *by Ken Moreno*

1   Your heart races. Your blood is pumping. Every nerve feels alive. For thrill-seekers, the charge of extreme sports keeps them coming back for more. And, of course, along with the excitement there's the breathtaking rush of danger and risk. It's an almost irresistible combination!

2   Extreme sports enthusiasts are always aware of the dangers. Most would agree that proper training and the right equipment are absolutely necessary to help minimize the risk. Yet even the most experienced participants will admit that training and equipment provide no guarantees when it comes to safety, so it's important to know what you're getting into.

3   Take whitewater rafting, for example. The raft is an inflatable boat designed to float down a rapidly flowing river. Split decisions must be made as rushing water shoots the raft past boulders, toward hidden snags, and over waterfalls. Controlling a raft's course can be exhausting. Still, rafting provides thrills at every turn and a wild ride!

4   Bungee jumping is another high-risk activity. Attached to a long, stretchy elastic cord, bungee daredevils jump from a high location, such as a bridge. They experience the thrill of freefall until the cord suddenly jerks them skyward again.

5   So what is it that attracts people to extreme sports? Most people have few chances in their daily lives to feel the rush that comes from pushing themselves to their limits and winning against great odds. Extreme sports can fulfill the need for that adrenaline rush and the satisfaction that comes from meeting a personal challenge.

Hints

Reread the title of the essay. Then reread the essay's last paragraph. Which answer choice connects most closely with these sections?

Which sentence describes the author's feelings about whitewater rafting?

What details and phrases does the author use to describe extreme sports and the feelings they create?

Use the Hints on this page to help you answer the questions.

1 With which statement would the author most likely agree?

   A   Interest in extreme sports comes from people's need for excitement and adventure.

   B   Extreme sports are dangerous only for people who are not physically fit.

   C   Whitewater rafting is more exciting and more unpredictable than bungee jumping.

   D   People who are thrill-seekers must be willing to prepare themselves for exhaustion and hard work.

2 Which sentence from the essay best shows the author's point of view about whitewater rafting?

   A   "The raft is an inflatable boat designed to float down a rapidly flowing river."

   B   "Split decisions must be made as rushing water shoots the raft past boulders, towards hidden snags, and over waterfalls."

   C   "Still, rafting provides thrills at every turn and a wild ride!"

   D   "Controlling a raft's course can be exhausting."

3 Describe the author's point of view toward extreme sports. Include at least two details from the essay to support your description.

_____

_____

_____

_____

_____

_____

_____

_____

_____

_____

Read the article. Then answer the questions that follow.

Flying Above the Water

by Tyrone Schenkel

1   Most people try to avoid risk as much as possible. For extreme-sport athletes, risk is their business. They put their careers, their bodies, and often their lives on the line to participate in their sport. The payoff is the indescribable rush that comes from doing what they do, as well as the knowledge that people watching are saying, "Can you believe that?"

2   One of the newest extreme sports is called kitesurfing. Mat Colefax is the sport's pioneer. In the early 1990s, he began experimenting with the sport in Australia. Colefax explained how he got the idea: "I caught a glimpse on TV of large kites being used with beach karts and I immediately [pictured] using such kites with my surf and snowboards. The idea of kiteboarding flashed into my mind and my imagination ran wild." In the early days of the sport, Mat sold a kite to Rebecca Nicholson, a young woman he met on the beach. She taught herself to fly it, and in 2003 became the first female world champion kitesurfer. She had become Rebecca Colefax by then. Today she and Mat spend their time promoting the thrilling sport.

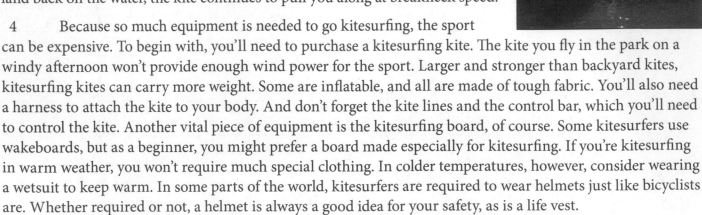

3   Kitesurfers ride the waves on a board like surfers do, but they're towed along by large kites flying in the wind. The sport is related to several other water sports. It's like surfing and wakeboarding because of the board the riders use. It's like waterskiing and windsurfing, too, but the wind in the kite, not a boat or a sail, provides the power. It's also similar to parasailing in that when a parasail rider builds up enough speed, he or she is pulled into the air. Kitesurfers can get airborne, too. In fact, that's one of the goals of the sport—to fly off the surface of the water and do tricks. One minute you're on the water, and the next your heart skips a beat as you're soaring through the air, performing aerial tricks with your feet still attached to the board. When you land back on the water, the kite continues to pull you along at breakneck speed.

4   Because so much equipment is needed to go kitesurfing, the sport can be expensive. To begin with, you'll need to purchase a kitesurfing kite. The kite you fly in the park on a windy afternoon won't provide enough wind power for the sport. Larger and stronger than backyard kites, kitesurfing kites can carry more weight. Some are inflatable, and all are made of tough fabric. You'll also need a harness to attach the kite to your body. And don't forget the kite lines and the control bar, which you'll need to control the kite. Another vital piece of equipment is the kitesurfing board, of course. Some kitesurfers use wakeboards, but as a beginner, you might prefer a board made especially for kitesurfing. If you're kitesurfing in warm weather, you won't require much special clothing. In colder temperatures, however, consider wearing a wetsuit to keep warm. In some parts of the world, kitesurfers are required to wear helmets just like bicyclists are. Whether required or not, a helmet is always a good idea for your safety, as is a life vest.

5   This adventurous sport is sure to provide an adrenaline rush as you enjoy the freedom of the wind blowing in your face. But kitesurfing isn't an activity you can take up on a whim. It's a tough sport that can be dangerous for a beginner. After all, you could find yourself flying 40 feet in the air at a fairly frightening rate

of speed. Most kitesurfers recommend that beginners get professional instruction so they'll be certain to obtain the right equipment and know how to use it.

6   If you're ready to try this exciting sport, you'll want to know that Australia is the world's top kitesurfing hot spot. Since it's also popular in Brazil, some surfers hope that kitesurfing events might be added to the 2016 Summer Olympics, which will be held in that country. In the United States, the Hawaiian island of Maui and the North Carolina coast off Cape Hatteras both offer good kitesurfing conditions.

7   It can certainly be worth your while to explore the sport of kitesurfing. If you're looking for the incredible rush of a new and exciting challenge, find a way to experience this extreme sport.

Answer the questions. Mark your answers to questions 1–4 on the Answer Form to the right.

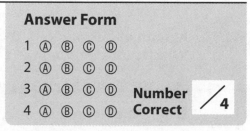

Answer Form

1 Ⓐ Ⓑ Ⓒ Ⓓ
2 Ⓐ Ⓑ Ⓒ Ⓓ
3 Ⓐ Ⓑ Ⓒ Ⓓ   **Number**
4 Ⓐ Ⓑ Ⓒ Ⓓ   **Correct** /4

1   Read this sentence from the article.

> One minute you're on the water, and the next your heart skips a beat as you're soaring through the air, performing aerial tricks with your feet still attached to the board.

Based on this sentence, with which statement would the author **most likely** agree?

A   Only professionals should attempt to perform kitesurfing tricks.

B   Kitesurfing is too dangerous for most people to attempt.

C   Performing aerial tricks while kitesurfing is as easy as doing tricks on waterskis.

D   Kitesurfing is a challenging but highly exciting water sport.

2   Which sentence from the article **best** illustrates how the author views kitesurfing?

A   "'The idea of kiteboarding flashed into my mind and my imagination ran wild.'"

B   "Kitesurfers ride the waves on a board like surfers do, but they're towed along by large kites flying in the wind."

C   "This adventurous sport is sure to provide an adrenaline rush as you enjoy the freedom of the wind blowing in your face."

D   "After all, you could find yourself flying 40 feet in the air at a fairly frightening rate of speed."

3 Which sentence **most accurately** describes the author's purpose for writing this article?

 A He wants to inform readers about the appeal and challenges of kitesurfing.

 B He wants to help readers to understand why kitesurfing can be very expensive.

 C He wants to compare kitesurfing to other types of extreme water sports.

 D He wants to encourage readers to help make kitesurfing an Olympic event.

4 In spite of his warnings, the author believes the thrill of kitesurfing is well worth the effort. Which sentence from the article **best** supports this statement?

 A "Because so much equipment is needed to go kitesurfing, the sport can be expensive."

 B "Whether required or not, a helmet is always a good idea for your safety, as is a life vest."

 C "If you're ready to try this exciting sport, you'll want to know that Australia is the world's top kitesurfing hot spot."

 D "If you're looking for the incredible rush of a new and exciting challenge, find a way to experience this extreme sport."

5 Although the author is enthusiastic about kitesurfing, he also wants readers to know what they're getting into. What are some of the details that help him achieve this goal?

_____

_____

_____

_____

_____

_____

_____

_____

 **Self Check** *Go back and see what you can check off on the Self Check on page 94.*

Read the biography. Then answer the questions that follow.

James Madison: The Forgotten Founder

by Mark Dziak

1   The presidents of the United States have made many great contributions to American history. These brave leaders charted the course for the nation by establishing the laws that would guide citizens for years to come. The first several presidents even led the fight for independence and helped lay the foundation for the country. One of these important leaders was James Madison: a president, a Founding Father, and one of history's greatest thinkers. Although Madison worked hard for the country, he is not very well known. His friend Thomas Jefferson, who was also a president, is far more famous. Examining the facts of Madison's life shows that he deserves more praise for all he did for our country.

A Founding Father

2   When he was only twenty-five years old, James Madison became a representative of the Virginia colony. This job helped Madison start his career in politics. It was in this position that he first met Thomas Jefferson, who would become Madison's lifelong friend and ally. During this time, Madison also exhibited his dedication to independence by passing new laws that would give the colonists freedom of religion.

3   In 1780, during the Revolutionary War, Madison was invited to join the Continental Congress, the group of leaders that helped form the new country. The youngest representative in the group, Madison attended the congress meetings for four years beginning in 1780. He helped make many critical decisions during these meetings. Meanwhile, his friend Thomas Jefferson only attended congress for about two years.

4   James Madison's service with the Continental Congress contributed to its greatest accomplishment. During the summer of 1787, a group of leaders began to review and change the laws that were already in place in America. The result of their work was the Constitution of the United States. This document set up the country's populist government, which allows citizens to express their individual ideas and beliefs. This accomplishment may never have occurred without the hard work and dedication of Madison. In fact, Madison is known as the Father of the Constitution because he played such an important part in its creation.

5   Not only was Madison important in drafting the ideas for the Constitution, but he also wrote much of the document. Madison wrote the Bill of Rights, which was designed to preserve the freedoms of American citizens. In addition, Madison joined Alexander Hamilton and John Jay in writing *The Federalist Papers*, essays that convinced leaders across the country to support the Constitution.

6   It is surprising that the person who added so much to the Constitution is not more popular today. By comparison, Thomas Jefferson became world famous for writing the Declaration of Independence, which helped the American colonies break away from Great Britain. Jefferson's work is legendary, even though the Declaration now has less effect on the everyday lives of American citizens than the Constitution does.

A National Leader

7   When Thomas Jefferson was elected the nation's third president, Madison became his secretary of state. In this position, Madison did something significant that helped expand America. In 1803, he oversaw the Louisiana Purchase, the purchase of a vast area of land from France. Part of this land was eventually divided into fifteen states. The Louisiana Purchase doubled the size of the United States and ensured that the country would grow stronger. Although Madison played a crucial role in the deal, few people remember the work he did. Instead, most people give credit for the Louisiana Purchase to Thomas Jefferson.

8   In 1809, Madison became the nation's fourth president. A few years later, problems between the United States and Great Britain led to the War of 1812. This was the first American war since the Revolutionary War, and it tested the strength of the young nation. President Madison faced enormous challenges during this time, including a shocking setback. In 1814, British soldiers marched into Washington, DC, and burned down the White House and other government buildings.

9   Unfortunately, many people remember Madison primarily for this tragic event. However, Madison did not hide when the British army invaded. During the attack on Washington, the courageous president went into the streets to gather soldiers to fight back. Madison also helped citizens endure the long, difficult war and rebuild the country when the fighting ended. Even Thomas Jefferson never faced such a great challenge during his presidency.

10   James Madison was known to his friends and fellow leaders as a brave decision maker and a brilliant politician. He strongly supported citizens' rights, and he later worked against slavery as well. Madison wrote the Bill of Rights and played a critical part in the creation of the Constitution. He also helped expand the country through the Louisiana Purchase, and he preserved the nation after the War of 1812. James Madison truly deserves as much appreciation as any other American leader.

1 Answer Parts A and B below.

Answer Form

1A Ⓐ Ⓑ Ⓒ Ⓓ
1B Ⓐ Ⓑ Ⓒ Ⓓ
2 Ⓐ Ⓑ Ⓒ Ⓓ
3 Ⓐ Ⓑ Ⓒ Ⓓ
4 Ⓐ Ⓑ Ⓒ Ⓓ
5 Ⓐ Ⓑ Ⓒ Ⓓ **Number**
6 Ⓐ Ⓑ Ⓒ Ⓓ **Correct** /7

Part A

What does the phrase "charted the course for the nation" mean as it is used in paragraph 1 of the passage?

A ran for an office

B fought for more freedom

C moved to a country

D planned for the future

Part B

Which of the phrases from the passage best helps the reader understand the meaning of "charted the course for the nation"?

A "made many great contributions"

B "establishing the laws"

C "guide citizens for years to come"

D "one of history's great thinkers"

2 The author thinks that Madison has not been recognized enough for his accomplishments, while other presidents may have been recognized too much for theirs. Which sentence from the passage **best** supports the above statement?

A "It was in this position that he first met Thomas Jefferson, who would become Madison's lifelong friend and ally."

B "When Thomas Jefferson was elected the nation's third president, Madison became his secretary of state."

C "Instead, most people give credit for the Louisiana Purchase to Thomas Jefferson."

D "Unfortunately, many people remember Madison primarily for this tragic event."

3   Read the sentence below.

Madison also helped citizens endure the long, difficult war. . . .

What does the word "endure" **most likely** mean?

A   live through

B   plan for

C   fight in

D   escape from

4   Read these sentences from the passage.

The youngest representative in the group, Madison attended the congress meetings for four years beginning in 1780. He helped make many critical decisions during these meetings. Meanwhile, his friend Thomas Jefferson only attended congress for about two years.

Why does the author **most likely** include these lines in the passage?

A   to suggest that Madison did more than Jefferson

B   to describe the decisions made by leaders of the past

C   to compare leaders from long ago with leaders today

D   to show that Madison and Jefferson were friends

5   How does paragraph 10 help to develop the ideas in the passage?

A   It introduces important new arguments into the passage.

B   It offers readers an alternative view of the author's opinions.

C   It reminds readers of the author's most important points.

D   It compares two different people mentioned in the passage.

6 Which graphic **best** represents the structure of "James Madison: The Forgotten Founder"?

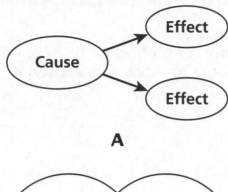

A

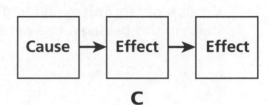

C

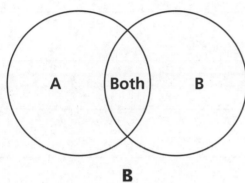

B

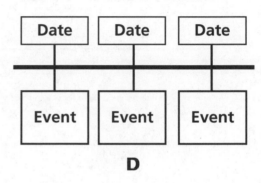

D

7 Read this sentence from the passage.

> During this time, Madison also exhibited his dedication to independence by passing new laws that would give the colonists freedom of religion.

Write a paragraph explaining how this sentence contributes to the development of ideas in the passage. Use details from the passage to support your answer.

_____

_____

_____

_____

_____

8 Read this sentence from paragraph 4 of the passage.

> In fact, Madison is known as the Father of the Constitution because he played such an important part in its creation.

Write a paragraph explaining how this sentence contributes to the development of ideas in the passage. Use details from the passage to support your answer.

_____

_____

_____

_____

9 Write a paragraph explaining why the author most likely included paragraph 9 and how that paragraph reflects the author's point of view. Use details from the passage to support your answer.

_____

_____

_____

_____

_____

Performance Task—Extended Response

10 Think about how the author compares James Madison and Thomas Jefferson. In what ways does he feel that these leaders were alike and different? What effect does this comparison have on the passage? How does it support the author's point of view? Write an essay of two to three paragraphs explaining your response. Be sure to include details from the passage in your answer.

In your answer, be sure to
- explain how the two leaders were alike and different
- explain how the author's comparison affects the passage
- explain how the comparison supports the author's point of view
- use details from the passage in your answer

Check your writing for correct spelling, grammar, capitalization, and punctuation.

_____

_____

_____

_____

_____

_____

_____

_____

_____

_____

_____

Unit 4
Craft and Structure in Literature

An artist is at work on a painting. She mixes the colors to get just the right tone, adding highlights and shadows to the canvas. Through the painting, the artist expresses her viewpoint about a subject. Like a painter, an author **crafts** a text, using words and phrases like brushstrokes on the page. The author carefully chooses words, phrases, lines, and stanzas as the artist chooses colors, to craft the **structure** of the text. Through the narrator in a story or speaker in a poem, the author expresses a point of view or perspective. This adds color and texture to the work, just like in a painting.

In this unit, you will learn how poets and writers of stories make deliberate choices about the language they use to create tone and meaning. In a similar way, they choose a form and structure that best suit their purpose and express their point of view. Writers are artists, so look for the pictures they have painted with their words as you read the literature in this unit!

✓ **Self Check** **Fill out the Self Check on the next page.** ▶

Before starting this unit, check off the skills you know below. As you complete each lesson, see how many more you can check off!

✓ Self Check

I know how to:	Before this unit	After this unit
explain the meanings of words and phrases in a text.	☐	☐
describe how the author's word choice affects meaning and tone.	☐	☐
explain how elements such as lines and stanzas contribute to the meaning or theme of a poem.	☐	☐
describe the structure of a story, and explain how each part contributes to the plot.	☐	☐
describe how the author expresses the narrator's point of view in a text.	☐	☐

Determining Word Meanings: Figurative and Connotative

CCLS

RL.6.4: Determine the meaning of words and phrases as they are used in a text, including figurative and connotative meanings. . . .

Theme: *Out in the Elements*

Would you rather trudge through the snow or stroll through the snow? The verbs have similar meanings, but each has a different **connotative meaning**, the feeling suggested by a word or phrase. *Trudge* connotes a struggle, but *stroll* suggests a relaxing walk.

Writers also use words in imaginative ways to create interesting effects. This kind of language is called **figurative language**. Figurative language often makes unusual comparisons between things or ideas that help readers imagine a subject in vivid or unexpected ways.

Look at the cartoon below. Think about why the writer of the text is using figurative language.

Tears fell from her face like rain from the sky.

Why do you think the writer compared the girl's tears to rain? It's not likely that water is pouring from the girl's eyes. But the writer wants us to know that she is crying hard.

Read the following chart to understand some different types of figurative language.

Figurative Language	Definition	Example
Simile	a comparison using *like* or *as*	She has a smile like sunshine.
Metaphor	a comparison that doesn't use *like* or *as*	He is a bear of a man.
Personification	giving human qualities to something nonhuman	The boiling tea kettle screeched its complaint.

Readers identify which ideas are being compared and what they have in common. They also consider the feelings that words create to appreciate what an author is trying to say.

Read the beginning of the short story below.

Genre: **Realistic Fiction**

The Gold Watch *by Matthew Allen*

Sunlight burst through the window and woke Gabriel that bright summer day. He felt disoriented, as if he'd been sleeping for years. He didn't even know what time it was! But that was no surprise—he was always late. He pulled on his clothes and went out to the yard, where he found his mother sorting through boxes of old things.

"Why did you get all that junk out of the garage?" Gabriel asked.

"It's not 'junk'," his mother answered. "These are things I've saved over the years, but it's time to have a yard sale and let them go."

Gabriel's mother pulled a broken coffee maker out of one box, the electrical cord trailing behind it like a tail. Next, his mother held up a pocket watch as golden as a tiny sun.

(continued)

Explore how to answer this question: *"To what does the author compare the electrical cord, and how does this make you imagine the coffee maker?"*

The author compares the cord to a tail, which gives the coffee maker the qualities of an animal. Review the chart on the previous page. What type of figurative language does the author use here?

Read the chart below. Use what you know about figurative language to complete it.

What's Being Compared	How They Are Alike	Meaning
a pocket watch and the sun		The watch is _____.

In the last sentence, the author compares the watch to the sun to suggest how Gabriel feels about the watch. How does this comparison suggest Gabriel's feelings about the watch? Write your answer on the lines below.

_____

_____

_____

Continue reading the short story. Use the Close Reading and the Hint to help you answer the question

Close Reading

Circle positive words describing the watch. **Draw a box** around the negative words. Think about the feelings the words suggest.

(continued from page 130)

"This old thing was your grandfather's," she said, smiling at the watch like it was a familiar friend. "I don't think it works. I suppose people would think it's pretty worthless."

But Gabriel asked his mother for the time, wound up the watch, and let it swing from its chain like a pendulum. The ticking sound it made was as steady as a heartbeat. Just then, some storm clouds crossed the sun, heavy with the rain of a summer storm. But Gabriel now had a new treasure, which he polished until it shined, and he tucked it carefully into his pocket so he would always know the time.

Hint

Review the words you marked above. Does the boy see the watch in a positive or negative way?

Circle the correct answer.

Which word from the story best describes how Gabriel feels about the watch?

A treasure

B worthless

C heartbeat

D familiar

Show Your Thinking

Identify any similes and metaphors you can find in the second paragraph. How do they help show how the boy feels about the watch?

_____

_____

_____

_____

 With a partner, discuss what Gabriel and his mother say about "junk" at the start of the passage. What is the connotation of *junk*? What does his mother's response reveal about her feelings?

Read the lyric poem. Use the Study Buddy and Close Reading to guide your reading.

I wonder how the speaker feels about this storm. As I read, I'm going to underline words with strong connotations.

Close Reading

What does the speaker compare the lightning to? **Underline** any lines that make a comparison.

Remember that a simile is a comparison using *like* or *as*. **Circle** a simile used in the poem.

Genre: **Lyric Poem**

A Thunder–Storm *by Emily Dickinson*

The wind begun to rock the grass
With <u>threatening</u> tunes and low,—
He flung a <u>menace</u> at the earth,
A <u>menace</u> at the sky.

5 The leaves unhooked themselves from trees
And started all abroad;
The dust did scoop itself like hands
And throw away the road.

The wagons quickened on the streets,
10 The thunder hurried slow;
The lightning showed a yellow beak,
And then a livid[1] claw.

The birds put up the bars to nests,
The cattle fled to barns;
15 There came one drop of giant rain,
And then, as if the hands

That held the dams had parted hold,
The waters wrecked the sky,
But overlooked my father's house,
20 Just quartering[2] a tree.

_____

[1] **livid:** dark blue
[2] **quartering:** reaching

Hints

Use the Hints on this page to help you answer the questions.

> The wind "flung a menace." Something that is "flung" is thrown hard and perhaps dangerously.

1 Which of the lines from the poem best helps the reader understand the meaning of the word "menace"?

   A "With threatening tunes and low,—"

   B "The thunder hurried slow"

   C "There came one drop of giant rain,"

   D "But overlooked my father's house"

> These lines mention the features of birds—but are the lines talking about actual birds?

2 Read the lines from the poem.

   The lightning showed a yellow beak,
   And then a livid claw.

   Which of the following best describes the meaning of these lines?

   A The lightning is striking wagons, nests, and barns.

   B The bolts of lightning seem to be dangerously alive.

   C At night, flashes of lightning show the features of birds.

   D The storm is pushing eagles and hawks into their nests.

> What does it mean for dust to "throw away the road"? Is the road really being thrown? What is happening in this stanza?

3 Identify the two forms of figurative language that are used in lines 7 and 8. Explain what these lines mean. Use two details from the poem in your response.

_____

_____

_____

_____

_____

_____

_____

_____

_____

_____

Read the story. Then answer the questions that follow.

from "To Build a Fire"

by Jack London

1   The man flung a look back along the way he had come. The Yukon lay a mile wide and hidden under three feet of ice. On top of this ice were as many feet of snow. . . . North and south, as far as his eye could see, it was unbroken white, save for a dark hair–line that curved and twisted from around the spruce–covered island to the south, and that curved and twisted away into the north, where it disappeared behind another spruce–covered island. . . .

2   But all this . . . made no impression on the man. It was not because he was long used to it. He was a new–comer in the land . . . and this was his first winter. The trouble with him was that he was without imagination. . . . Fifty degrees below zero was to him just precisely fifty degrees below zero. That there should be anything more to it than that was a thought that never entered his head. . . .

3   At the man's heels trotted a dog, a big native husky. . . . The animal was depressed by the tremendous cold. It knew that it was no time for travelling. Its instinct told it a truer tale than was told to the man by the man's judgment. . . . The dog had learned fire, and it wanted fire. . . .

4   Empty as the man's mind was of thoughts, he was keenly observant, and he noticed the changes in the creek, the curves and bends and timber–jams, and always he sharply noted where he placed his feet. . . .

5   And then it happened. At a place where there were no signs, where the soft, unbroken snow seemed to advertise solidity beneath, the man broke through. It was not deep. He wetted himself half–way to the knees before he floundered out to the firm crust.

6   He was angry, and cursed his luck aloud . . . . for he would have to build a fire and dry out his foot–gear. This was imperative at that low temperature—he knew that much; and he turned aside to the bank, which he climbed. On top, tangled in the underbrush about the trunks of several small spruce trees, was a high–water deposit of dry firewood. . . . He threw down several large pieces on top of the snow. . . . The flame he got by touching a match to a small shred of birch–bark that he took from his pocket. . . .

7   He worked slowly and carefully, keenly aware of his danger. Gradually, as the flame grew stronger, he increased the size of the twigs with which he fed it. He squatted in the snow, pulling the twigs out from their entanglement in the brush and feeding directly to the flame. He knew there must be no failure. When it is seventy–five below zero, a man must not fail in his first attempt to build a fire—that is, if his feet are wet. . . .

8   There was the fire, snapping and crackling and promising life with every dancing flame. He started to untie his moccasins. They were coated with ice; the thick German socks were like sheaths of iron half–way to the knees; and the moccasin strings were like rods of steel all twisted and knotted. . . . For a moment he tugged with his numbed fingers, then, realizing the folly of it, he drew his sheath–knife.

9   But before he could cut the strings, it happened. It was his own fault or, rather, his mistake. He should not have built the fire under the spruce tree. . . . Now the tree under which he had done this carried a

weight of snow on its boughs. . . . It grew like an avalanche, and it descended without warning upon the man and the fire, and the fire was blotted out!

Answer the questions. Mark your answers to questions 1–4 on the Answer Form to the right.

Answer Form

1 Ⓐ Ⓑ Ⓒ Ⓓ
2 Ⓐ Ⓑ Ⓒ Ⓓ
3 Ⓐ Ⓑ Ⓒ Ⓓ   Number
4 Ⓐ Ⓑ Ⓒ Ⓓ   Correct /4

1 In paragraph 1, what connotation does the word *flung* add to the first sentence?

A caution

B haste

C terror

D anger

2 Read this example of personification from paragraph 3.

Its instinct told it a truer tale than was told to the man by the man's judgment.

What does it mean that the dog's instinct "told it a truer tale"?

A The dog did not believe that the man could build a fire.

B The dog's sharper hearing could tell where the ice was thin.

C The dog had a better sense of the danger they were in.

D The dog remembered another time when the man got wet.

3 Which phrase from the passage best helps the reader to understand the meaning of the phrase "keenly observant"?

A "Empty as the man's mind was"

B "always he sharply noted"

C "cursed his luck aloud"

D "worked slowly and carefully"

4 Read this sentence from the story.

They were coated with ice; the thick German socks were like sheaths of iron half–way to the knees; and the moccasin strings were like rods of steel all twisted and knotted. . . .

What do the two similes in this sentence show?

A The man's feet are stuck in the frozen ground.

B The man is too weak to remove his own socks.

C The man's socks and laces are made of metal.

D The man's wet clothes have frozen solid.

5 In paragraph 5, the author says that "the soft, unbroken snow seemed to advertise solidity beneath." State what type of figurative language is this, and explain what it means. Support your answer with at least **two** details from the story.

_____

_____

_____

_____

_____

_____

_____

_____

_____

_____

_____

 **Self Check** *Go back and see what you can check off on the Self Check on page 128.*

Lesson 14   Part 1: Introduction

Analyzing Word Choice

CCLS

RL.6.4: . . . analyze the impact of a specific word choice on meaning and tone.

Theme: Surprise Endings

Have you ever heard someone say "It's the little things that matter"? In everyday life, little things can make you happy, sad, annoyed, or excited. In literature and poetry, the little things that matter are words, chosen carefully by the author.

Words affect meaning and establish the **tone**, or the attitude of the narrator or speaker. Word choice also is important because it can create the **mood**, or atmosphere, in a story or poem.

Read the poem below, paying close attention to poet's choice of action verbs and descriptive words.

> Murky Monday. Lockers slam,
>
> Doorways clog and hallways jam.
>
> Sweetest Ruby smiles so wide—
>
> She can't see me shyly hide . . .
>
> Wondrous Monday. Lockers shine.
>
> Ruby smiled at me in line.

Circle words in each line that help you understand the speaker's feelings.

Read the chart below to help you analyze the poet's word choices in each line.

Lines	Words with Positive Meaning	Words with Negative Meaning
1–2		murky, slam, clog, jam
3–4	sweetest, smiles	shyly, hide
5–6	wondrous, shine, smiled	

Just as movie directors pay attention to the smallest details when setting up each scene, authors pay attention to each word when they create poems and stories. In this poem, the poet uses words to show how the speaker's whole attitude changes after Ruby smiles.

Analyzing an author's choice of words will help you more fully understand a text's meaning, mood, and tone.

Read this story about a girl named Carmen who is awakened by a strange sound.

Genre: **Mystery**

A Fright in the Night   by Tasha Gilden

Carmen squinted through the thin curtains on her window, seeking the source of the sound that had awakened her. Unable to focus through the fabric, she pinched the hem with two fingertips and pulled the curtain aside slowly. She held her breath and her whole body completely still—but there was nothing.

I know I heard something; I thought it was the wind out in the old oak tree. But the tree was still and Carmen's chest pounded a little and her palms went sweaty because something had made a noise, and it wasn't the tree.

Carmen settled back into her blankets but stayed upright and scanned her room. The moonlight created an eerie glow on her bookshelves, and the rainbow mobile cast shadows more snakelike than serene.

(continued)

Explore how to response to this prompt: *"Describe the mood of this part of the story. Identify specific words that help to produce this mood."*

First, identify words that the author uses to describe the character and the setting. Circle these words in the passage. Then, tell what kind of feeling each word is intended to express.

Words the Author Uses	Feelings the Words Convey
squinted	uncertainty

Now, use the information in the chart to write a short paragraph. First, describe the mood of the story so far. Then, explain how the author's words help to create that mood.

_____

_____

_____

_____

Continue reading about Carmen. Use the Close Reading and the Hint to help you answer the question.

Close Reading

Find and **underline** some words and phrases in this part of the story that convey the mood.

(continued from page 138)

Carmen swallowed the lump in her throat when she heard the sounds again—*rustle, rustle, thump*—coming clearly now from the opposite side of the room. She pulled her toes in tight, as if that could prevent something from grabbing them. Her mouth opened as she prepared to yell, because there just shouldn't be anything rustling in her room in the night. And then—*rustle, rustle, scratch*—Carmen's cat finished pushing its way out of the bottom drawer of her dresser!

Carmen's near-yell turned into a laugh. "Dandy-Lion, you must have been more scared than I was!"

Hint

Which phrase helps you understand the story's surprise ending?

Circle the correct answer.

Which group of words from the story best reflects the change in mood?

A "swallowed the lump in her throat"

B "near-yell turned into a laugh"

C "pushing its way out"

D "more scared than I was"

✎ **Show Your Thinking**

Look at the answer that you chose above. Explain why you think it is the correct answer.

_____

_____

 With a partner, list phrases from the story that you think are the strongest in creating a menacing mood.

Read the poem. Use the Study Buddy and the Close Reading to guide your reading.

I know poets choose words carefully. I'm going to pay close attention to descriptive words and how they make me feel about the boys in the poem.

Close Reading

What kind of boy was Jim? **Circle** words in stanzas 3 and 4 that describe him.

Reread stanzas 1 and 2, paying close attention to the words the speaker uses to describe Bill. **Underline** words that describe Bill's traits.

Genre: **Narrative Poem**

Those Two Boys   *by Franklin P. Adams*

1   When Bill was a lad he was terribly bad.
    He worried his parents a lot;
    He'd lie and he'd swear and pull little girls' hair;
    His boyhood was naught[1] but a blot.

2   At play and in school he would fracture each rule—
    In mischief from autumn to spring;
    And the villagers knew when to manhood he grew
    He would never amount to a thing.

3   When Jim was a child he was not very wild;
    He was known as a good little boy;
    He was honest and bright and the teacher's delight—
    To his mother and father a joy.

4   All the neighbors were sure that his virtue'd endure,
    That his life would be free of a spot;
    They were certain that Jim had a great head on him
    And that Jim would amount to a lot.

5   And Jim grew to manhood and honor and fame
    And bears a good name;
    While Bill is shut up in a dark prison cell—
    You never can tell.

[1] **naught:** nothing

Hints

What kinds of actions are described in stanza 1?

Which words create the most positive feelings?

Look carefully at your marked-up text in the first three stanzas. What words and phrases did you circle? What did you underline?

Use the Hints on this page to help you answer the questions.

1 Why did the author use the word *blot*, which can mean "a dark stain," in line 4?

   A It suggests that Bill's behavior was always bad.

   B It shows that Bill's misdeeds were accidental.

   C It illustrates that Bill's mischief was truly criminal.

   D It shows that Bill's bad acts marked him for life.

2 Which words from the poem best help you understand Jim?

   A child, good, boy

   B honest, bright, delight

   C mother, father, neighbors

   D wild, free, spot

3 Explain how the poet's choice of words helps create a judgmental tone. Cite examples from the text to support your explanation.

_____

_____

_____

_____

_____

_____

_____

_____

_____

_____

_____

_____

Read the story. Then answer the questions that follow.

from "The Eyes Have It"

by Philip K. Dick

1   It was quite by accident I discovered this incredible invasion of Earth by life-forms from another planet. As yet, I haven't done anything about it; I can't think of anything to do. . . .

2   I was sitting in my easy–chair, idly turning the pages of a paperbacked book someone had left on the bus, when I came across the reference that first put me on the trail. For a moment I didn't respond. It took some time for the full import to sink in. After I'd comprehended, it seemed odd I hadn't noticed it right away.

3   The reference was clearly to a nonhuman species of incredible properties, not indigenous to Earth. A species, I hasten to point out, customarily masquerading as ordinary human beings. Their disguise, however, became transparent in the face of the following observations by the author. It was at once obvious the author knew everything. Knew everything—and was taking it in his stride. The line (and I tremble remembering it even now) read:

4   . . . *his eyes slowly roved about the room.*

5   Vague chills assailed me. I tried to picture the eyes. Did they roll like dimes? The passage indicated not; they seemed to move through the air, not over the surface. Rather rapidly, apparently. No one in the story was surprised. That's what tipped me off. No sign of amazement at such an outrageous thing. . . .

6   The eyes had clearly come apart from the rest of him and were on their own. My heart pounded and my breath choked in my windpipe. I had stumbled on an accidental mention of a totally unfamiliar race. Obviously non–Terrestrial. Yet, to the characters in the book, it was perfectly natural—which suggested they belonged to the same species.

7   And the author? A slow suspicion burned in my mind. The author was taking it rather *too easily* in his stride. Evidently, he felt this was quite a usual thing. He made absolutely no attempt to conceal this knowledge. The story continued:

8   . . . *presently his eyes fastened on Julia.*

9   Julia, being a lady, had at least the breeding to feel indignant. She is described as blushing and knitting her brows angrily. At this, I sighed with relief. They weren't *all* non-Terrestrials. The narrative continues:

10   . . . *slowly, calmly, his eyes examined every inch of her.*

11   Great Scott! But here the girl turned and stomped off and the matter ended. I lay back in my chair gasping with horror. . . .

12   Trembling, I read the next revealing passage:

13   . . . *he put his arm around Julia. Presently she asked him if he would remove his arm. He immediately did so, with a smile.*

14   It's not said what was done with the arm after the fellow had removed it. Maybe it was left standing upright in the corner. Maybe it was thrown away. I don't care. In any case, the full meaning was there, staring me right in the face.

15   Here was a race of creatures capable of removing portions of their anatomy at will. Eyes, arms—and maybe more. Without batting an eyelash. My knowledge of biology came in handy, at this point. Obviously they were simple beings, unicellular, some sort of primitive single-celled things. Beings no more developed than starfish. Starfish can do the same thing, you know. . . .

16   There was no doubt of the thing in the next passage. Julia, whom I had thought to be the one normal person, reveals herself as also being an alien life form, similar to the rest:

17   *. . . quite deliberately, Julia had given her heart to the young man. . . .*

18   Flushing crimson, I slammed the book shut and leaped to my feet. But not in time to escape one last reference to those carefree bits of anatomy whose travels had originally thrown me on the track:

19   *. . . her eyes followed him all the way down the road and across the meadow. . . .*

20   I had had enough of the thing. I want to hear no more about it. Let them come on. Let them invade Earth. I don't want to get mixed up in it.

21   I have absolutely no stomach for it.

Answer the questions. Mark your answers to questions 1–3 on the Answer Form to the right.

Answer Form

1 Ⓐ Ⓑ Ⓒ Ⓓ

2 Ⓐ Ⓑ Ⓒ Ⓓ **Number**

3 Ⓐ Ⓑ Ⓒ Ⓓ **Correct**   /3

1   Read this sentence from the story.

> It was quite by accident I discovered this incredible invasion of Earth by life-forms from another planet.

Which statement **best** describes the intended effect of the author's word choice?

A It instills terror in the reader.

B It provokes a feeling of amusement.

C It hints at the narrator's madness.

D It creates a sense of amazement.

2 Throughout the story, the narrator includes excerpts from the book he is reading. How are these excerpts **most likely** intended to affect your understanding of the story?

  A They show that the narrator is wrong about the alien invasion.

  B They add tension as the narrator finds more proof of the aliens.

  C They tell a separate story about Julia's romance with an alien.

  D They demonstrate the narrator's ability to find hidden messages.

3 Which of the following sentences from the story **best** conveys the narrator's growing sense of fear in the text?

  A "It took some time for the full import to sink in."

  B "My heart pounded and my breath choked in my windpipe."

  C "A slow suspicion burned in my mind."

  D "In any case, the full meaning was there, staring me right in the face."

4 In the last sentence from the story, the narrator states, "I have absolutely no stomach for it." Explain how the author's word choice adds a humorous meaning to the story. Use text evidence to support your answer.

_____

_____

_____

_____

_____

_____

_____

 **Self Check** *Go back and see what you can check off on the Self Check on page 128.*

Lesson 15   Part 1: Introduction

Analyzing the Structure of a Poem

CCLS
RL.6.5: Analyze how a particular sentence . . . or stanza fits into the overall structure of a text and contributes to the development of the theme. . . .

Theme: *Capturing Memories*

A poem is a little like a photograph. It captures an important moment or expresses a strong feeling. To get the most out of a poem, it helps to know that poems have a special **structure**, or type of organization. Structure can refer to how the lines or ideas of a poem are organized. Each line and stanza has its place. You need to put together the meaning of all of the individual lines to find the **theme**, or message, that the poem is trying to convey.

Read the the poem below, paying close attention to its meaning and structure.

> A boat beneath a sunny sky,
> Lingering onward dreamily
> In an evening of July—
>
> Children three that nestle near,
> Eager eye and willing ear,
> Pleased a simple tale to hear—
>
> Long has paled that sunny sky:
> Echoes fade and memories die:
> Autumn frosts have slain July.

How is the poem organized? What is the poem's message?

The poet organizes the poem into stanzas of three lines. Think about what each stanza means. Then compare your ideas with those in the chart.

Stanza	Main Idea
1	A boat drifts peacefully as night draws near on a warm July day.
2	Children gather happily to enjoy a story.
3	Cold autumn weather has destroyed summer fun.

Each line of a poem contributes to the overall theme of the poem. Look again at the main ideas in the chart. Taken together, they convey the message that the speaker has fond, pleasant memories of summer and misses the fun and peacefulness of July.

Read the poem below in which the speaker talks about things he likes.

Genre: **Lyric Poem**

Motto   *by Langston Hughes*

I play it cool
and dig all jive.
That's the reason
I stay alive.

My motto,
As I live and learn,
         is:
Dig And Be Dug
In Return.

Explore how to answer this question: *"What do you notice about the structure, or organization, of this poem?"*

Poems are often organized into stanzas. A **stanza** is a group of lines that form a unit in a poem. Like a paragraph, each stanza has its own main idea. Taken together, these main ideas develop the poem's theme.

Complete the chart below by filling in the main idea for the poem's second stanza. Then explain a theme of this poem.

Stanza	Main Idea	Theme
1	Being relaxed and getting along with people is the key to life.	
2		

With a partner, take turns rereading the poem aloud. Then discuss how the poem's structure contributes to the poem's theme.

Read the poem below. Use the Close Reading and the Hint to help you answer the question.

Close Reading

Each stanza conveys a different feeling. **Underline** at least two details in each stanza that help create those feelings.

Genre: **Lyric Poem**

The Heart of a Woman   *by Georgia Douglas Johnson*

The heart of a woman goes forth with the dawn,
As a lone bird, soft winging, so restlessly on,
Afar o'er life's turrets and vales does it roam
In the wake of those echoes the heart calls home.

The heart of a woman falls back with the night,
And enters some alien cage in its plight,
And tries to forget it has dreamed of the stars
While it breaks, breaks, breaks on the sheltering bars.

Hint

Reread the first stanza. What message do the first and second lines of the stanza suggest?

Circle the correct answer.

Which of the following best describes a theme, or central message, of the poem?

A The heart of a woman is strong and can never be broken.

B The heart of a woman is restless and often feels trapped.

C The heart of a woman is happy and free to dream of the stars.

D The heart of a woman is dark and dreary like the night sky.

✎ **Show Your Thinking**

Look at the answer you chose above. What words in that answer choice helped you know that it is the correct answer?

_____

_____

 In a small group, list the words and phrases the poet uses to describe "the heart of a woman." Then discuss how the poem's structure helps support the theme.

Read the poem below. Use the Study Buddy and the Close Reading to guide your reading.

The speaker mentions the passage of time, which may be a clue about the poem's theme. I'll look for words in each stanza that relate to time and may contribute to the theme.

Close Reading

The speaker repeats the phrase "I sit beside the fire and think of" in the first stanza. **Underline** words in the first stanza that explain what time frames the speaker is thinking about.

The speaker begins the second stanza with thoughts about the future. **Circle** the phrase that shows how the speaker feels about the future at the beginning of this stanza.

Genre: **Lyric Poem**

I Sit by the Fire and Think   *by J. R. R. Tolkien*

I sit beside the fire and think of all that I have seen,
of meadow-flowers and butterflies in summers that have been;
Of yellow leaves and gossamer in autumns that there were,
with morning mist and silver sun and wind upon my hair.
5   I sit beside the fire and think of how the world will be
when winter comes without a spring that I shall ever see.

For still there are so many things that I have never seen:
in every wood in every spring there is a different green.
I sit beside the fire and think of people long ago,
10 and people who will see a world that I shall never know.
But all the while I sit and think of times there were before,
I listen for returning feet and voices at the door.

Hints

Which choice describes the speaker's thoughts in the opening and closing lines of the first stanza?

Use the Hints on this page to help you answer the questions.

1 Which best describes the first stanza?

   A The speaker looks back on past events with sadness and deep regret.

   B The speaker looks ahead to future events with excitement.

   C The speaker thinks about the past and wonders about the future.

   D The speaker thinks about all he has to do in the months ahead.

Which sentence in the second stanza best describes the speaker's thought process from the start of the poem to the end?

2 How does the idea of time contribute to the poem's structure?

   A The speaker thinks about the past and then the future, and at the end he returns to the present.

   B The speaker first thinks about what will happen in the future, wonders about the present, and then the past.

   C The speaker thinks about the present autumn, then wonders what winter without spring would be like.

   D The speaker recalls sitting by the fire during his youth, and remembers the sound of feet and voices.

What does the speaker think about in the last two lines of the poem?

3 State the theme of the poem. Give at least one example of a sentence from the poem that develops the poem's theme.

_____

_____

_____

_____

_____

_____

_____

_____

_____

Read the ballad. Then answer the questions that follow.

Brennan on the Moor

a traditional Irish ballad

It's of a famous highwayman a story I will tell;
His name was Willy Brennan, in Ireland he did dwell;
And on the Kilworth mountains he commenced his wild career,
Where many a wealthy gentleman before him shook with fear.

5   Brennan on the Moor, Brennan on the Moor,
       Bold and undaunted stood young Brennan on the Moor. . . .

One day, on the highway, as Willy he sat down,
He met the Mayor of Cashel a mile outside the town;
The Mayor, he knew his features—"I think, young man," said he,
10   "Your name is Willy Brennan—you must come along with me."

       Brennan on the Moor, Brennan on the Moor,
       Bold and undaunted stood young Brennan on the Moor.

As Brennan's wife had gone to town provisions for to buy,
When she saw her Willy, she began to weep and cry;
15   He says, "Give me that tenpenny." As soon as Willy spoke,
She handed him a blunderbuss, from underneath her cloak.

       Brennan on the Moor, Brennan on the Moor,
       Bold and undaunted stood young Brennan on the Moor.

Then with his loaded blunderbuss—the truth I will unfold—
20   He made the Mayor tremble, and robbed him of his gold;
One hundred pounds were offered for his apprehension there,
And he, with his horse and saddle, to the mountain did repair.

       Brennan on the Moor, Brennan on the Moor,
       Bold and undaunted stood young Brennan on the Moor.

25   Then Brennan being an outlaw, upon the mountain high,
With cavalry and infantry to take him they did try;
He laughed at them with scorn, until at length, it's said;
By a false-hearted woman he basely was betrayed.

       Brennan on the Moor. Brennan on the Moor.
30   Bold and undaunted stood young Brennan on the Moor. . . .

So they were taken prisoners, in irons they were bound,
And conveyed to Clonmel Jail, strong walls did them surround;
They were tried and found guilty—the Judge made this reply:
"For robbing on the king's highway, you're both condemned to die."

35   Brennan on the Moor, Brennan on the Moor,
        Bold and undaunted stood young Brennan on the Moor.

When Brennan heard his sentence, he made this reply;
"I own that I did rob the rich, and did the poor supply;
In all the deeds that I have done I took no life away;
40   The Lord have mercy on my soul against the judgment day."

        Brennan on the Moor, Brennan on the Moor,
        Bold and undaunted stood young Brennan on the Moor. . . .

Answer the questions. Mark your answers to questions 1–3 on the Answer Form to the right.

Answer Form

1 Ⓐ Ⓑ Ⓒ Ⓓ
2 Ⓐ Ⓑ Ⓒ Ⓓ   **Number** ⟋3
3 Ⓐ Ⓑ Ⓒ Ⓓ   **Correct**

1 Which of the following **best** describes the poem's organization?

   A stanzas of two lines in which the end words of each line rhyme

   B stanzas of four lines throughout with every other end word rhyming

   C a pattern of two-, four-, and six-line stanzas with a changing rhyme scheme

   D alternating stanzas of four lines and two lines with a consistent rhyme scheme

2 Which **best** describes a purpose of the four-line stanzas in the poem?

   A Each adds a new theme to the poem's meaning.

   B Each describes an episode that advances the story.

   C Each marks a new time and place in the chronology.

   D Each repeats the same phrase about the main character.

3 The structure of the poem uses lines of consistently similar length. Which **best** describes a reason this text feature is used in the poem?

A It shows all events in the poem are equally important.

B It makes it easier for the poet to find rhyming end words.

C It allows the poet to create a steady rhythm throughout.

D It makes the sometimes difficult phrasing easier to read.

4 Explain what effect the repetition of the lines "Brennan on the Moor, Brennan on the Moor, / Bold and undaunted stood young Brennan on the Moor" has on the meaning of the poem. Use at least **two** details from the text to support your answer.

_____

_____

_____

_____

5 The poet organizes the poem into stanzas that have four lines or only two lines. Explain why the poet structured the poem in this way by comparing the content presented in the four-line and two-line stanzas. Support your answer with at least **two** details from the poem.

_____

_____

_____

_____

_____

_____

_____

✓ **Self Check** *Go back and see what you can check off on the Self Check on page 128.*

Analyzing the Structure of Stories

CCLS

RL.6.5: Analyze how a particular sentence, chapter [or] scene . . . fits into the overall structure of a text and contributes to the development of the theme, setting, or plot.

Theme: *Wilderness Adventures*

Stories are made of words. Authors build those words into sentences and paragraphs and—if the story is really long—chapters. This is pretty obvious. What's less obvious is how these parts work together to develop a story's theme, setting, and plot. When you think about how a story's parts work together, you're thinking about the story's **structure**.

One way to analyze a story's structure is ask yourself this question: How does a specific sentence or chapter help develop this story? You can do something similar with cartoons.

Read the cartoon below. The two panels are part of a longer story. Ask yourself: What does each panel contribute to the setting and the plot of the longer story?

Complete the chart. It will help you analyze what each panel contributes to the story.

Panel	Contribution to Setting	Contribution to Plot	Contribution to Theme
Left	The characters are in a forest.	• The characters have been walking for hours. •	The panels, when taken together, suggest the story's theme is about how people should act when in danger.
Right	The forest is not safe.	• The boy has broken his ankle. •	

As you read, stop and ask yourself: How does this section of the story build on what came before? How do these pieces help develop the theme, setting, or plot? Doing this sort of analysis will help you understand not just what a story tells but how it tells it.

Read the first two paragraphs of an adventure about encountering an animal in the wild.

Genre: Adventure Story

A Moose Encounter   by Lucy Barrett

Jill quietly slipped out of the faded orange tent and into the cool fall air of a Minnesota morning. Though the sun had just begun to rise, she could hear woodland creatures scurrying on the ground. Jill glanced back to make sure her father was still asleep inside. He had told her not to wander around alone, but she *had* to see a moose. They had been making this camping trip for three years now, and though this was supposed to be moose territory, they had yet to actually see one. Jill was determined to change that.

Moving swiftly, Jill eventually found herself at the river. She decided to wait, hoping that a moose might come and drink. A short time later, Jill saw a brown animal in the distance, and she held her breath as the creature approached. It was a moose calf! Grinning broadly, Jill began walking toward it, but before she could get very far, a giant female moose appeared out of nowhere and came charging toward her.

(continued)

Explore how to answer this question: *"What role does each paragraph play in helping to develop the story?"*

Each paragraph plays its own part in telling a story. Reread each paragraph and ask yourself: What does it add to the story?

Complete the chart below. It will help you analyze what each paragraph contributes to the story.

Paragraph	Contribution to Setting	Contribution to Plot
First	It establishes the setting: a fall morning in Minnesota	It starts the story: Jill wants to see a moose so badly that she disobeys her father to see one.
Second		

With a partner, discuss what the theme of this story might be. Then discuss what roles paragraphs 1 and 2 play in developing that theme.

Continue reading the adventure story. Use the Close Reading and the Hint to help you answer the question.

Close Reading

Circle details that show what happens to Jill after the calf's mother comes running toward her. How does this moose encounter contribute to the story's plot and theme?

(continued from page 154)

Petrified, Jill could only stare as the animal galloped closer and closer. She knew the worst place to be was between a mother animal and her young, especially an animal as massive as a moose.

Suddenly, Jill felt herself being yanked out of the moose's path, and she held on tightly as her father pulled her behind some trees to hide from the moose's view. They watched as the mother became distracted by her calf, and Jill sighed in relief.

Later, when she had finally returned to the safety of the campsite, Jill was full of apologies. "I learned my lesson," she vowed to her father. "No more moose encounters for me."

Hint

A story's falling action occurs after the climax has been reached. It leads to the resolution, when the story's conflict is resolved.

Circle the correct answer.

Which statement best describes the role the second paragraph on this page plays in the story's plot?

A It details the story's turning point, when Jill's father scolds her.

B It presents a new problem that Jill and her father must face.

C It shows that Jill has learned to always listen to her father.

D It explains how Jill's father saves her and sets up the resolution.

✏️ **Show Your Thinking**

Explain your answer. Why is the second paragraph on this page necessary to the story?

_____

_____

 Discuss the story's overall theme with a partner. Which sentences are most important in developing this theme?

Read the following excerpt from a novel. Use the Study Buddy and the Close Reading to guide your reading.

According to the introduction, John is looking for a deer. I wonder if he's going to find one. I'll look for signs of a deer in the story.

Close Reading

In this excerpt, the setting is not directly stated. **Circle** clues in paragraph 2 that suggest the setting.

How does hunting the deer help John? **Draw a box** around details in paragraph 5 that show how the deer encounter affects him.

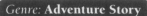

Genre: **Adventure Story**

from *Tracker*   *by Gary Paulsen*

John Borne always hunts with his grandfather, but this year his grandfather is dying of cancer. John can think of little else. As he goes looking for a deer alone, he hears a noise.

1   It was a releasing sound, as if a branch or tree which had been held had been turned loose—a kind of *swoosh*—in back of him, back to his right, and he froze, waiting for another sound to guide him. None came.

2   He turned and took two steps, then two more, and so covered a distance of perhaps thirty yards until he came to a deer bed. It was about a yard across, where snow had been melted down to bare swamp grass in a cupped little warm place under a stand of willows. . . .

3   He knelt next to the bed and felt the grass and it was still warm. That had been the sound. A deer had been here in its storm bed . . . and he had walked past it and it had jumped up, apparently hitting the willow on the way.

4   It must have surprised the deer, his coming, because the first tracks were more than ten feet from the bed. The deer had bounded up and away. The next tracks were twenty feet from the first ones, out into a clearing and across, craters in the new snow where the deer had run.

5   *Well*, he thought. *I was close to one, anyway, even if I didn't know it.* . . . It came to him suddenly that he hadn't thought about his grandfather for nearly an hour and he didn't know if that was good or if that was bad.

Hints

How do the clues about the deer lead into the rest of the story?

Use the Hints on this page to help you answer the questions.

1 In the first sentence, John hears a swoosh and looks around. How does this sentence contribute to the story?

    A It shows that John is not very good at hunting by himself.

    B It introduces a theme about the thrill of deer hunting.

    C It establishes that John's conflict will be with the deer.

    D It creates suspense about whether John will find a deer.

Which answer fits best with the clues you circled in paragraph 2?

2 How does paragraph 2 develop the setting of this story?

    A It shows snow and swamp grass on the ground.

    B It reveals how far from home John has walked.

    C It helps readers understand what a deer bed is.

    D It explains what time of day it is in the story.

What does the last sentence tell you about the main conflict of the story?

3 Describe how the final sentence contributes to the plot of the story. Use details from the story to support your answer.

_____

_____

_____

_____

_____

_____

_____

_____

_____

_____

_____

Read the following excerpt from a novel. Then answer the questions that follow.

from *Hatchet*

by Gary Paulsen

Thirteen-year-old Brian Robeson is stranded in the Canadian wilderness after a plane crash, and now he must study his environment to survive. In this part of the novel, he has been dreaming of his father. Now he dreams of his friend Terry.

1   He was not gesturing to Brian but was sitting in the park at a bench looking at a barbecue pit and for a time nothing happened. Then he got up and poured some charcoal from a bag into the cooker, then some starter fluid, and he took a flick type of lighter and lit the fluid. When it was burning and the charcoal was at last getting hot he turned, noticing Brian for the first time in the dream. He turned and smiled and pointed to the fire as if to say, see, a fire.

2   But it meant nothing to Brian, except that he wished he had a fire. He saw a grocery sack on the table next to Terry. Brian thought it must contain hot dogs and chips and mustard and he could think only of the food. But Terry shook his head and pointed again to the fire, and twice more he pointed to the fire, made Brian see the flames, and Brian felt his frustration and anger rise and he thought, All right, all right. I see the fire but so what? I don't have a fire. I know about fire; I know I need a fire.

3   I know that.

4   His eyes opened and there was light in the cave, a gray dim light of morning. He wiped his mouth and tried to move his leg, which had stiffened like wood. There was thirst, and hunger, and he ate some raspberries from the jacket. They had spoiled a bit, seemed softer and mushier, but still had a rich sweetness. He crushed the berries against the roof of his mouth with his tongue and drank the sweet juice as it ran down his throat. A flash of metal caught his eye and he saw his hatchet in the sand where he had thrown it at the porcupine in the dark.

5   He scooched up, wincing a bit when he bent his stiff leg, and crawled to where the hatchet lay. He picked it up and examined it and saw a chip in the top of the head.

6   The nick wasn't too large, but the hatchet was important to him, was his only tool, and he should not have thrown it. He could keep it in his hand, and make a tool of some kind to help push an animal away. Make a staff, he thought, or a lance, and save the hatchet. Something came then, a thought as he held the hatchet, something about the dream and his father and Terry, but he couldn't pin it down.

7   "Ahhh . . ." He scrambled out and stood in the morning sun and stretched his back muscles and his sore leg. The hatchet was still in his hand, and as he stretched and raised it over his head it caught the first rays of the morning sun. The first faint light hit the silver of the hatchet and it flashed a brilliant gold in the light. Like fire. That is it, he thought. What they were trying to tell me.

8   Fire. The hatchet was the key to it all. When he threw the hatchet at the porcupine in the cave and missed and hit the stone wall it had showered sparks, a golden shower of sparks in the dark, as golden with fire as the sun was now.

9   The hatchet was the answer. That's what his father and Terry had been trying to tell him. Somehow he could get fire from the hatchet. The sparks would make fire.

10   Brian went back into the shelter and studied the wall. It was some form of chalky granite, or a sandstone, but imbedded in it were large pieces of a darker stone, a harder and darker stone. It only took him a moment to find where the hatchet had struck. The steel had nicked into the edge of one of the darker stone pieces. Brian turned the head backward so he would strike with the flat rear of the hatchet and hit the black rock gently. Too gently, and nothing happened. He struck harder, a glancing blow, and two or three weak sparks skipped off the rock and died immediately.

11   He swung harder, held the hatchet so it would hit a longer, sliding blow, and the black rock exploded in fire. Sparks flew so heavily that several of them skittered and jumped on the sand beneath the rock and he smiled and struck again and again.

12   There could be fire here, he thought. I will have a fire here, he thought, and struck again—I will have fire from the hatchet.

Answer Form

1 Ⓐ Ⓑ Ⓒ Ⓓ
2 Ⓐ Ⓑ Ⓒ Ⓓ   **Number**
3 Ⓐ Ⓑ Ⓒ Ⓓ   **Correct** /3

1   How does Brian's dream contribute to the plot of the story?

    A   The dream suggests that Brian needs to find food.

    B   The dream shows what Brian's normal life was like.

    C   The dream reveals that Brian is feeling lonely.

    D   The dream provides clues to help Brian survive.

2   In paragraph 10, the author describes the setting in detail. Why is this paragraph important to the story?

    A   The rock wall of the cave can make sparks.

    B   The cave provides a place for Brian to rest.

    C   The wilderness presents a huge challenge.

    D   The wilderness offers different types of fuel.

3   Read this sentence from paragraph 11.

> He swung harder, held the hatchet so it would hit a longer, sliding blow, and the black rock exploded in fire.

What does this sentence contribute to the plot?

A   It is the resolution, because Brian has solved his problem, ending the conflict.

B   It represents the rising action, because the problem is becoming even worse.

C   It serves as the climax, because after this Brian begins to solve the problem.

D   It is part of the falling action, because it is the solution to Brian's problem.

4   Describe how paragraphs 8 through 12 contribute to the development of the story's theme. Use details from the text to support your answer.

_____

_____

_____

_____

_____

_____

_____

_____

_____

_____

_____

_____

_____

 **Self Check**   *Go back and see what you can check off on the Self Check on page 128.*

Lesson 17 Part 1: Introduction

Explaining Point of View

CCLS

RL.6.6: Explain how an author develops the point of view of the narrator or speaker in a text.

RL.6.6.a: Explain how an author's geographic location or culture affects his or her perspective.

Theme: *Culture Shock*

Have you ever had two friends tell you about the same event but hear two very different stories? That's because each one told you how the event looked from his or her **point of view**, or perspective. When you read a story or poem, you get a point of view, too. Sometimes it's the point of view of the author, but often it's the point of view of the **narrator**, or speaker—the voice that tells the story. At other times, you might even experience the events through the eyes of one or more of the characters.

Think about how a narrator would describe the scene below from the boy's point of view. How would the description differ if it were told from the woman's perspective?

Read the chart below. Think about how the details in the illustration suggest each character's point of view.

Details	Character's Point of View
The boy is leaning against a tree. He looks like he's taking a nap.	The boy is peaceful and content. He feels like it's a lovely, lazy day.
The woman has her hands on her hips and an angry expression on her face.	The woman is angry because the boy is resting instead of painting.

The two characters in the illustration above are having two very different experiences. This results in two very different points of view about the same situation. The boy in the picture might not care that he's not working, but the woman definitely does!

Good readers understand that *how* an event is described is directly affected by *who* is describing it. Thinking about the point of view of the storyteller can help you understand how an author develops characters' attitudes, feelings, or beliefs.

Read the first three paragraphs of a historical fiction story.

Genre: **Historical Fiction**

The Settlers   *by Rowena Jackson*

Little Bear crept closer and closer through the tall grass until he had a better vantage point to watch the trail of wagons pass. He'd never seen white people before, though his father sometimes traded skins and bows with the men. Little Bear had heard all the warnings, but he still wanted to see what they looked like.

One wagon fell behind the rest of the caravan. The rains of the past few days had turned the trail to thick mud, and the wagon's oxen were tired. They made it another few minutes before Little Bear heard a loud crack, and the back corner of the wagon crashed to the ground.

Two people from the wagon inspected the broken wheel. Little Bear froze when one pulled out a rifle and fired it into the air. He crouched into a small ball in the weeds, his heart drumming in his ears. But then he saw other people running to help the stranded travelers, and he knew that the rifle shot had just been a signal.

(continued)

Explore how to answer this question: *"The narrator describes the scene from Little Bear's point of view. What do you find out as a result?"*

In order to understand Little Bear's point of view, first identify words and phrases that reveal his thoughts, feelings, or attitudes in this scene.

Look for details suggesting how Little Bear feels toward the settlers. Then complete the chart.

Evidence from the Text	Character's Point of View
	Little Bear is curious about the white settlers but not necessarily afraid of them.
He freezes at the sound of the rifle; he crouches into a ball and his heart beats fast.	

On the lines below, explain how the narrator's description of Little Bear's experiences influences the reader's understanding of events.

_____

_____

_____

Continue reading about Little Bear. Use the Close Reading and Hint to help you complete the chart.

Close Reading

What is Little Bear's attitude toward the white settlers in the last paragraph? **Circle** any clues that suggest how Little Bear feels.

(continued from page 162)

   Just then, there was a rustle in the grass beside Little Bear. He let out the long breath he'd been holding when he saw it was just his older brother, White Deer, who silently signaled that they needed to return home before the settlers spotted them.

   Little Bear followed, but he paused a moment to glance back. Traveling out on the open prairie was dangerous, and the settlers were just people. He hoped the pioneer family got their wagon wheel fixed soon.

Hint

Little Bear was curious about the white settlers and then became startled by the rifle. How does he feel now?

Complete the following chart by using evidence to explain Little Bear's point of view at the end of the story.

Evidence from the Text	Character's Point of View

✎ **Show Your Thinking**

Explain how the evidence from the text helped you determine Little Bear's point of view.

_____

_____

 With a partner, discuss how the author revealed Little Bear's changing attitude toward the settlers.

Read the following story. Use the Study Buddy and the Close Reading to guide your reading.

This story is in the form of a girl's diary. As I read, I'll underline details that help me understand more about her point of view.

Close Reading

How does Anya feel during her time at Ellis Island? **Draw a box** around any details that express or suggest her emotions.

What is Anya's attitude toward America in the last paragraph? **Circle** details that reveal what she thinks about her new home now.

Genre: **Historical Fiction**

Landing at Ellis Island   *by Stuart Crowley*

1   ***From the diary of Anya Bulgakov, age 13:***

2   *August 24, 1912:* I'm <u>not speaking to my parents.</u> This afternoon we were standing at the railing on the ship's deck, mother and father cheering and pointing out at the island approaching across the waves. They hugged me <u>(I didn't hug back)</u> and told me <u>AGAIN</u> how our wonderful new home in America was going to be full of opportunities. I didn't speak English, I reminded them, only Russian, and I wouldn't know any of their customs. I <u>miss my real home.</u>

August 25, 1912: The Ellis Island Great Hall where we waited for five hours to be processed thundered with strange voices and terrifying faces. Finally, I wedged myself under my mother's arm to escape the distant cries of a child. At last, a stern medical examiner inspected each of us. We were not marked with chalk, thank goodness. That would have been a sign that we were ill and had to be deported. Relieved, we moved on to another line. Then we came to a table where the impatient man who also spoke Russian asked us question after question. He recorded the details in his ledger, and to my great relief, we were done.

3   *September 9, 1912:* The city is a bustling and amazing place! We've rented rooms in a building with other Russian immigrants, and my new friend Katya has promised to help me learn English. Father has secured work at a printer's shop, and mother has made my favorite *shashlyk* and *pirozhki* dishes for our new neighbors—New York City might just become a home for me after all!

Hints

Which choice is supported by Anya's behavior on the ship?

What kinds of words and phrases does Anya use to describe her experience at Ellis Island?

Trace the shifts in Anya's attitude throughout the story by looking back at the details you marked.

Use the Hints on this page to help you answer the questions.

1 At the beginning of the story, what is the narrator's point of view about immigrating to America?

    A   Anya is angry and upset about having to leave Russia.

    B   Anya is anxious about having to learn English.

    C   Anya is excited to be making a home in a new country.

    D   Anya is grateful that there will be new opportunities for her.

2 What text evidence supports the idea that Anya feels afraid during her day at Ellis Island?

    A   She and her family had to wait for five hours to be processed.

    B   She was not marked with the chalk that meant she was ill.

    C   She says that the Great Hall was filled with "terrifying faces."

    D   She describes the man who asks her questions as "impatient."

3 Describe how Anya's attitude toward her new home changes by the end of the story. Include at least two details from the text that show how the author develops Anya's point of view.

_____

_____

_____

_____

_____

_____

_____

_____

_____

_____

Read the following excerpt from a novel. Then answer the questions that follow.

The Japanese-American author of this story, Yoshiko Uchida, was raised to appreciate her parents' culture and language, yet she was often excluded by her classmates as a result. Later she traveled to Japan, and her appreciation for her heritage became stronger. When writing her novels, Yoshiko always emphasized the need for readers to look past labels and appreciate people as human beings.

from *A Jar of Dreams*

by Yoshiko Uchida

1   That summer turned special from the day Mama got the letter that caused her strange behavior. It was on a Tuesday, one of the days Mama went to work for Mrs. Phillips to clean her house and scrub her floors. The minute I got home from school and walked into the kitchen, I knew something was wrong. Well, not wrong exactly, but strange. I felt the way I do when I've got one sweater button in the wrong hole or when I put my left slipper on my right foot.

2   In the first place, water was dripping from the kitchen faucet and splashing on dishes Mama had left in the sink. Ordinarily Mama never leaves the house without checking the faucets to see that they're turned off good and tight. And she never leaves dirty dishes sitting in the sink when she goes to work.

3   But that wasn't all. She'd left so many things scattered over the kitchen table, I couldn't even see the yellow oilcloth cover. The Japanese newspaper was spread out on the table with a square hole in it where Mama had cut out the recipe for the day. And she hadn't bothered to put away the scissors she'd used. There were two or three bills Mama hadn't opened and a five-page letter from Japan that hadn't been put back in its envelope. The table was a mess, and if I had left it that way, or my brother, Joji, we sure would have heard about it from Mama.

4   I looked at the Japanese writing in the letter, squiggling up and down the soft rice paper like a lot of skinny black spiders, and wished I could read it. But of course I couldn't, because I don't study very hard at Japanese Language School, and besides I'm not far enough advanced to read that kind of writing. All I could read were the numbers that said first day of the fifth month, 1935. I had a hunch, though, that whatever was in the letter was the reason Mama had gone off acting like Joji instead of her own neat self. And I couldn't bear to wait until she got home to tell me what was in the letter.

5   I stuffed the letter in the envelope, grabbed an apple from the bin in the sunporch, and headed for Papa's barbershop. It was a hot day, but I ran all the way to Shattuck Avenue and forgot to wait until I'd gotten to Channing Way before crossing Shattuck. That meant I'd have to walk by the Starr Laundry, which I usually avoided like a nest of cobras because of Mr. Wilbur J. Starr, the owner.

6   The reason I hate and despise Wilbur J. Starr is because he is so mean and nasty. Once when I was in the fourth grade, Joji and I walked by his laundry on the way home from Papa's shop. Old Wilbur J. Starr was standing in the doorway of his laundry, and when Joji and I walked by minding our own business, he yelled, "Get outta here you . . . Jap kids!"

7   Joji dropped my hand and began to run. "Come on, Rinko," he yelled. "He's gonna git us." And he went steaming on ahead of me, pounding hard on his fat legs.

8   I wanted to run with him, but when I heard Wilbur Starr laughing behind us, I just held up my head and said to Joji, "Pretend you never heard him." But my knees were shaking so hard, I could barely walk home.

9   Ever since that day, I try never to walk by the Starr Laundry if I can help it, because I hated the way I felt when Wilbur Starr called me a Jap. It made me really mad, but it also made me feel as though I was no good. I felt ashamed of who I was and wished I could shrink right down and disappear into the sidewalk.

10   There are a few white girls in my class at school who made me feel that way too. They never call me "Ching Chong Chinaman" or "Jap" the way some of the boys do, but they have other ways of being mean. They talk to each other, but they talk over and around and right through me like I was a pane of glass. And that makes me feel like a big nothing. Some days I feel so left out, I hate my black hair and my Japanese face. I hate having a name like Rinko Tsujimura that nobody can pronounce or remember. And more than anything, I wish I could just be like everybody else.

Later, Rinko finds out about the contents of the letter—her Aunt Waka in Japan is coming to visit them. During her stay, Aunt Waka teaches Rinko to appreciate her Japanese culture and traditions, to preserve her heritage, and above all, to value herself.

Answer the questions. Mark your answers to questions 1–3 on the Answer Form to the right.

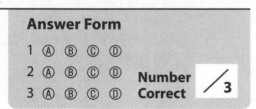

Answer Form

1 Ⓐ Ⓑ Ⓒ Ⓓ
2 Ⓐ Ⓑ Ⓒ Ⓓ   **Number**
3 Ⓐ Ⓑ Ⓒ Ⓓ   **Correct** / 3

1   How does Rinko's point of view about the letter reflect the author's perspective as a Japanese American?

   A   Like the author, Rinko knows why a letter from Japan might upset a family member.

   B   Like the author, Rinko wishes she were better at reading Japanese writing.

   C   Like the author, Rinko doesn't study hard at a Japanese language school.

   D   Like the author, Rinko has a hunch about details in a letter.

2   How does the author reveal Rinko's feelings about her mother's behavior?

   A   by telling how Rinko's mother goes to clean house for Mrs. Phillips

   B   by telling how Rinko couldn't wait to hear more about the letter from her mother

   C   by telling how Rinko's mother was acting like Joji instead of her neat self

   D   by telling how Rinko's mother checks the faucets before leaving for work

3   The author develops Rinko's point of view in the story to show that she sees herself as an outsider who feels left out of the community around her. Which sentence from the story **best** supports this conclusion about how the author develops Rinko's point of view?

    A   "The minute I got home from school and walked into the kitchen, I knew something was wrong."

    B   "But of course I couldn't, because I don't study very hard at Japanese Language School, and besides I'm not far enough advanced to read that kind of writing."

    C   "I wanted to run with him, but when I heard Wilbur Starr laughing behind us, I just held up my head and said to Joji, 'Pretend you never heard him.'"

    D   "They talk to each other, but they talk over and around and right through me like I was a pane of glass."

4   Explain how the author's culture influences the way she was able to develop Rinko's point of view. Use at least **three** details from the text to support your response.

_____

_____

_____

_____

_____

_____

_____

_____

_____

_____

_____

 **Self Check**   *Go back and see what you can check off on the Self Check on page 128.*

Read the poem. Then answer the questions that follow.

The Migration of the Grey Squirrels

by William Howitt

1   When in my youth I traveled
throughout each north country,
Many a strange thing did I hear,
And many a strange thing to see.

5   But nothing was there pleased me more
Than when, in autumn brown,
I came, in the depths of the pathless woods,
To the grey squirrels' town.

    There were hundreds that in the hollow boles[1]
10   Of the old, old trees did dwell,
And laid up store, hard by their door,
Of the sweet mast as it fell.

    But soon the hungry wild swine came,
And with thievish snouts dug up
15   Their buried treasure, and left them not
So much as an acorn cup.

    Then did they chatter in angry mood,
And one and all decree,
Into the forests of rich stone-pine
20   Over hill and dale to flee.

    Over hill and dale, over hill and dale,
For many a league they went,
Like a troop of undaunted travelers
Governed by one consent.

[1] **boles:** tree trunks

Answer Form

1A Ⓐ Ⓑ Ⓒ Ⓓ **Number**
1B Ⓐ Ⓑ Ⓒ Ⓓ **Correct** / 2

1 Answer Parts A and B below.

Part A

Read the lines below from the poem "The Migration of the Grey Squirrels."

There were hundreds that in the hollow boles
Of the old, old trees did dwell,
And laid up store, hard by their door,
Of the sweet mast as it fell.

What does the word "mast" mean in these lines?

A fruit

B branch

C rain

D night

Part B

Which word from the lines of text in Part A **best** helps the reader to understand the meaning of "mast"?

A door

B dwell

C hollow

D sweet

2 Describe the structure of the poem. How does the structure help to develop the theme? Use details from the poem to support your answer.

_____

_____

_____

_____

Read the story. Then answer the questions that follow.

The Campsite

by Rupert Menosa

1   Tom and I took turns pounding in the stake pegs, the dull thwack thwack of the mallet the loudest sound in the forest. We were pitching the tent in a small clearing less than an eighth of a mile from a stream. We had pored over the map of the state park for hours, trying to select a campsite close to water but not too close to the lodge where less seasoned park visitors would stay. Both of us were entirely confident of our abilities, having worked as Boy Scout leaders for over a decade. We were strong, able men, and there wasn't much about forest or wildlife that we didn't know.

2   I paused to gaze at the August sky, a beautiful if eerie sight. An orangey-red glare hung over the horizon, making me think of wildfires. Rays of light filtered through the pines, casting a crimson pool at our feet.

3   "What's that?" Tom asked, turning from the tent to scan the area.

4   I heard it too, then: a muffled noise that sounded like something heavy being dragged through the brush. Other campers? Maybe, maybe not.

5   Automatically, my eyes searched out the pine trees that encircled the clearing. The pines were stubby, nothing like the giant redwoods of northern California or the towering oak trees of my hometown back East. However, they were trees, and trees were perfect for climbing.

6   "I don't hear it anymore," Tom offered, brushing at a cloud of gnats that swirled through the darkening air. "Whatever it was, it's gone now."

7   "Then let's get this tent up and start a campfire," I replied. I didn't remark that a canvas structure was little protection against the kind of dangers that lurked in a forest. We both knew that, and besides, the lodge was a scant two miles away.

8   We heated several cans of beans and pork over the fire, washing the meal down with water from our canteens. There were only familiar sounds, now: the faint splashing of the nearby creek, the hooting of an owl, the crackle of twigs on the glowing fire. I relished this peace, far away from the bustle of towns and cities where the predominant noises came from blaring trucks and deafening sirens.

9   "Let's turn in," Tom suggested, yawning. We doused the fire, careful not to leave any burning embers that could start up a blaze, and then packed up food that might attract animals.

10   Worn out from the strenuous trek up the mountain, I was asleep within minutes, heedless of the lumpy pillow formed from a rolled sweatshirt. Tom settled down quickly too and began snoring.

11   I don't know how long we'd been out before a loud snuffling woke me with a jolt. Something rocked the damp canvas of the tent, and there was a strong odor that I knew could only be bear— grizzly bear.

12   Silently, I nudged Tom into consciousness. "Bear!" I whispered. "We've got to get out of this tent. Tree."

13   There was no time to get into specifics and in any case, we both realized there was only one possible escape route. It lay past the roaming bear, and that is where the chief danger also lay.

14   Tom unzipped the tent and we crawled out as stealthily as possible, a pair of crabs scuttling for safety. I cannot speak for my friend, but I was drenched in the clammy sweat of terror.

15   The bear, a shaggy dark shadow, was rummaging through the remains of our dinner. Finding little, it snorted and lumbered over to the tent. While the animal was occupied, Tom and I sprinted to the pines.

16   The trees closest to the tent had been scorched by a forest fire; the lower branches were either stripped or completely destroyed. I scolded myself for having failed to notice this before, but this was no time for reflection. Tom ran to one tree while I headed for another, and for several minutes the only things I heard was my own panting and gasping.

17   During the bleak hours of that long night, we clung to the uppermost branches of the pines. There was simply no way of telling whether the bear was truly gone, or whether the fierce predator still lurked near the clearing.

18   A pale sun rose over the forest, and I began to hope for the best. But there was nothing better, I can assure you, than the roar of an engine rumbling up the mountain. Strong hands helped us down from our perches, and soon we were safe in the truck of two park rangers.

19   "You men should have stayed at the lodge—didn't you see the caution signs posted along the trail?" one of the rangers asked. "Bears have been active in this area. A couple of humans aren't much good against an angry grizzly on the rampage."

20   We had to agree with them: apparently, there are some things that even a seasoned woodsman should fear. Next time we're in bear country, we'll stay in the lodge with its cheerful lamps, cozy companionship, and stout wooden doors.

3 How does the last paragraph contribute to the plot of the story?

A It helps the reader understand the danger that the men face.

B It summarizes the problem and solution in the story.

C It reveals how the rangers know where to look for the two men.

D It shows how the narrator learns a lesson and changes his point of view.

4 At the beginning of "The Campsite," the author develops the narrator's point of view to show that he is confident in his abilities as an outdoorsman. Which sentence from the story **best** supports this conclusion?

A "Tom and I took turns pounding in the stake pegs, the dull thwack thwack of the mallet the loudest sound in the forest."

B "We were pitching the tent in a small clearing less than an eighth of a mile from a stream."

C "We were strong, able men, and there wasn't much about forest or wildlife that we didn't know."

D "I paused to gaze at the August sky, a beautiful if eerie sight."

5 Which event is most important to the development of the plot of the story?

A The campers build a fire for cooking.

B The narrator hears the noise of an engine.

C The campers choose a spot far from the lodge.

D The narrator observes the sounds of the forest.

6 In the story, the words "a dark, shaggy shadow" are used to describe the bear. What is the connotation of the phrase?

    A something unusual

    B something menacing

    C something weak

    D something imagined

7 In the story, what is the effect of the figurative language comparing the men to "a pair of crabs scuttling"?

    A It indicates panic.

    B It expresses humor.

    C It suggests the men are clumsy.

    D It means the men are cowardly.

8 How does the narrator's attitude change during the course of the story? Use details from the story to support your answer.

_____

_____

_____

_____

_____

_____

Performance Task—Extended Response

9 How does the setting contribute to the development of the story? Which details about the campsite are important to the plot? Be sure to include details from the story in your answer.

In your answer, be sure to
- describe the setting of the story, including the details that make it important
- explain how the characters' choice of a campsite develops the plot of the story
- use details from the story in your answer

Check your writing for correct spelling, grammar, capitalization, and punctuation.

_____

_____

_____

_____

_____

_____

_____

_____

_____

_____

_____

_____

_____

_____

_____

_____

_____

_____

_____

_____

_____

_____

_____

_____

Unit 5
Integration of Knowledge and Ideas in Informational Text

Have you ever heard a speech given by a candidate running for office? Candidates make claims about how the country should be run or how to improve their communities. Smart voters try to learn all they can about the candidates before they cast their vote. They listen to the candidates' speeches, read articles expressing different viewpoints, and follow reports in the media. Only after **integrating** all of that information do they decide how to vote. A smart reader, like a smart voter, collects **knowledge** and **ideas** from a variety of sources and **integrates** it, or puts it together, to thoroughly understand a topic. Then the reader, like a voter, can make an informed choice about what to believe.

In this unit, you will learn to find and use information from a variety of sources, both print and media. You will look for an author's claims in a text and decide whether they are supported by reasons. You will read different texts on the same subject, making connections across the texts and comparing the differerent viewpoints of the authors. You'll even learn how to write an essay in response to texts that you've read.

✓ **Self Check**   **Fill out the Self Check on the next page.** ▶

Before starting this unit, check off the skills you know below. As you complete each lesson, see how many more you can check off!

✓ Self Check

I know how to:	Before this unit	After this unit
follow the argument an author makes and identify its claims.	☐	☐
tell whether an author's claims are supported by reasons.	☐	☐
describe the similarities and differences between two authors' presentations of the same events.	☐	☐
follow the steps involved in writing an extended-response essay	☐	☐
find and use information from different media, such as websites and video, to learn about a topic.	☐	☐

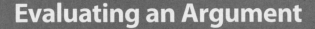
Evaluating an Argument

CCLS

RI.6.8: Trace and evaluate the argument and specific claims in a text, distinguishing claims that are supported by reasons and evidence from claims that are not.

Theme: *Weighing the Evidence*

An **argument** states an author's position about a topic and tries to get readers to agree with it. As a reader, it's your job to **evaluate**, or judge, whether the author's argument is sound—that is, whether it presents clear thinking and sensible ideas.

Begin evaluating an argument by tracing, or figuring out, how the author has "built" it. First, identify the author's position on the topic. Then study any claims. **Claims** are statements the author presents as true in order to support his or her position. Also note any reasons and evidence the author gives to support each claim.

Look carefully at the cartoon below. Try to figure out the girl's argument.

This chart shows details about the girl's argument. Add the evidence she gave in the cartoon to support Claim 1. Then add a sensible reason or evidence to support Claim 2.

Argument: The girl should have a dog.

Claim 1: Having a dog will make her more responsible.	**Claim 2:** A dog will be a good friend and companion to her.
Reason or Evidence:	**Reason or Evidence:**

After you trace how an author develops an argument, evaluate it further to decide if it is sound. Ask: Does each claim support the author's argument and make sense? Does the author give reasons and evidence that support each claim? If you can ask and answer such questions, you'll be able to distinguish strong, sound arguments from weak ones.

Read the following persuasive essay about whether hip-hop should be taught in English classes.

Genre: **Persuasive Essay**

Today's Lesson: Hip-Hop　　*by Anita Perry*

　　Year after year, most literature classes cover the same authors and genres. It's time that educators made a change. For teachers to keep current and engage students, we must allow students to read diverse texts from their own generation. As a first step, hip-hop should be included in the literature curriculum.

　　This suggestion is not as odd as it may seem. After all, hip-hop is simply another form of poetry, as are all song lyrics. The verses of hip-hop have rhyme schemes, rhythms, and meters. In addition, hip-hop lyrics deal with the same timeless themes as other forms of poetry, including heartache and the challenges of growing up. In many ways, today's hip-hop artists are contemporary versions of William Shakespeare and Emily Dickinson, only with a modern, fresh perspective.

(continued)

Explore how to answer this question: *"What is the author's argument, and how does she support it with claims, reasons, and evidence?"*

First, identify what the author wants to convince you about. Then, find the claims she uses to show *why* her position is sound. Finally, identify reasons or evidence she gives to support each claim.

Analyze the author's argument by completing the chart below. State what her argument is. Then add one reason and one claim she gives to support her position on hip-hop.

Argument:

Claim 1: Hip-hop is a form of poetry. **Reason:**	**Claim 2:** **Reason:** Hip-hop lyrics deal with topics such as heartache and the challenge of growing up.

With a partner, take turns evaluating the author's argument. Does it seem sensible? Has the author provided support for her claims? Use reasons and evidence to support your evaluation.

Continue reading the essay. Use the Close Reading and Hint to help you answer the question.

Close Reading

On page 180, the author makes two claims to support her argument about hip-hop. **Underline** another claim she gives in the first paragraph on this page.

(continued from page 180)

Examining hip-hop songs in class can help teachers identify more closely with their students' interests, cultures, and life experiences. The subject matter or lyrics of some hip-hop songs may be objectionable, but teachers can find plenty of acceptable options to explore.

Additionally, teachers can help students think critically about the lyrics and messages of their favorite songs. Exploring hip-hop will strengthen students' analytical skills and their ability to connect old and new forms of literature. Our students will therefore become more engaged, challenged, and informed.

Hint

How does the author think hip-hop will help teachers understand their students?

Circle the correct answer.

What claim does the author make in the first paragraph on this page to support her argument that hip-hop should be taught in literature classes?

A Hip-hop is more interesting than classic poetry.

B Lyrics for hip-hop songs can teach students life lessons.

C Teachers can better relate to their students' experiences.

D Students can learn to write hip-hop lyrics.

✎ Show Your Thinking

Evaluate the essay you just read. Judge whether or not the author provides enough strong reasons and evidence to support her claims and argument. Use text details in your response.

_____

_____

_____

_____

 With a partner, discuss other reasons the author could have included to support her claims.

Read the following editorial about the censorship of school yearbooks. Use the Study Buddy and the Close Reading to guide your reading.

As I read, I'll figure out the author's claims about censorship and the reasons and evidence he uses to support his claims.

Close Reading

What is the author's argument? **Underline** it, and **circle** the first claim the author gives as support.

What is the second claim the author gives? **Circle** the second claim and label it "2." Then **underline** the evidence—if any—the author provides.

Genre: **Editorial**

Say No to Censorship *by Marcos Suarez*

1   A yearbook is a special collection of memories that will be treasured by students for decades. However, some school authorities insist on dictating what students can and cannot include in yearbooks. Teachers often remove articles and images they feel are inappropriate. Authorities should not ruin this treasure by censoring yearbooks and removing what they believe to be unsuitable.

2   Educators need to respect students' right to free speech. Everyone needs to be reminded that the First Amendment of the Constitution protects "freedom of expression." This fundamental right should be upheld and appreciated.

3   School authorities also need to acknowledge how much students learn when they can express themselves freely. Students need more opportunities to develop their creativity. Creative expression will allow students to create interesting yearbooks that capture all of their school experiences.

4   Those who feel that yearbooks should be censored need to explain their goals. They may claim that they want to protect students, but aren't they really trying to promote their own values? Authorities need to be open and honest about what they want to accomplish by censoring yearbooks.

5   Teachers should work together with students to define and discuss the word *objectionable*. Respecting students' opinions on censorship will empower students and allow school yearbooks to be the treasure they deserve to be.

Hints

Which answer choice restates the author's position and claims that you marked on the previous page?

Use the Hints on this page to help you answer the questions.

1 Which statement best summarizes the author's argument?

A School authorities need the freedom to practice censorship upon the content of yearbooks.

B School authorities are obligated to remove objectionable material from yearbooks to protect their students.

C School authorities should work together with students to delete objectionable material from yearbooks.

D School authorities should not censor school yearbooks because it limits students' rights and creativity.

Reread the second paragraph of the editorial. Which answer choice matches closely with the author's ideas in this paragraph?

2 The author mentions the First Amendment in the editorial. What purpose does this reference serve?

A to explain why yearbooks should be censored by school authorities

B to support the idea that students have a right to express themselves

C to point out why yearbook censorship is a controversial topic

D to emphasize the problem of objectionable school materials

Does the author give strong reasons and evidence to support each of the claims in his argument?

3 In the editorial, the author explains his position on censorship of school yearbooks. How well do you think the text supports his ideas about censoring yearbook materials? Cite details from the text to support your evaluation.

_____

_____

_____

_____

_____

_____

_____

_____

Read the article. Then answer the questions that follow.

Longer school day: Expanded learning time pros and cons

by Bethany Bray, The Andover Townsman

ARGUMENTS IN FAVOR

- **More time to cover the curriculum.**

1   "I'm always hearing from teachers that there's not enough time," Superintendent Claudia Bach said. "We really need more time to do the academic things, not just extracurricular."

2   The extra time allotted with ELT [expanded learning time] would allow teachers to expand current lessons, introduce special projects, provide new enrichment and have time for more teacher workshops and development, supporters say.

3   "If you look at the curriculum, you say, 'Oh my gosh, how can a teacher possibly get this done?' ELT will allow us to do so much more, for all our kids," said Brad Heim, a High Plain Elementary parent. "There's always room for improvement, and we have the luxury of being out front and being able to decide how we want to do it."

- **Provide students global, 21st century skills.**[1]

4   "Andover's looking at 21st century skills like cultural awareness, communication skills. For Andover, it's making education all it can be . . . The big vision is that the world is changing, education is changing, and how can the schools meet the needs of the children and society?" said Lisa Glickstein, grant coordinator for the district. "Kids are doing reading and math that we didn't do at their age."

5   But Glickstein added, "Parents are justifiably concerned. . . . We're still figuring out if this grant program is right for Andover."

- **State money is growing.**

6   Although ELT grants guarantee money for only one year, school districts can reapply year after year, and preference is given to districts that have ELT programs, Glickstein said.

7   ELT funding has increased substantially in the three years it's been offered by the state, Heim said. What started as $500,000 has increased to $13 million this year, and Gov. Deval Patrick and Sen. Edward Kennedy are in favor of ELT, he said.

---

[1] **21st century skills:** The skills students need to succeed in a highly technological workplace.

8   "With such tremendous support from our legislature, even in these economic times, (ELT funding) is being increased," Heim said. "It's being funded because it works."

ARGUMENTS AGAINST

- **If it ain't broke, why fix it?**

9   Andover is already one of the top districts in the state. In the past, ELT grants have helped underperforming districts such as Boston and Worcester with low state test scores and high dropout rates, problems Andover does not have.

- **Only one year of funding guaranteed.**

10   "As the political atmosphere changes, there's no promise of long-term funding," said Karen Lu, a High Plain Elementary parent. "Realistically, we cannot support this kind of budget long term, and it's almost practically a certainty that funding would be dropped eventually."

11   Lisa Glickstein, grant coordinator for Andover, said, "It is a legitimate concern that the grant will go away. There really is no way that the town budget would be able to support that amount of time in a long-term way."

- **Takes time away from families.**

12   Bancroft Elementary mother Dawn Kalinowski, who also teaches at Pentucket Regional High School, believes ELT could eliminate the positive effect of parental involvement.

13   "We may be taking away the very thing that makes Andover such a great district," she said.

14   She switched careers from engineering to teaching to have more time with her kids. Being able to put her kids on the bus in the morning is priceless, she said.

15   Also, Andover parents, including Kalinowski herself, provide very specific extracurricular activities and lessons tailored to their children. School districts can't provide something each youth likes.

---

1   What evidence does the article provide to support one claim in favor of adding expanded learning time?

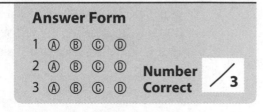

Answer Form

1 Ⓐ Ⓑ Ⓒ Ⓓ
2 Ⓐ Ⓑ Ⓒ Ⓓ   **Number**   /3
3 Ⓐ Ⓑ Ⓒ Ⓓ   **Correct**

A   Andover schools are already top performers in the state.

B   Funding for longer school days is only guaranteed for one year.

C   Some are convinced that ELT will encourage positive parent involvement.

D   More time is needed for current academic lessons and special projects.

2 Why does the author include the fact that the amount available for expanded learning time [ELT] programs has increased to $13 million?

A It proves that starting an ELT program is a good way for Andover to raise money.

B It suggests that ELT programs are growing rapidly, so Andover should add one.

C It shows that ELT is too expensive a program for Andover to fund on its own.

D It supports the idea that state funding for Andover's ELT program will not run out.

3 Which statement **best** summarizes the argument against expanded learning time?

A Andover should not begin ELT because Andover is a high-performing district, the funding might run out, and ELT takes time away from families.

B There is no point in starting ELT in Andover because grant money to fund it might run out after a single year, and the town could not pay for it.

C ELT is most useful in districts where test scores are low and dropout rates are high, but Andover does not have these problems.

D Adding extra time to the school day would allow less time for parents to help their own children, so students' performance might actually suffer from ELT.

4 In her article, the author intends to show that future funding of an ELT program in Andover is uncertain. Explain how the text supports this idea about the uncertain future of ELT in the town. Use at least **two** details from the text to support your response.

_____

_____

_____

_____

_____

_____

 **Self Check** *Go back and see what you can check off on the Self Check on page 178.*

Lesson 19   Part 1: Introduction 👥

Comparing and Contrasting Texts

CCLS
RI.6.9: Compare and contrast one author's presentation of events with that of another (e.g., a memoir written by and a biography on the same person).

Theme: *American Icons*

If you've ever read two articles about a movie star, you often come away with two different impressions. Even if two pieces of writing are about the same topic, they don't always present the same ideas. Each author might have a different purpose for writing, a different point of view about the topic, or access to different information. For example, an author writing a **biography**, or a true account of a person's life, will have a different perspective than the person writing his or her own **autobiography** that tells about the same events from personal experience.

Read the following texts. The first describes the 1969 moon landing from the viewpoint of a woman who saw the event. The second is from a student's history report.

> I'll never forget the day that *Apollo 11* landed on the moon. It was July 20, 1969, and I had just turned 12. Although it took place late on a Sunday night our time, my parents let me stay up past my bedtime to join the millions of people watching Neil Armstrong take the first step on the moon's surface. I still recall how my imagination raced. Would I be able to live on the moon one day? At that moment, anything seemed possible.

> At 10:56 PM Eastern Daylight Time on Sunday, July 20, 1969, Neil Armstrong became the first person to set foot on the surface of the moon. Astronaut Buzz Aldrin followed Armstrong onto the lunar surface 20 minutes later. These historic events were broadcast from the moon's surface and watched by perhaps the largest television audience ever—approximately half a billion people around the world.

Now read both accounts a second time. Circle information that is similar in both texts. Then underline details in each text that do not appear in the other.

Both texts discuss the same event, but each author wrote for a different purpose. The first author discusses her personal experience. The second author writes to inform readers.

When reading different texts on the same topic, you can compare and contrast the authors' purposes and points of view. This can help you understand why each author chose to include certain details and leave out others.

Read the following short biography of Amelia Earhart.

Genre: **Biography**

Born to Fly   *by Ann Randall*

Amelia Earhart didn't always dream of becoming an aviator. While she had seen airplanes growing up, it wasn't until her early twenties that she realized she was born to fly. When Earhart was 20 years old, she and a friend attended a stunt-flying contest. Their fun ended, however, when one of the planes came zooming toward them. In spite of the danger, Earhart stood firm, displaying the same fearlessness that she would continue to show all her life. This encounter proved to be a sign of things to come: just a few years later, Earhart found herself flying inside an airplane.

On December 28, 1920, pilot Frank Hawks changed Earhart's life by taking her on her first plane ride. It was then that she knew she was meant to be in the air. Earhart attended her first flying lesson just five days later, and by 1922, she was already setting records: She became the first woman to fly to an altitude of 14,000 feet. Over the next 15 years, Earhart would continue to make her mark on the record books time and time again, proving that flying was truly in her blood.

Explore how to answer this question: *"How does the author's purpose influence the focus of the text and the details presented?"*

The author wants to focus on the early part of Earhart's life to explain her passion for flying. Which facts has the author presented to show how Earhart's experiences started her on the path to becoming a famous and fearless aviator?

On the lines below, explain the author's purpose. Find evidence from the text to support your answer.

_____

_____

_____

_____

With a partner, discuss the author's point of view about Amelia Earhart and how these feelings are shown throughout the text. How might the author's point of view toward Earhart have affected her choice of details and her presentation of events?

Read another biography of Amelia Earhart. Use the Close Reading and the Hint to complete the activity.

Genre: **Biography**

Earhart on Equality   *by Brian Vargas*

As a famous female aviator, Amelia Earhart did much to advance equality for women. In 1928, she became the first woman to fly across the Atlantic, and she spent the rest of her life fearlessly flying farther, faster. Earhart was first to fly many long, dangerous routes, and she encouraged other women to fly. She championed women in the sciences as a guest professor at Purdue University. She said, "Women must try to do things as men have tried. When they fail, their failure must be but a challenge to others."

Close Reading

Underline important facts about Amelia Earhart that the author includes in this biography. What do they help you understand about Earhart? Why might the author have chosen to include them?

Hint

Both biographies contain some of the same facts, but the authors use them differently. How does this help convey different messages about Amelia Earhart?

Fill in the chart below based on the two biographies you read.

Write facts that are different under the title of each biography. Write facts that are similar in the two biographies under Both.

"Born to Fly"	Both	"Earhart on Equality"

✎ **Show Your Thinking**

On a separate piece of paper, write two paragraphs comparing and contrasting the information provided in the biographies on pages 188 and 189.

 With a partner, discuss why these two biographies about Earhart are different. Consider the authors' purposes for writing, their points of view, and the information they chose.

Read the following memoir and biography about Helen Keller. Use the Study Buddies and the Close Readings to guide your reading.

As I read, I'll think about how Helen Keller's memory and emotions influence her writing.

Close Reading

Circle words in the title and first two sentences that tell you who is writing this passage.

Underline words and phrases that show Keller's thoughts and feelings. What do you think she wants the reader to understand?

Genre: **Memoir**

from *The Story of My Life*   by Helen Keller

1   My teacher had been with me several weeks before I understood that everything had a name. One day, while I was playing with my new doll, Miss Sullivan put my big rag doll into my lap also, spelled "d-o-l-l" and tried to make me understand that "d-o-l-l" applied to both. Earlier in the day we had had a tussle over the word "m-u-g." Miss Sullivan had tried to impress it upon me that "m-u-g" is *mug* and that "w-a-t-e-r" is *water*, but I persisted in confounding the two. In despair she had dropped the subject for the time, only to renew it at the first opportunity. I became impatient at her repeated attempts and, seizing the new doll, I dashed it upon the floor. I felt my teacher sweep the fragments to one side of the hearth, and I had a sense of satisfaction that the cause of my discomfort was removed. She brought me my hat, and I knew I was going out into the warm sunshine.

2   We walked down the path to the well-house. Some one was drawing water and my teacher placed my hand under the spout. As the cool stream gushed over one hand she spelled into the other the word *water*, first slowly, then rapidly. I stood still, my whole attention fixed upon the motions of her fingers. Suddenly I felt a misty consciousness as of something forgotten—a thrill of returning thought; and somehow the mystery of language was revealed to me. I knew then that "w-a-t-e-r" meant the wonderful cool something that was flowing over my hand. That living word awakened my soul, gave it light, hope, joy, set it free!

I wonder why the author wanted to write this biography of Helen Keller. I'm going to look for clues that help me understand her purpose.

Close Reading

What event is described in Keller's memoir on page 190? **Box** the information about the same event in this biography.

Underline at least three important facts that the author of this biography includes that are not present in Helen Keller's memoir. How do these facts help you know the author's purpose for writing is different than Keller's?

Genre: **Biography**

A Remarkable Life   *by Mary Wilkes*

1   For a year and a half after Helen Keller's birth on June 27, 1880, she was a healthy, bright child. She started to talk at six months old and walked at one. However, all of that changed when, in February of 1882, she came down with a high fever. Although she survived, her family soon discovered that the illness had left her blind and deaf.

2   Young Helen found ways to cope with her new situation, such as developing a limited system of signs with a playmate. By the time she was seven, though, she had also become wild and undisciplined. Desperate, her family finally contacted the Perkins Institute for the Blind, which recommended a recent graduate, Anne Sullivan, to work with Helen. Of course, most people know the story of how Sullivan helped Helen realize that "w-a-t-e-r" meant the liquid running over her hand. Helen learned thirty new words that first day and went on to quickly master finger signs, touch-lip reading, and Braille reading and typing.

3   Determined to complete college, Helen graduated with high honors from Radcliffe in 1904; she also wrote and published her autobiography, *The Story of My Life,* in 1903. She wrote ten other books and many articles in her lifetime. Her greatest achievements, however, were her efforts to help others around the country and throughout the world. Many of her visits prompted the creation of new resources for blind and deaf-blind individuals. Because she could relate to people's difficulties, she worked with leaders to improve their situations. Everywhere she went, she spread a message of strength and courage, a legacy that stands to this day.

Hints

Think about the kinds of facts provided by each author. Why do they include these facts? What do they each hope to achieve?

Use the Hints on this page to help you answer the questions.

1 How does Helen Keller's purpose for writing her memoir differ from that of the biographer who wrote about her life?

  A Helen tries to inform people about the facts of her life, but the biographer wants people to know about Helen's personality.

  B Helen tries to explain her childhood actions, while the biographer writes to tell people about Helen's wild childhood.

  C Helen wants to reflect on her experiences, while the biographer writes to inform people about events in Helen Keller's life.

  D Helen wants to entertain people by describing her point of view, but the biographer wants to amaze people with facts.

What text did you draw a box around in the biography on page 191?

2 What event appears both in Helen Keller's memoir and the biography of Helen Keller?

  A how she lost both her hearing and sight

  B how she learned that things have names

  C how she learned to touch-read people's lips

  D how she helped the blind all over the world

What do you learn from a memoir that you can't from a biography? How does learning about many parts of a person's life in a biography help you understand one part?

3 Describe how the two accounts of Helen Keller's life are different. Think about the event they both describe. Explain what you learn from the memoir compared to what you learn from the biography. Use at least two details from the text in your response.

_____

_____

_____

_____

_____

_____

_____

_____

_____

Read the two articles about the creation of Spider-Man. Then answer the questions that follow.

Stan Lee and Spider-Man

by Simmi Patel

1   Spider-Man is a popular comic book superhero who continues to delight his fans some 50 years after his creation. In the autobiography *Excelsior! The Amazing Life of Stan Lee*, his creator, Stan Lee explains his version of how Spider-Man came to life.

2   Stan Lee had been working in the comic book business for over twenty years. He wanted to create a hero who had a realistic life in addition to superpowers. Lee presented his idea to his boss and publisher, Martin Goodman.

3   "I told Martin I wanted to feature a hero who had just a touch of super strength but his main power was that he could stick to walls and ceilings," Lee says.[1] Lee explained that his hero, Spider-Man, would also be a normal teenager. Spider-Man would be raised by his Aunt May and Uncle Ben and have all the normal problems of an adolescent. The hero would be worried about money, allergies, girls, and anything else that Lee could think of.

4   According to Lee, the creation of Spider-Man had sprung from his reading as a child. One of his favorite magazines was called *The Spider—Master of Men*, and Lee loved that name. He remembers the character wearing a slouch hat and a special spider ring. If The Spider hit someone, he would leave the impression of a spider on his victim. Although Lee remembers The Spider vividly, he clarified that this character never had superpowers like Spider-Man.

5   According to Lee, Martin Goodman hated his idea. Goodman felt that a superhero couldn't be a teenager with personal problems. He said that Spider-Man seemed more like a comedy character than a powerful superhero. Since most people don't like spiders, Goodman thought that the name "Spider-Man" was a terrible choice.

6   But Lee couldn't give up on his idea of Spider-Man. He gave artist Jack Kirby a plot line for Spider-Man and asked him to illustrate it. As Lee tells it, "Jack started to draw, but when I saw that he was making our main character, Peter Parker, a powerful-looking, handsome, self-confident typical hero type, I realized that wasn't the style I was looking for. So I took Jack off the project. He couldn't care less because he had so many other strips to draw at the time, and Spider-Man wasn't exactly our top-of-the-line character."[2]

7   Lee reassigned the project to Steve Ditko, who used a more subtle and stylized style of drawing. Ditko's rendition was exactly what Lee had in mind. They finished the comic strip, and it was published in the last issue of *Amazing Fantasy* in 1962. When sales figures of that publication came in, they showed that the Spider-Man issue was a huge success. According to Lee, Goodman ran into Lee's office to congratulate himself

---

[1] Stan Lee and George Mair. *Excelsior! The Amazing Life of Stan Lee* (New York: Fireside, 2002) p. 126.

[2] Lee and Mair, p. 127.

and Lee on the new character. Lee says, "I can still hear his now-classic comment, 'Stan, remember that Spider-Man idea of yours that I liked so much? Why don't we turn it into a series?'"[3]

8   Spider-Man became one of the most successful comic book characters ever. When Spider-Man headed up Marvel comic books' line of heroes, sales increased from 7 million copies in 1961 to 13 million copies in 1962.[4]

9   After Steve Ditko stopped drawing Spider-Man, artist John Romita took over. He slowly incorporated his own style, and Peter became tall and handsome as he grew up. The characters gradually took on a new look, and the Spider-Man comic strip continued to increase in popularity.

[3] Lee and Mair, p. 128.

[4] Lee and Mair, p. 132.

The Birth of Spider-Man

by Max Bruno

1   What do you think of when you hear the name Spider-Man? A superhero who can cling to almost anything? Devices that shoot spider webs? A "spider sense" to outwit enemies?

2   Since his appearance in the early 1960s, Spider-Man has been different than other comic book superheroes. Initially, he was a teenager who had to deal with loneliness, rejection, and other realistic problems. Over the years, Peter Parker went to college, got married, taught high school, and became a freelance photographer. By 2011, he had become a member of two superhero teams, the Avengers and the Fantastic Four. But how did Spider-Man crawl into existence?

3   In his autobiography, *Excelsior! The Amazing Life of Stan Lee*, Lee explains his version of the birth of Spider-Man. Stan Lee had been working in the comic book business since 1939. Lee always wanted to be a writer, and he began by writing comic book text filler. Later, he wrote features and became an editor before he was 20. According to Lee, he had been trying to develop a superhero who also needed to deal with the normal problems of daily life. He presented his idea to his boss, Martin Goodman. Lee maintains that Goodman thought Spider-Man was a terrible idea.

4   Lee claims he asked artist Jack Kirby to illustrate his plot line but later reassigned the job to artist Steve Ditko. Lee liked Ditko's stylized approach. The comic strip was published in 1962, and it became a huge success.

5   Others, however, have called Lee's version of events into question. In the book *Stan Lee and the Rise and Fall of the American Comic Book*, authors Jordan Raphael and Tom Spurgeon take a different viewpoint. They claim that the original Spider-Man was the result of the work of several artists and writers. Stan Lee wanted to create a spider superhero, but artist Jack Kirby also wanted to draw an insect superhero. Raphael and Spurgeon explain, "Stan Lee expressed the desire to do a teenage superhero using the spider motif. Jack Kirby had long wanted to do an insect-related superhero." Kirby started to put together a slightly different version of the tale. He rejected "some of the more fantastic Lee story elements," instead adding "a kindly aunt and uncle, and giving the superhero a secret origin revolving around a neighbor who happened to be a scientist."[1]

[1] Jordan Raphael and Tom Spurgeon, *Stan Lee and the Rise and Fall of the American Comic Book* (Chicago Review Press, 2003), p. 93.

6   The character of Spider-Man was eventually given to artist Steve Ditko. He worked from a story summary and Kirby's ideas, and eventually he created the drawings of Spider-Man and Peter Parker with "bottle-thick glasses, slumped shoulders, and a homemade costume. Ditko was nearly as sharp as Kirby when it came to shaping characters in ways that would make them effective on the page. The Spider-Man millions of readers came to know and love got his youth and voice from Stan Lee and his human frailty from Steve Ditko."[2] And the first cover drawing of Spider-Man was drawn by Jack Kirby.

7   According to Raphael and Spurgeon, Lee often built on contributions from other artists. Comic book publishers tried to produce as many books as possible in a short amount of time, and Lee encouraged everyone to contribute ideas. As more writers and artists were hired, everyone shared ideas. Later, legal and financial questions arose regarding who actually created which comic book character. But during the early 1960s, superhero comic books flourished through this collaborative process.

[2] Raphael and Spurgeon, pp. 93–94.

---

1   How does the author's purpose for writing the first article, "Stan Lee and Spider-Man," differ from the author's purpose for writing "The Birth of Spider-Man"?

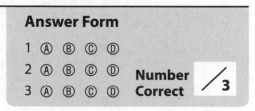

Answer Form

1 Ⓐ Ⓑ Ⓒ Ⓓ
2 Ⓐ Ⓑ Ⓒ Ⓓ   **Number**
3 Ⓐ Ⓑ Ⓒ Ⓓ   **Correct** /3

   A   The first author describes Stan Lee's version of the creation of Spider-Man. The second explains that there are different versions of how Spider-Man was created.

   B   The first author wants readers to understand why Stan Lee is so popular. The second wants readers to understand why Spider-Man is so popular.

   C   The first author wants readers to reflect on Stan Lee's point of view. The second wants readers to reflect on facts about Stan Lee's career.

   D   The first author wants to describe Stan Lee's vision of Spider-Man. The second wants to describe Jack Kirby's vision of Spider-Man.

2   What did **both** authors want the reader to understand about Martin Goodman and the creation of the Spider-Man character?

   A   Martin Goodman headed the team who developed the Spider-Man concept.

   B   Martin Goodman respected Stan Lee's decisions as a writer.

   C   Martin Goodman shaped the character to make him effective on the page.

   D   Martin Goodman didn't deserve credit for the creation of Spider-Man.

3   Which fact appears in **both** articles?

    A   Martin Goodman felt that the name "Spider-Man" was a terrible choice.

    B   Spider-Man was probably the result of several writers' ideas.

    C   Steve Ditko created the art for the character of Spider-Man.

    D   Jack Kirby also wanted to create a superhero that looked like an insect.

4   Compare and contrast the way the two authors present information about Spider-Man in these articles. Describe similarities and differences in the authors' purposes, their points of view, and the facts they chose. Use at least **four** details from the articles to support your response.

_____

_____

_____

_____

_____

_____

_____

_____

_____

_____

_____

_____

_____

_____

✓ **Self Check**   *Go back and see what you can check off on the Self Check on page 178.*

CCLS
RI.6.9: Compare and contrast one author's presentation of events with that of another . . .
W.6.2: Write informative/explanatory texts to examine a topic and convey ideas, concepts . . .
W.6.9: Draw evidence from literary or informational texts to support analysis, reflection, and research.

Introduction By now, you've probably answered many kinds of questions on school tests. You've chosen the correct letter, filled in the blank, completed charts, matched one thing to another, and so on.

Answering any kind of test question takes knowledge. But writing an essay about what you have read takes some extra skills. Writing an essay doesn't have to be difficult, if you know how to go about it. Just remember to follow these simple steps each time you write.

What Are the Steps?	What Do I Do?
1. Analyze the Prompt	• Read the prompt carefully. • Identify the type of writing you need to do, for example, comparing and contrasting how two different authors present the same events. • Notice what kinds of details you must include.
2. Gather Text Evidence	• Carefully reread the passages named in the prompt. • Find evidence that will support the ideas you want to present.
3. Organize Your Ideas	• Make a plan for your essay. • Decide how many paragraphs you will write and what evidence to include in each one.
4. Draft Your Essay	• Write your essay, following the plan you made. • Use transition words and phrases such as *however*, *similarly*, and *on the contrary* to link your ideas. • Use precise vocabulary, for example *towering* instead of *tall*, to explain your ideas clearly.
5. Check Your Work	• Be sure you have written about each topic in the prompt. • Revise your draft by changing or adding details. • Proofread to find any mistakes in grammar, capitalization, punctuation, and spelling.

Before you begin, reread "Stan Lee and Spider-Man" and "The Birth of Spider-Man" on pages 193–195.

Step 1 | Analyze the Prompt You might be tempted to jump right in and start writing when you come to a prompt on a test. But you should take a moment to analyze the prompt before you begin. Be sure you understand clearly what you're being asked to write. Here are some tips:

1. Read the prompt slowly and carefully.

2. Underline any key words or phrases that give important clues about how you should write your essay.

3. Read the prompt again. Ask yourself questions about what you're supposed to do: What passages do I need to write about? What kind of essay am I supposed to write? Do I need to give my opinion? Should I be comparing and contrasting? What kind of evidence will I need to include?

Modeled Instruction **Read the following prompt. Then fill in the blanks to explain what the underlined key words and phrases tell.**

Prompt 1

Both articles discuss the problems Stan Lee had in getting people to accept his ideas for a new kind of superhero. <u>Which article</u> do you think <u>best explains why Lee had trouble convincing people to accept his ideas</u> for Spider-Man? Using specific details from both articles, discuss how each author presents the challenges Lee faced in developing Spider-Man.

In your response, be sure to:

- <u>describe how the author of "Stan Lee and Spider-Man"</u> presents the challenges Lee faced

- <u>describe how the author of "The Birth of Spider-Man"</u> presents the challenges Lee faced

- <u>tell which article</u> you think <u>best describes Lee's challenges</u> and explain your reasons for that choice

- use <u>details from both articles</u> in your response

These key phrases explain that the essay must describe how both authors present the challenges Lee faced.

These clue words tell you to write about which article best explains _____ _____ _____ _____.

This is a reminder that your essay must include details from _____ articles.

Now imagine that you are asked to write about these articles on a test. Use what you just learned to analyze the prompt.

Read the following prompt carefully. Underline key words and phrases that are the most important clues for helping students understand what to write. Then answer the questions that follow.

Prompt 2

Both articles show Stan Lee as the main creator of Spider-Man. But how much did other people contribute to the character? Compare and contrast the two reports about how much help Lee received from others in creating Spider-Man.

In your response, be sure to:

- describe what "Stan Lee and Spider-Man" says about other people helping Lee
- describe what "The Birth of Spider-Man" says about other people helping Lee
- compare and contrast what the two articles report about others' contributions
- use details from both articles in your response

1 What are two questions you should ask yourself after reading this prompt?

_____

_____

2 What kind of essay am I being asked to write?

I am being asked to write a compare and _____ essay.

3 When you write your essay, what is the main question from the prompt that you will be trying to answer?

_____

_____

4 When you write your essay, what is something you should contrast?

_____

_____

 Tell your partner what you learned about analyzing a writing prompt.

Step 2 | Gather Text Evidence Once you've figured out what the prompt is asking you to do, you're ready for the next step. It's time to start gathering evidence from the texts you've read.

When you write your essay, support the things you say with solid evidence. That will take a bit of detective work on your part. You need to sort through information in the texts for the evidence that supports your case. Evidence can take many forms, including details, facts, quotations, and examples. To find the right evidence for your essay, take a close look at the passages. Underline the information you might want to use to support and explain ideas in your essay.

Modeled Instruction **Prompt 2 asks students to describe what the first author says about how other people may have helped Lee create Spider-Man.**

- describe what "Stan Lee and Spider-Man" says about other people helping Lee

Read the excerpt below from "Stan Lee and Spider-Man." Then fill in the blanks to explain what the underlined evidence shows about other people helping Lee.

But Lee couldn't give up on his idea of Spider-Man. He gave artist Jack Kirby a plot line for Spider-Man and asked him to illustrate it. As Lee tells it, "Jack started to draw, but when I saw that he was making our main character, Peter Parker, a powerful-looking, handsome, self-confident typical hero type, I realized that wasn't the style I was looking for. So I took Jack off the project. He couldn't care less because he had so many other strips to draw at the time, and Spider-Man wasn't exactly our top-of-the-line character."

Lee reassigned the project to Steve Ditko, who used a more subtle and stylized style of drawing. Ditko's rendition was exactly what Lee had in mind. They finished the comic strip, and it was published in the last issue of *Amazing Fantasy* in 1962. When sales figures of that publication came in, they showed that the Spider-Man issue was a huge success. According to Lee, Goodman ran into Lee's office to congratulate himself and Lee on the new character. Lee says, "I can still hear his now-classic comment, 'Stan, remember that Spider-Man idea of yours that I liked so much? Why don't we turn it into a series?'"

This is evidence that Lee relied on artists to create drawings of his ideas for Spider-Man.

This shows that Kirby's drawings helped Lee realize he didn't want Parker to look like a

_____

_____

_____ .

These details show that with Ditko's help, Lee got a Spider-Man that was _____

_____

_____ .

Prompt 2 also asks students to describe what the second author says about others helping Lee.

> • describe what "The Birth of Spider-Man" says about other people helping Lee

Read the passage below from "The Birth of Spider-Man." Underline three sentences or phrases that show how other people may have helped Lee in creating Spider-Man. Explain what each piece of evidence proves about other people helping Lee.

. . . "Stan Lee expressed the desire to do a teenage superhero using the spider motif. Jack Kirby had long wanted to do an insect-related superhero." Kirby started to put together a slightly different version of the tale. He rejected "some of the more fantastic Lee story elements," instead adding "a kindly aunt and uncle, and giving the superhero a secret origin revolving around a neighbor who happened to be a scientist."

The character of Spider-Man was eventually given to artist Steve Ditko. He worked from a story summary and Kirby's ideas, and eventually he created the drawings of Spider-Man and Peter Parker with "bottle-thick glasses, slumped shoulders, and a homemade costume. . . ."

What the Evidence Shows
1 _____
_____
_____
_____
2 _____
_____
_____
_____
3 _____
_____
_____
_____

4 What are two questions you might ask yourself when you are looking for evidence?

_____

_____

5 What conclusion can you draw about others helping Lee from the evidence you underlined?

_____

_____

 Tell your partner what you learned about how to find the right kind of evidence to respond to a writing prompt.

Step 3 Organize Your Ideas You've already taken two important steps in the essay-writing process. You've analyzed the prompt, and you've gathered evidence from the text. Your next step will be to organize your ideas. Most essays are organized in a standard order that makes it easier for readers to follow what's being said.

A good essay has three parts: the introduction, the body, and the conclusion.

Introduction	Body	Conclusion
The introduction tells readers what the essay will be about. It states the writer's opinion or main idea.	The body presents evidence that supports the main idea stated in the introduction.	The conclusion sums up the writer's thoughts. It often restates the main idea of the essay.

Think about how you will organize your essay *before* you begin writing. If you study the way a writing prompt is arranged, it will often guide you in knowing how many paragraphs to write. It can also help you decide which details you might include in each paragraph.

 Modeled Instruction **Read Prompt 2 again. Then fill in the blanks to explain what the body of an essay for this prompt should include.**

Prompt 2

Both articles show Stan Lee as the main creator of Spider-Man. But how much did other people contribute to the character? Compare and contrast the two reports about how much help Lee received from others in creating Spider-Man.

In your response, be sure to:

- describe what "Stan Lee and Spider-Man" says about other people helping Lee
- describe what "The Birth of Spider-Man" says about other people helping Lee
- compare and contrast what the two articles report about others' contributions
- use details from both passages in your response

Introduction

The first paragraph should state the main idea and explain what you are going to compare and contrast.

Body

Describe what the first article reports about how others helped Lee.

Describe what the second article reports about _____

_____.

Another paragraph should compare and contrast _____

_____.

Conclusion

The last paragraph should restate the main idea and sum up the similarities and differences.

Write notes that describe what you would include in each part of an essay that responds to Prompt 2. Look again at the articles "Stan Lee and Spider-Man" and "The Birth of Spider-Man" on pages 193–195 to find specific evidence. Don't write the essay—just make notes!

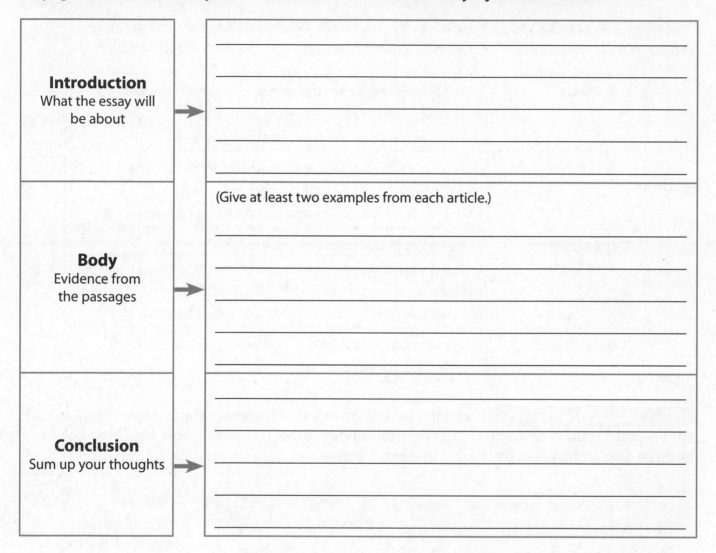

Introduction What the essay will be about	_____
Body Evidence from the passages	(Give at least two examples from each article.) _____
Conclusion Sum up your thoughts	_____

Step 4 | Draft Your Essay Once you've organized your ideas, it's time to start writing! As you draft your essay, follow your outline. Use one like you've made in the chart above.

- Remember to use transition words and phrases such as *in a like manner*, *similarly*, *on the contrary*, or *whereas* to show your readers how your ideas are connected.

- Choose your words carefully. Your sentences will be easier to understand if you use precise language, such as *threatening* instead of *mean* or *strenuous* instead of *difficult*.

 Discuss with your partner what you learned about the three main parts of an essay.

Step 5 | Check Your Work After you've drafted your essay, the hardest part is behind you. But don't stop yet! It's important to read your work carefully.

- First, look back at the big stuff—the content of your essay. See if your writing might be improved by adding supporting details or by cutting information that doesn't really belong.

- Proofread your essay. Correct mistakes in spelling, punctuation, capitalization, or grammar.

Following is a checklist you can use to review your work. When you write an essay for a test, reviewers will read it and give it a score. The checklist they use will cover the same points.

Ideas	☐ Did I write an introduction that clearly introduces my topic? ☐ Have I responded to each part of the prompt? ☐ Did I demonstrate an understanding of what I read?
Evidence	☐ Did I support my ideas with appropriate evidence from the text? ☐ Have I included enough details to make my points? ☐ Have I used a variety of evidence, such as facts and quotations?
Organization and Style	☐ Are my ideas organized clearly and logically? ☐ Did I use various transition words and phrases to connect my ideas? ☐ Did I use vocabulary that is formal and specific? ☐ Did I write an interesting conclusion that sums up my topic?
Conventions	☐ Have I used correct grammar, capitalization, and punctuation? ☐ Is each word spelled correctly?

Modeled Instruction **Read the paragraph one student wrote about what "Stan Lee and Spider-Man" reports about the help Lee received from others. Then fill in the blank to explain how the paragraph could be revised to make it better.**

In "Stan Lee and Spider-Man," author Simmi Patel tells how Stan Lee sought help from artists in ~~making~~ his new superhero. He first asked artist Jack Kirby to draw Spider-Man. But Kirby's Peter Parker wasn't what Lee was looking for. ^ So next, Lee tried another artist ^ who used a different style of drawing. This time, the character "was exactly what Lee had in mind." He finally had a picture that matched his own ideas about Parker and Spider-Man.

Style

Use more exact language. Replace *making* with "designing."

Evidence

Why wasn't Kirby's Parker what Lee wanted? Use a sentence from the article.

Evidence

Include more detail about the second artist. Add the words "named _____."

Read the essay one student wrote to respond to Prompt 2. Did the student do a good job? Use the checklist on page 204 to judge the writing. Put a check beside each item that was done well.

　　The first article tells how Stan Lee got help from artists when he was making up Spider-Man. Lee asked Jack Kirby to draw Spider-Man and Peter Parker. Kirby did that, but it wasn't what he wanted. He tried another artist and this time he got what he wanted.

　　The second article tells about Lee and the same two guys. In this one, Kirby already wants to draw an insect superhero. He also wants to change things about Lee's story because he has some better ideas. He finally gets to illustrait the cover of the first Spider-Man comic so it wasn't all a big waste of time for him. The other artist is the one who draws the Spider-Man and Peter Parker that Lee and everybody else likes.

　　The articles are similar because they show Lee got some help from others. They are different because of what they have to say about all that.

The essay could use an opening paragraph, instead of jumping right into a discussion of the first article.

The writer says Lee got what he wanted from the second artist. But what did he like about those drawings? Who drew them?

Where's the evidence that shows how the articles are different?

How could the essay you just read be improved? Write one suggestion in each part of the chart.

Ideas	Organization and Style
My suggestion: _____ _____ _____ _____	My suggestion: _____ _____ _____ _____
Evidence	**Conventions**
My suggestion: _____ _____ _____ _____	My suggestion: _____ _____ _____ _____

Below is the last paragraph from the student essay you just read. Reread the paragraph. Think about how it can be improved.

> The articles are similar because they show Lee got some help from others. They are different because of what they have to say about all that.

Now revise the paragraph. Rewrite it so that it does a better job of responding to the points in the prompt below. Be sure you include evidence from the articles on pages 193–195.

> - compare and contrast what the two articles report about others' contributions
> - use details from both articles in your response

_____

_____

_____

_____

_____

_____

_____

_____

_____

_____

_____

_____

_____

_____

 Share your revised paragraph with a partner. Explain what you added or changed and why.

 **Go back and see what you can check off on the Self Check on page 178.**

Integrating Information

CCLS

RI.6.7: Integrate information presented in different media or formats (e.g., visually, quantitatively) as well as in words to develop a coherent understanding of a topic or issue.

Have you ever wanted to learn everything you could about some topic? Maybe it was a pet you wanted to get, or the next installment in your favorite movie series, or a place you wanted to visit. Where would you go to learn as much as you could about the topic?

There is so much information available these days, and you can find it in many different places and formats. There's print, video, images, charts, graphs, interactive displays—but which do you use to get the information you need? Understanding the different types of media and what you can find in each can help you **integrate**, or pull together, information from a variety of sources to develop a strong understanding of a topic.

Let's say you're thinking about getting a gecko for a pet. Here are different types of media you might research to find out more about geckos.

Print
Books, magazines articles, website articles
What you'll get
- detailed information
- facts and statistics

Your New Pet Gecko

Images
Photos and illustrations
What you'll get
- a clear understanding of what the subject looks like
- labels and captions providing additional information

The leopard gecko is the most popular lizard among pet owners.

Visual Aids
Charts, graphs, maps, and diagrams
What you'll get
- a lot of facts in an easy-to-read format

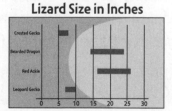

Lizard Size in Inches

Crested Gecko
Bearded Dragon
Red Ackie
Leopard Gecko

0 5 10 15 20 25 30

Videos and Multimedia
Films, documentaries, slide shows, newscasts, animations
What you'll get
- an interesting and engaging presentation
- verbal (words) and visual (images) information

 Brainstorm some questions that would help you decide whether or not a gecko would make a good pet. Then talk about how the different types of media shown above could help you find answers to your questions.

One important question you might have brainstormed about a gecko is, "How hard is it to care for?" Here are some answers you might find in different sources.

Look carefully at each of these sources. Underline or circle details that, taken together, would help give you the answer to your question.

Chart	
Leopard Gecko Facts	
Average adult size:	6–9 inches long
Average life span:	20+ years with special care
Diet:	Insectivore (eats crickets, small mealworms, waxworms)
Habitat:	10–20 gallons for one gecko, multiple hiding places with non-toxic plants, no less than 50% humidity
Behavior:	Nocturnal

Diagram

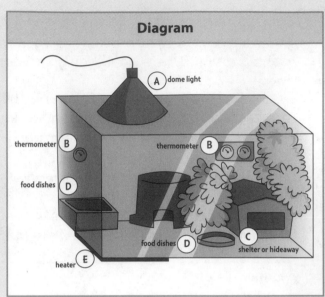

Book

Most geckos are nocturnal, meaning they are active at night. But some species of gecko are active during the day. These geckos are called diurnal. No matter the type of gecko you get, you need to give it a habitat in which it can thrive.

Geckos need warm temperatures. This is easily accomplished by making sure you have a terrarium equipped with a heat lamp that warms one side of the gecko's habitat. It is important to establish a hot zone and a cool zone for your gecko, as well as at least two structures for the gecko to hide in. Put one on the warm side and one on the cool side.

Geckos prefer to eat live food. Crickets are a favorite; you can usually purchase them from a pet store for a relatively cheap price. It is important that you introduce only live crickets (or similar insects) into the habitat. Some species of gecko will also eat bits of fruit.

Geckos need moisture and water to thrive. Spray the habitat daily. Some geckos will drink the water droplets they find in the habitat. Others will need a small bowl of water.

—from *All About Geckos!* by Salvatore A. Manndeer

 Use the information above to make notes about what you would need to set up a gecko habitat for your new pet.

Unit 6
Integration of Knowledge and Ideas in Literature

Have you ever met a pair of twins who are nothing alike? They might look the same on the outside, but their personalities and likes and dislikes might be totally different. The same is true in literature. Think about how many stories you know in which a brave hero triumphs over evil. The stories may take place in different time periods, they may be realistic or fantasy, but like the twins, they have something important in common despite their differences. The more you read, the more **knowledge** and **ideas** you gain about themes in literature and about the different ways in which authors can address a similar theme. By **integrating**, or putting together, this knowledge, you will learn how to appreciate literature in a whole new way.

In this unit you will read literature from a variety of genres and compare the ways in which different authors express the same theme or topic. You will even compare a film based on a book to the original text. You may be surprised to learn how all these works can be both similar and different—just like the twins!

 **Self Check** **Fill out the Self Check on the next page.** ▶

Before starting this unit, check off the skills you know below. As you complete each lesson, see how many more you can check off!

✓ Self Check

I know how to:	Before this unit	After this unit
compare and contrast literary texts in different genres that have similar themes or topics.	☐	☐
describe how different authors treat the same theme or topic.	☐	☐
compare and contrast a story with its movie version.	☐	☐

Comparing and Contrasting Genres

CCLS
RL.6.9: Compare and contrast texts in different forms or genres (e.g., stories and poems; historical novels and fantasy stories) in terms of their approaches to similar themes and topics.

Theme: *Courage*

A reluctant hero saves a village. An unhappy kid learns a secret that changes his life. How many books or movies have you seen with one of these storylines? Many "new" stories are actually old stories retold in new ways, and sometimes in a different genre. A **genre** is a specific category of literature, such as poetry, drama, fantasy, or historical fiction.

Study each picture below. Think of one way in which they are similar and one way in which they differ.

Now look at the diagram below. Complete it by noting the scenes' similarities and differences.

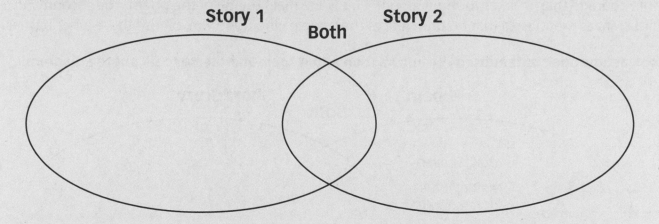

A similar **theme**, or message, may appear in an ancient myth, a modern play, or a classic poem. When you read, be mindful of how the author's choice of genre affects the storyline and the development of the theme. Think about why the author used a particular genre to approach a theme and how another author might approach the same theme in another genre.

Read the poem, in which the speaker talks about a kind of bravery.

Genre: **Lyric Poem**

To Fight Aloud Is Very Brave   *by Emily Dickinson*

To fight aloud is very brave,
But gallanter, I know,
Who charge within the bosom,
The cavalry of woe.

5   Who win, and nations do not see,
Who fall, and none observe,
Whose dying eyes no country
Regards with patriot love.

We trust, in plumed procession,
10 For such the angels go,
Rank after rank, with even feet
And uniforms of snow.

Explore how to answer this question: *"What are the topic and the theme of this poem?"*

This poem compares the courage to face our daily struggles with the bravery shown by soldiers at war. In the first stanza, the speaker notes that fighting battles against sorrow in our hearts requires more courage than it takes to "fight aloud." This is the main theme of the poem. The second and third stanzas emphasize that no one notices the people who fight, win, or lose these inner battles.

Look at how one student used the information about topic and theme to fill out the diagram.

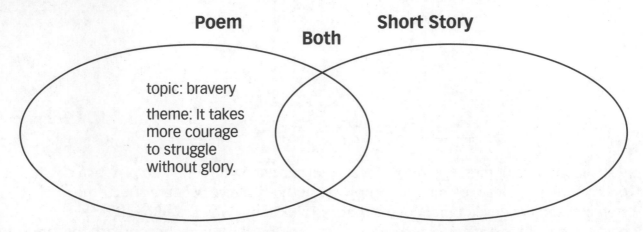

Poem   Both   Short Story

topic: bravery

theme: It takes more courage to struggle without glory.

Read the short story. Then read and answer the questions that follow.

Genre: **Realistic Fiction**

Brave Soldiers   *by Lin Mori*

When Tasha came downstairs early Saturday morning, her father was dressed in full military uniform. His duffle bag was leaning against the front door, and his smile didn't seem quite real. When he kneeled down, Tasha fit into his arms like a key in a lock.

"Remember," he said calmly, "that it's my job to protect our country, and it's your job to be strong and brave at home."

Tasha nodded in agreement, but she could feel her eyes swelling. Some tears escaped, but Tasha knew she couldn't show her father how afraid she was. She would have to be brave for him now, and for herself, until he returned.

Close Reading

Think about what this story has in common with the poem.
Underline a phrase that shows Tasha is similar to the speaker in the poem.

Hint

In what ways are Tasha and her dad showing bravery?

How does the story approach the topic of bravery?

_____

_____

_____

_____

_____

_____

Complete the diagram on page 220 by adding details about the story.

✎ Show Your Thinking

On a separate sheet of paper, compare the types of bravery presented in the poem and story.

💬 Discuss with a partner two similarities and two differences between the story and the poem.

Read the texts. Use the Study Buddies and Close Readings to guide your reading.

As I read, I'm going to think about the theme, or main message, of the story.

Close Reading

What type of person is Chief Joseph? **Underline** the phrase in the sixth paragraph that helps readers understand his character.

Circle the phrases in the final paragraph that show how the author approaches the topic of courage.

Genre: **Historical Fiction**

Fort Fizzle   *by Robert Ingalls*

1   Chief Joseph huddled with the other Nez Perce leaders in the shadow of the nearby mountains, listening quietly.

2   "We have to fight and defend our people," said White Feather. "The white soldiers began this war, not us. And now they are the ones refusing to let us leave peacefully."

3   "They're frightened," said Lean Elk. "So are the settlers in Bitterroot Valley. That is why the soldiers built that foolish fort in the canyon. But this is a battle we can win."

4   "A battle just means more deaths," Joseph retorted.

5   "Better to die fighting than to wait here like cowards!" White Feather exclaimed angrily. He looked away.

6   "I am not saying we should wait," explained Chief Joseph patiently. "But my plan requires another form of courage."

7   That night, Chief Joseph instructed the tribe to pack up their belongings and leave as silently as possible. Then, instead of heading through the canyon, the entire tribe climbed the steep mountain and crossed over a ridge above the fort, following a path barely wide enough for a mountain goat. Several hours later, they reached the valley on the far side and continued peacefully on their journey.

8   By showing wisdom and braving the mountains instead of the soldiers, Chief Joseph and his people avoided conflict and saved many lives. And the fort in the canyon became known as Fort Fizzle, after the battle that never happened.

This story is a fantasy. As I read, I'm going to think about how the author uses fantastic events to deal with the topic of courage.

Close Reading

Compare the characters in this story with the characters in "Fort Fizzle." **Circle** phrases in the sixth paragraph that show how Eli is like Chief Joseph and his tribe.

Think about this story's ending and the final events of "Fort Fizzle." **Underline** the sentence that shows how Eli and his friends avoid conflict. How is this different from Chief Joseph's solution?

Genre: **Fantasy**

Ogel's Tear   *by Ana Smith*

1   Kate, Eli, and Juan sat together in Juan's room, glued to the latest issue of their favorite comic book: *Gilda the Great*. Gilda was strong and fearless, fighting off enemies and performing amazing feats to protect her people from harm.

2   In this issue, Gilda learned that an enormous, gremlin-like creature named Ogel was rampaging through villages, tearing down trees and scaring families from their homes.

3   The trio eagerly turned the page to see how Gilda would defeat Ogel. Kate cleared her throat and read aloud. Just as Kate began reading, a flash of light lit up the room, and the pages of the comic book fluttered excitedly. Moments later, Kate, Eli, and Juan found themselves standing beside Gilda in the midst of a mountain forest.

4   "I'm so glad you've arrived!" Gilda yelled as she raised her sword. "We must join forces to vanquish Ogel!"

5   But just as Juan tried to process what Gilda had said, he noticed one large tear rolling down Ogel's cheek. Juan said, "Gilda, wait! Look at Ogel—I think he's . . . um . . . crying."

6   Suddenly Eli stepped forward and began speaking to Ogel so softly his friends could not hear. Eli's tone was soothing, and he slowly inched closer to Ogel. Baffled, everyone shouted, imploring Eli to stop, but he refused to turn back.

7   Moments later, Ogel dropped to his knees and began sobbing uncontrollably. Eli explained that Ogel was lost and scared, and the creature was desperate to find his family. The group was stunned for a moment, but then they helped Ogel to his feet and assured him that they would help him.

Hints

Don't focus on the different settings of the stories. What lesson do both stories teach?

Use the Hints on this page to help you answer the questions.

1 Which statement best describes the theme of both stories?

   A Sometimes it takes more courage not to fight.

   B When you cannot win a fight, sneak away and hide.

   C True bravery comes from understanding one's enemy.

   D Only cowards refuse to take on a necessary fight.

Look back at the stories to see what you marked about Chief Joseph and Eli. How are they alike?

2 Which traits best describe Chief Joseph and Eli?

   A obedient and shy

   B loyal and honest

   C intelligent and funny

   D brave and kind

What are the key events of each story? How does each story end?

3 Compare and contrast the ways the two stories approach the topic of courage. Explain how each author resolves the conflict. Include at least three details from the texts to support your answer.

_____

_____

_____

_____

_____

_____

_____

_____

_____

_____

_____

_____

Read the excerpt from a novel and then the short story. Then answer the questions that follow.

from *Before We Were Free*

by Julia Alvarez

Twelve-year-old Anita and her family live in a compound in the Dominican Republic in the 1960s, after most of their friends have fled to the United States. Anita learns that her father is involved in the underground resistance to the Dominican dictatorship. In order to stay safe, the girls must keep their family's political beliefs a secret.

1   The night before going back to school, I spend a long time picking out my outfit, as if I'm getting ready for the first day of classes. Finally, I settle on the parrot skirt Mami made me in imitation of the poodle skirt all the American girls are wearing. But even after everything is laid out, I feel apprehensive about going back. Everyone will be asking me why I've been absent for over two weeks. I myself don't understand why we weren't able to go to school just because the SIM were on our doorstep. After all, Papi still went to work every day. But Mami has refused to even discuss it.

2   I go next door to Lucinda's room. My sister is setting her hair in rollers. Talk about torture! How can she sleep with those rods in her hair? For her outfit, she also picked out her skirt just like my parrot skirt, but she insisted on a poodle when Mami made hers.

3   "*Linda* Lucinda," I butter her up. "What are we going to tell everyone at school? You know they're going to be asking us where we were."

4   Lucinda sighs and rolls her eyes at herself in the mirror. She motions for me to come closer. . . .

5   "If people ask, just tell them we had the chicken pox," Lucinda says.

6   "But we didn't."

7   Lucinda closes her eyes until she regains her patience with me. "I know we didn't have the chicken pox, Anita. It's just a story, okay?"

8   I nod. "But why didn't we really go to school?"

9   Lucinda explains that after our cousins' departure, too many upsetting things have been happening and that's why Mami hasn't wanted us out of her sight. Raids by the SIM, like the one we had; arrests; accidents.

10   "I heard Papi talking about some accident with butterflies or something," I tell her.

11   "*The* Butterflies," Lucinda corrects me, nodding. "They were friends of Papi. He's really upset. Everyone is. Even the Americans are protesting."

12   "Protesting what? Wasn't it a car accident?"

13   Lucinda rolls her eyes again at how little I know. "'Car accident,'" she says, making quote marks in the air with her fingers, as if she doesn't really mean what she's saying.

14   "You mean, they were—"

15   "Shhh!" Lucinda hushes me.

16   Suddenly, I understand. These women were murdered in a pretend accident! I shiver, imagining myself on the way to school, tumbling down a cliff, my parrot skirt flying up around me. Now I feel scared of leaving the compound. "So why send us to school at all?"

17   "The Americans are our friends," Lucinda reminds me. "So for now, we're safe."

18   I don't like the sound of "for now," or how Lucinda makes those quote marks in the air again when she says "we're safe."

Raven's Song

by Mista Ward

1   Since she could remember, Raven had loved music. When she was just a child, her grandfather let her sit in the closet of their apartment and listen to old recordings using strange earpieces he called headphones. Eventually, the precious headphones had broken and her grandfather had passed away. Raven still kept the recordings in her closet, but without headphones, there was no way to play music without danger of a neighbor reporting her to the guards. The guards could arrest Raven and her parents for breaking the music ordinance, and those who were arrested rarely returned.

2   Raven found it hard to believe that just over fifty years ago, music had been legal. She imagined the days when cars filled the street, sweet songs blaring from those things her grandfather called radios.

3   Raven took the floating bus to school that day. In her notebook, she drew five lines with music notes on them. She'd learned to write music. She could hear the notes in her head. Suddenly, she caught herself humming a tune aloud. A boy next to her caught her wrist. "Quiet," he said.

4   These days, even humming was dangerous. Sometimes Raven wondered if anyone else sang songs in their head all day. Sometimes she wondered if anyone remembered music at all, or if it had simply died along with the birds and trees and streams.

5   Raven stepped onto a giant moving walkway that moved her briskly to her first class: genetics. There, they learned how to manipulate the cellular structure of food so that it could be grown quickly, indoors, in shallow ground. The class took place in an old auditorium. Instead of a teacher, a movie screen took center stage, flashing information for students to memorize.

6   As Raven sat in the auditorium, she imagined what wonderful musical performances happened there long ago. She kept recording the notes of her song, holding her paper low so no one could see the markings. Lost in thought, Raven began to hum again. The other students turned to her with eyes wide as distant suns, but she didn't stop humming the tune she had written. Soon, she heard another voice join in, then another, and another. For the first time in their lives, Raven and her peers felt the vibrations of music in the air. There was no turning back now.

Answer the questions. Mark your answers to questions 1–3 on the Answer Form to the right.

1   What topic do **both** texts address?

    A   the dangers of an oppressive government

    B   the way scientific developments change society

    C   the need to fit in with classmates at school

    D   the importance of music in people's lives

2   Which sentence **best** captures the theme of both stories?

    A   Accept things the way they are even if you don't agree.

    B   Defying authority, even in secret, is an act of bravery.

    C   It is foolish to challenge people in power for childish reasons.

    D   Only weak, spineless people endure unfair treatment.

3   How do the stories approach the idea of courage in different ways?

    A   The first story shows courage over a long time. The second story shows courage in a single moment.

    B   The first story shows courage as a good quality. The second story shows it as a problem.

    C   The first story shows the courage of a single person. The second story shows the courage of a group.

    D   The first story shows the courage to keep silent. The second story shows the courage to express oneself.

4 In both *Before We Were Free* and "Raven's Song," the main characters must keep secrets because of the harsh governments they live with. Using at least **two** details from **each** story, explain how Anita and Raven feel about their secrets in ways that are alike and different.

_____

_____

_____

_____

_____

_____

_____

_____

_____

_____

_____

_____

_____

_____

_____

_____

_____

_____

_____

_____

 **Self Check** *Go back and see what you can check off on the Self Check on page 218.*

Read the Greek myth and the story. Then answer the questions that follow.

Phaethon and Helios

by Siri Glasoe

1   Long ago in ancient Greece, a teenage boy named Phaethon lived alone with his mother. Although they enjoyed a happy existence, Phaethon felt the absence of his father as he grew older. From a young age, Phaethon had pleaded with his mother to identify his father. Finally, when she felt Phaethon was old enough, Phaethon's mother confided that his father was the sun god, Helios. Helios could not live with them because he had an important job. He drove the chariot of the sun around the earth to herald the arrival of each new day.

2   Phaethon was so impressed by this news that he was determined to meet his father. He left his mother and began a long journey to the ends of the earth, where the gods lived. The trip took many months, and Phaethon often thought about turning back, but he kept going. When Phaethon finally located Helios, he introduced himself as the god's son. Helios, who had not seen Phaethon since he was a baby, was unsure if the youth was his child. Eager to prove he was his father's son, Phaethon begged Helios to let him drive the chariot.

3   Helios hesitated, knowing the horses were too wild and difficult to be controlled by a young and inexperienced boy. He told Phaethon, "Not even Zeus, the king of the gods, is able to drive the wild beasts."

4   Still, Phaethon refused to back down. "If you are really my father," he said, "you will let me try." Helios finally agreed.

5   Helios showed Phaethon how to drive the chariot and made the boy promise to use extreme caution. Phaethon took the reins and started at an easy pace. Ignorant of the skill it took to drive the chariot and overconfident in his abilities, Phaethon soon urged the horses to run faster. The horses stormed across the sky, and the ride quickly turned into a nightmare.

6   At first, the horses ran too high in the sky, making the earth cold and dark. Then they got too close to the ground and burned everything in their path. To prevent the earth's destruction, Helios asked Zeus to throw a thunderbolt to stop the chariot. Frightened by the thunderbolt, the horses stopped, and Helios took control of the chariot. Although Phaethon could not control the horses, Helios acknowledged that he had attempted to steer them back on course and had not cried out for help. "You are a brave boy, " he said. "And you are truly my son."

Handling Hermes

by Kelsey Green

1   Every year, my dad is the most popular speaker at my school's career day. He's a distinguished bareback rider in the rodeo, and his riding skills are admired throughout the rodeo circuit. My friends love hearing about his courageous acts during competitions. Did I mention that Dad is a terrific storyteller in addition to being a great rider?

2   The downside to having such an amazing father is that he travels frequently for his job, and when he's not traveling, he's usually riding somewhere on our property. He believes that to be a great bareback rider, you have to be "one with your horse," which means he is always riding his prized stallion, Hermes, who is named for a Greek god. I inherited my love of riding from my dad, and I want to be part of his thrilling world of rodeos one day.

3   I had begged Dad to let me ride Hermes many times, but he always responded with a firm no. He'd say, "Sara, a great horse like Hermes is a little bit wild, just like the West." I believed him because there were many skilled riders on our ranch, but only Dad was able to control Hermes. Even so, I'd been around Hermes since I was a little girl, and I had been riding for almost as long as I had been walking. I was certain that I could handle this horse.

4   One day, after another round of relentless pleading on my part, Dad agreed to let me sit on Hermes but not ride him. After I successfully mounted Hermes, I foolishly thought I had him under control. Before I could think about what I was doing, I gently nudged Hermes with my heel. Suddenly, it was like I was riding a tornado. I clung desperately to Hermes's back as he spun me around, but it was clear who was in charge.

5   Just when I thought I would fall, Hermes stumbled slightly on a loose rock in the riding ring. Dad's commands caught his attention, and he slowed to a stop. Dad iced Hermes's leg and said he'd be fine after a rest, but he was clearly upset with me. I thought it was because I'd hurt Hermes, but Dad explained that all he could think about was what would have happened if I had fallen and been injured. But then he gave me an affectionate smile and said, "You know what I just realized? You stayed on the whole time!"

6   After we went back inside, Dad said would not let me ride Hermes again. I was discouraged, but he promised to start teaching me to ride bareback on another horse. One day, I hope I can become a rodeo champion and make my dad proud.

Answer the questions. Mark your answers to questions 1–4 on the Answer Form to the right.

1 How did both authors develop their stories in a similar way?

A Both stories are set in the distant past.

B Both stories include the use of dialogue.

C Both stories could happen in real life.

D Both stories are told from the main character's point of view.

2 What theme is common to both stories?

A It is important to know your limitations.

B It is important to spend time with family.

C People should work hard to achieve their goals.

D People should focus on the positive things in life.

3 How are Phaethon and Sara's lives different?

A Phaethon grew up riding horses; Sara did not.

B Sara grew up knowing her father; Phaethon did not.

C Sara is confident in her ability to control horses; Phaethon is not.

D Phaethon feels guilty about the mistakes he made; Sara does not.

4   Which statement **best** describes a difference in the development of the plots of the two stories?

    A   Phaethon is afraid to drive the horses, but Sara is not.

    B   Phaethon is successful with his ride, but Sara is not.

    C   Phaethon gets his father's permission for his ride, but Sara does not.

    D   Phaethon is safe during his ride, but Sara is injured during hers.

5   Answer Parts A, B, and C below.

Part A

Circle **one** word that describes both Phaethon and Sara based on evidence from the text. There is more than one correct choice listed below.

    determined   experienced   powerful

    clever   careful   brave

Part B

Find a sentence in "Phaethon and Helios" with details that support your answer to Part A. Write that sentence on the lines below.

_____

_____

Part C

Find a sentence in "Handling Hermes" with details that support your answer to Part A. Write that sentence on the lines below.

_____

_____

6   Explain briefly how both stories address the relationships between fathers and their children. Use details from the stories to support your answer.

_____

_____

_____

_____

_____

7   In both stories, the main characters are determined to accomplish a goal. Did their determination help them achieve that goal, or did it cause problems? Explain your answer, using details from **both** stories.

_____

_____

_____

_____

_____

8 Explain how the actions of Helios and Sara's father are similar. Use details from the stories to support your answer.

_____

_____

_____

_____

_____

_____

_____

_____

_____

_____

_____

_____

_____

Performance Task—Extended Response

9　In both stories, the main characters want the approval of their fathers. How does this affect their actions? Do these characters change in any way? Explain whether Phaethon and Sara's desire to win the approval of their fathers affected their actions or changed them.

In your response, be sure to
- explain how the desire to win his father's approval affected Phaethon's actions
- explain how the desire to win her father's approval affected Sara's actions
- explain how this need for approval changed Phaethon and Sara
- use details from both stories in your answer

Check your writing for correct spelling, grammar, capitalization, and punctuation.

_____

_____

_____

_____

_____

_____

_____

_____

_____

_____

Media Feature

Comparing and Contrasting
Reading to Viewing

CCLS

RL.6.7: Compare and contrast the experience of reading a story . . . to listening to or viewing an audio, video, or live version of the text, including contrasting what they "see" and "hear" when reading the text to what they perceive when they listen or watch.

You've read stories, and you've seen movies and plays. But have you ever read a book and then seen the movie version of it? Did you think, "Whoa, I really liked the book so much better"—or the reverse?

Writers can give readers information that a filmmaker cannot. But filmmakers can show you things a writer cannot. Whether you read a story or watch it unfold in a play or movie, though, all stories have the same important elements: character, setting, plot, and mood.

Use this chart to compare how books and movies present the elements of stories.

Element	In a Book, You Read...	In a Movie or Play, You See and Hear...
Character	• detailed descriptions of the characters' looks and actions • information about the main character's background • what the characters say and how they think	• how an actor interprets the character • the sound of the character's voice and the way the character speaks • the actions and reactions of several characters at once
Setting	• detailed descriptions of place and time • information about the specific elements of the settings: the color of a house or the smell of a meal	• images capturing the appearance and sounds of a setting all at once • close-up visual details, such as a rusty doorknob to a house, the fabric of a curtain
Plot	• the fine points of important events that keep the plot moving • details about the conflict: how it comes to be, and how it is resolved	• a version of the plot written to fit within a certain amount of time • the story told mainly by characters talking and doing things you can see
Mood/Tone	• imagery, figurative language, and descriptive details to help you create a mental picture of a scene	• lighting, camera angles, sound effects and music that combine to create a mood

 Reading words or watching images on a screen affects how you experience a story. With a partner, discuss your experiences reading a book and then seeing the movie.

On page 237 you learned how important storytelling elements are conveyed in print and in movies or plays. But is one way of telling a story better than another?

Think about why you like reading a story in a book and what you enjoy about seeing it on screen. Then think about what you don't like about each version. Add your own observations to each section. Include examples from books and movies you've read or seen.

Pros and Cons	Print Story	Movie Story
Pros	• Sometimes you can learn what a character is thinking. That helps me understand the character. • I get to imagine what characters and places look like. When I read *The Lightning Thief*, I really liked picturing the monsters. _____ _____ _____ _____	• A movie can make action scenes a lot more exciting. In *The Lord of the Rings*, one paragraph in the book turned into a great battle scene with the Orcs. • You actually get to see what the characters look like and hear how they sound. _____ _____ _____ _____
Cons	• Sometimes there's too much description, and I get bored. • Action scenes in a book can be hard to follow. In *The Maze Runner* I couldn't always figure out what was going on. _____ _____ _____ _____	• Sometimes large parts of the plot are cut out of the story. That happened a lot in the Harry Potter movies. • I don't like it when the characters don't look the way I imagined. _____ _____ _____ _____

 Find a partner and compare charts. Did your partner come up with some ideas you hadn't thought of? Do you agree with those ideas?

Ready® New York CCLS Language Handbook
Table of Contents

Conventions of Standard English

			CCLS
Lesson 1:	Subject and Object Pronouns	241	L.6.1.a
Lesson 2:	More About Subject and Object Pronouns	243	L.6.1.a
Lesson 3:	Possessive Pronouns	245	L.6.1.a
Lesson 4:	Reflexive and Intensive Pronouns	247	L.6.1.b
Lesson 5:	Shifts in Pronoun Number and Person	249	L.6.1.c
Lesson 6:	Correcting Vague Pronouns	251	L.6.1.d
Lesson 7:	Recognizing and Correcting Errors	253	L.6.1.e
Lesson 8:	Punctuating Parenthetical Elements	255	L.6.2.a

Knowledge of Language

Lesson 9:	Varying Sentence Patterns	257	L.6.3.a
Lesson 10:	Consistency in Style and Tone	259	L.6.3.b

Vocabulary Acquisition and Use

Lesson 11:	Using Context Clues	261	L.6.4.a
Lesson 12:	Greek and Latin Word Parts	263	L.6.4.b
Lesson 13:	Using a Dictionary or Glossary	265	L.6.4.c
Lesson 14:	Using a Thesaurus	267	L.6.4.c
Lesson 15:	Figures of Speech	269	L.6.5.a
Lesson 16:	Relationships Between Words	271	L.6.5.b
Lesson 17:	Denotation and Connotation	273	L.6.5.c

Subject and Object Pronouns

CCLS
L.6.1.a: Ensure that pronouns are in the proper case (subjective, objective, . . .).

Introduction

A pronoun takes the place of a noun. A **subject pronoun** is used as the subject of a sentence. An **object pronoun** is used as the direct object of a verb or as the object of a preposition. It is important to use them correctly when speaking and writing.

Subject	**I** am learning about the Mongolian ruler Genghis Khan.
Direct Object of Verb	The Mongol people admired **him**.
Object of Preposition	This fearsome warrior was a hero to **them**.

• Subject and object pronouns can be singular or plural.

Subject Pronouns		Object Pronouns	
Singular	**Plural**	**Singular**	**Plural**
I	we	me	us
you	you	you	you
he, she, it	they	him, her, it	them

• A pronoun can be part of a **compound subject** or **compound object**. Compound subjects and objects are made up of two or more nouns, pronouns, or both. If the pronoun *I* or *me* is included, it usually comes last.

Compound Subject	**Tricia and I** are reading about ancient China.
Compound Object	The teacher assigned the topic to **Fred and me**.

Guided Practice

Cross out each underlined word or phrase. Above it, write the correct subject or object pronoun to replace it.

Hint

The pronouns *it* and *you* can be used as either a subject or an object. But all other pronouns are used only as a subject or an object. Be careful to use them correctly!

Many historians have written about Genghis Khan. Often these historians describe Genghis Khan as a cruel warrior who captured land for the people of Mongolia. However, this fierce leader also united the people of Mongolia.

Tricia became interested in the Mongolian empire, and her and me wrote a report on the empire. Fred helped Tricia and I on the research. Fred, me, and Tricia learned a lot.

For numbers 1–5, which word or words correctly complete each sentence?

1 When Genghis Khan was a child, his mother kept _____ and the rest of the family safe in the Mongolian Desert.

  A we

  B him

  C they

  D he

2 This brave woman and her children often had little to eat, but _____ survived.

  A her and them

  B she and them

  C her and they

  D she and they

3 Genghis Khan's mother was a strong, smart woman. Her son's ability to lead probably came from _____.

  A her

  B she

  C he

  D they

4 As a leader, Genghis Khan promoted religious freedom because other people's beliefs were interesting to _____.

  A he

  B him

  C they

  D we

5 _____ also learned that Genghis Khan created the first Mongol written language.

  A Me and my friends

  B They and me

  C My friends and I

  D My friends and me

More About Subject and Object Pronouns

CCLS
L.6.1.a: Ensure that pronouns are in the proper case (subjective, objective . . .).

Introduction   **Subject pronouns** and **object pronouns** can be used to tell about or emphasize something mentioned in the sentence.

- Sometimes a **subject pronoun** follows a form of the linking verb *be (is, am, are, was, were)* to tell about the subject. The pronoun can be used alone or in a compound subject.

> It **was I**, not Zoey, who saw the boy fall off his bike.
>
> However, the first ones to reach the boy **were she and Terrance.**

- The plural pronouns *we* and *us* can also be used before a noun for emphasis. Use *we* if the noun is the subject of the sentence. Use *us* if the noun is the object of a verb or preposition.

> **We girls** kept the boy calm and called his mom.
>
> When the boy's mother arrived, she thanked **us girls** for our help.

Guided Practice   **Circle the correct pronoun to complete each sentence.**

Hint

If the pronoun is followed by a noun, try reading the sentence without the noun. For example, "We [doctors] care about health." You can tell that *We* sounds right and that *Us* would sound wrong.

Look for forms of the linking verb *be (is, am, are, was, were)*. If a pronoun comes after one of these forms, remember to use a subject pronoun.

1 The people in our class who want to become doctors are Zoey and (me, I).

2 (Us, We) students enjoyed meeting Dr. Higgs on Career Day.

3 It was (him, he) who won the Doctor of the Year award in our state.

4 Dr. Higgs inspired (we, us) kids to learn more about careers in medicine.

5 Terrance's parents are both doctors, and it was (they, them) who invited Dr. Higgs to speak to us.

For numbers 1–5, which pronoun correctly completes each sentence?

1 The Young Paramedic Program is perfect for _____ students.

   A we

   B them

   C us

   D they

2 The first people to sign up were Zoey, Paris, and _____.

   A me

   B I

   C them

   D him

3 It was _____ who noticed the sign-up sheet first.

   A us

   B I

   C me

   D them

4 The instructors are all paramedics, and it will be _____ who teach us basic first aid.

   A they

   B her

   C them

   D it

5 _____ young volunteers are eager to learn about saving lives.

   A Us

   B Them

   C They

   D We

Lesson 3
Possessive Pronouns

CCLS
L.6.1.a: Ensure that pronouns are in the proper case (. . . possessive).

 Introduction Possessive pronouns are pronouns that show ownership.

- Some possessive pronouns are used before nouns.

  Is that **my** notebook on **your** desk?   **Our** markers are on **their** table.

Possessive Pronouns Used Before a Noun	
Singular	my, his, her, your, its
Plural	our, your, their

- Other possessive pronouns can stand alone.

  I think that pencil is **mine**, not **yours**.   Is that stapler **ours** or is it **theirs**?

Possessive Pronouns That Can Stand Alone	
Singular	mine, his, hers, yours
Plural	ours, yours, theirs

Guided Practice Circle the possessive pronoun or pronouns that correctly complete each sentence.

Hint

Be careful not to confuse the possessive pronouns *its*, *their*, and *your* with the contractions *it's*, *they're*, and *you're*. Just remember that possessive pronouns do not have apostrophes.

1 (Our, Ours) teacher gives us weekly writing assignments.

2 "Don't forget to complete (yours, your) assignment by (it's, its) due date," Ms. Sanchez reminded us.

3 Levi and Ian work together on (their, theirs) assignments.

4 Annie and I often collaborate on (ours, our).

5 I usually like (her, hers) topic ideas better than (my, mine).

6 When will they finish (their, theirs) research?

7 (My, Mine) research will be completed by Friday.

For numbers 1–5, which pronoun correctly completes each sentence?

1 Raul is proud of _____ writing and always proofreads it carefully.

    A his

    B theirs

    C its

    D ours

2 Noah offered to let Shayla read his poem if he could read _____.

    A her

    B its

    C hers

    D their

3 Someday I hope to write as well as _____ favorite author, Christopher Paul Curtis.

    A hers

    B my

    C mine

    D ours

4 How do you come up with _____ unusual ideas for characters?

    A theirs

    B your

    C yours

    D ours

5 We brought our writing journals, but the twins forgot _____.

    A our

    B your

    C their

    D theirs

Lesson 4
Reflexive and Intensive Pronouns

CCLS
L.6.1.b: Use intensive pronouns (e.g., *myself*, *ourselves*).

Introduction **Reflexive** and **intensive pronouns** are pronouns that end in -*self* or -*selves*. They refer back to a noun or another pronoun in the same sentence.

- Reflexive and intensive pronouns can be singular or plural.

Singular	Plural
myself	ourselves
yourself	yourselves
himself, herself, itself	themselves

- A **reflexive pronoun** is an object pronoun that refers back to the subject and is important to the meaning of the sentence. If you leave out the reflexive pronoun, the sentence will not be clear.

Jake was mad at **himself** for dropping the ball during the game.

- An **intensive pronoun** can be used to emphasize, or *intensify*, a noun or pronoun. If you leave out the intensive pronoun, the sentence will still make sense.

I myself thought it wasn't his fault. His **teammates themselves** agreed.

Guided Practice **Cross out the incorrect pronoun or pronouns in each sentence. Then write the correct form above the incorrect one.**

Hint

A reflexive pronoun should not be used as the subject of a sentence. Use the correct subject pronoun instead.

Example:
Ben and **I** played.
NOT
Ben and **myself** played.

1 My family and myself were excited to see my brother's first ball game.

2 He itself was nervous about how he would play.

3 Dad drove us to the field at 1:00, although the game themselves did not start until 2:00.

4 Himself and I found themselves good seats in the bleachers.

5 My two sisters went to buy popcorn for herself.

6 Myself asked them to bring some for Dad and me.

7 When they returned, Dad told them, "You'll fill yourself with popcorn and miss dinner."

For numbers 1–3, which pronoun should replace the underlined pronoun to make the sentence correct?

1 When the team lost the game, the players blamed <u>ourselves</u>.

 A itself

 B themselves

 C himself

 D yourselves

2 The pitcher <u>itself</u> said that he had not pitched his best game.

 A myself

 B himself

 C yourself

 D themselves

3 Alonzo and <u>myself</u> agreed that the other team had simply played better.

 A I

 B me

 C himself

 D ourselves

For numbers 4 and 5, which revision uses a reflexive or intensive pronoun correctly?

4 Mayor Ramirez is a great fan and attends every single game.

 A Herself Mayor Ramirez is a great fan and attends every single game.

 B Mayor Ramirez themselves is a great fan and attends every single game.

 C Mayor Ramirez is a great fan itself and attends every single game.

 D Mayor Ramirez herself is a great fan and attends every single game.

5 She told the winning team, "All of you should be proud of yourself."

 A She told the winning team, "All of yourselves should be proud."

 B She told the winning team, "All of you should be proud of themselves."

 C She told the winning team, "All of you should be proud of yourselves."

 D She told the winning team, "All of you should be proud of you."

Shifts in Pronoun Number and Person

CCLS

L.6.1.c: Recognize and correct inappropriate shifts in pronoun number and person.

Introduction Pronouns have a **number** (singular or plural) and a **person** (first, second, or third person). When you use pronouns, be sure to keep them consistent in number and person with the noun or pronoun they refer to.

Person	Singular Pronouns	Plural Pronouns
First Person	I, me, my, mine	we, us, our, ours
Second Person	you, your, yours	you, your, yours
Third Person	he, him, his, she, her, hers, it, its	they, them, their, theirs

- Avoid shifts from singular to plural, or from plural to singular.

> **Faulty:** A **visitor** can't see the film unless **they** have a ticket.
>
> **Better:** **Visitors** can't see the film unless **they** have a ticket.

- Avoid shifts in person, such as from first person to second person.

> **Faulty:** As **we** watched the film, **you** were transported back in time.
>
> **Better:** As **we** watched the film, **we** were transported back in time.

Guided Practice Cross out each underlined pronoun. Above it, write a pronoun that is consistent with the word or words in bold type that it refers to.

Hint

You can use the pronoun phrase *he or she* or *him or her* to refer to a singular noun, such as *teacher*, that can stand for a man or a woman.

Example:
A **teacher** can bring **his or her** class to the film.

1. The **exhibit** was on Queen Nefertiti, and <u>they</u> included a film.

2. **Queen Nefertiti** was known for <u>its</u> beauty.

3. Since **my friends and I** love Egypt, the topic interested <u>them</u>.

4. The **Egyptians** saw rulers as gods, so in 1350 B.C.E., <u>we</u> worshipped Nefertiti.

5. A **ruler** in ancient Egypt could do as <u>they</u> pleased.

For numbers 1–5, which pronoun correctly completes each sentence?

1 Some unknown artist had tried to capture Nefertiti's face in _____ sculpture.

  A his and hers

  B its or his

  C his or her

  D its and hers

2 A few ancient Egyptian rulers were women, but usually _____ had to be male.

  A you

  B they

  C she

  D it

3 In 1912, archeologists dug up sculptures of Nefertiti and shared _____ with the world.

  A it

  B his

  C him

  D them

4 When we saw the sculptures, _____ could see why Nefertiti's name meant "the beautiful one has come."

  A you

  B we

  C it

  D us

5 If you have questions about Nefertiti after the film, the guide will answer _____.

  A it

  B us or them

  C him or her

  D them

Correcting Vague Pronouns

CCLS

L.6.1.d: Recognize and correct vague pronouns (i.e., ones with unclear or ambiguous antecedents).

Introduction   Pronouns help writers to avoid repetition, but when a pronoun is **vague**, or unclear, readers can't tell what or whom it refers to.

- A pronoun may be unclear if there is more than one noun to which the pronoun could be referring. For example:

> **Clear:** The cliff dwellings at Mesa Verde were built by the Ancestral Pueblo people.
> **Unclear: They** show us what life was like there thousands of years ago.

The pronoun *they* could refer to *cliff dwellings* or to *Ancestral Pueblo people*. You can fix the problem by changing the pronoun to the correct noun.

> **Clear: These dwellings** show us what life was like there thousands of years ago.

- A pronoun may also be unclear if there is no noun to which the pronoun refers.

> **Unclear:** Our days at Mesa Verde were long and full, and **it** taught us a lot.

> **Unclear:** At home, people sometimes asked questions, and **it** was hard.

You can fix the first sentence by replacing the pronoun with a noun phrase, such as *the trip*. However, the second sentence might need a bit more work.

> **Clear:** Our days at Mesa Verde were long and full, and **the trip** taught us a lot.

> **Clear:** At home, people asked questions that were hard to answer.

Guided Practice   **Read the paragraph. Cross out each vague (unclear) pronoun, and write your correction above it. You may want to revise more than the pronoun to make the sentence's meaning clear.**

Hint

Changing a vague pronoun to a noun is not always enough. You may need to revise the sentence to give a bit more information.

In 1888, during a heavy snowfall near what is now Mesa Verde National Park, two cowboys saw walls and towers off in the distance. They were unusual, and they decided to go and explore them. They found homes built right into the walls of the tall cliffs. They had ancient tools and pottery, and it was exciting.

Read the paragraph. For numbers 1–4, choose the revision that corrects the vague pronoun in each numbered sentence in the paragraph.

The Ancestral Pueblo people moved to Mesa Verde around 550 C.E., but the cliff dwellings weren't built until around 1200 C.E. **(1)** They showed a high degree of skill in stone masonry. **(2)** They do not know why the Ancestral Pueblo people moved into the cliffs. **(3)** They might have been safer in harsh weather. **(4)** Whatever the reason these people moved to the cliffs, it is amazing.

1

A They showed skill in stone masonry to a high degree.

B All showed a high degree of skill in stone masonry.

C A high degree of skill in stone masonry was shown by them.

D The Pueblo people showed a high degree of skill in stone masonry.

3

A In harsh weather, they might have been safer.

B Their safety might have been greater in harsh weather.

C Cliff dwellings might have been safer in harsh weather.

D It might be because of their safety in harsh weather.

2

A Archeologists are not sure why the Ancestral Pueblo people moved into the cliffs.

B The Ancestral Pueblo people do not know why they moved into the cliffs.

C It is unknown to them why the Ancestral Pueblo moved into the cliffs.

D Why the Ancestral Puebloans moved into the cliffs, they do not know.

4

A Whatever the reason they moved to the cliffs, they are amazing.

B Whatever the reason these people moved to the cliffs, they are amazing.

C Whatever the reason these people moved to the cliffs, you'd be amazed by them.

D Whatever the reason these people moved to the cliffs, their dwellings are amazing.

Lesson 7
Recognizing and Correcting Errors

CCLS
L.6.1.e: Recognize variations from standard English . . . in their own and others' writing. . . .

Introduction Mistakes in spelling, capitalization, grammar, and punctuation can make it difficult for your reader to understand what you have written. You should always **proofread** your writing and correct your errors. An easy way to show corrections is to use proofreading marks.

Proofreading Mark	Purpose	Example
و	to take out punctuation marks, letters, words, or sentences	A volcanoe is a mountain that can erupt and eject molten rock.
∧	to insert punctuation marks, letters, words, or sentences	Mount St. Helens erupted ⁱⁿ 1980 in the state of Washington.
⊙	to add a period	Some volcanoes occur on land Others, however, erupt on the ocean floor.
/	to change a capital letter to a lowercase letter	A recent Undersea eruption occurred off the Canary Islands.
≡	to change a lowercase letter to a capital letter	An undersea volcano near oregon produced 12-foot-thick layers of lava.

Guided Practice **Use proofreading marks to correct the errors in this paragraph. Then work with a partner to check each other's corrections.**

Hint

Sometimes you will need to use more than one proofreading mark to make a correction. For example, a spelling error may require that you use one mark to delete and another mark to insert the correct spelling.

Their are more than 3,000 volcanoes on the ocean floor.

Undersea volcanoes are caused by a crack. in the crust. Like land

Volcanoes, undersea volcanoes erupts and force out liquid rock

scientists now observed these volcanoes and try to predict

possible eruptions.

For numbers 1–5, select the correct way to revise the sentence.

1 Eruptions occur when Pressure in a volcano build up

A Eruptions occurs when Pressure in a volcano build up.

B Eruptions occurs when pressure in a volcano builds up

C Eruptions occur when pressure in a volcano builds up.

D Eruptions occur when Pressure in a volcano build up.

2 When undersea volcanoes erupt, they often caused powerfull waves.

A When undersea volcanoes erupt, they often cause powerfull waves.

B When undersea volcanoes erupt, they often caused powerful waves.

C When undersea volcanoes erupt, they often cause powerful waves.

D When undersea volcanoes erupt, They often cause powerful waves.

3 A tsunami is a series of waves it can move too shore at high speeds.

A A tsunami is a series of waves, it can move too shore at high speeds.

B A tsunami is a series of waves. it can move to shore at high speeds.

C A tsunami is a series of waves, It can move too shore at high speeds.

D A tsunami is a series of waves, and it can move to shore at high speeds.

4 If a tsunami strike land, she can cause sereous damage.

A If a tsunami strikes land, she can cause serious damage.

B If a tsunami strikes land, it can cause serious damage.

C If a tsunami strike land, it can cause serious damage.

D If a tsunami strike land, it can cause sereous damage.

5 In oregon, the undersea eruption themselves changed the seafloor.

A In oregon, the Undersea Eruption itselves changed the seafloor.

B In Oregon, the undersea eruption themselves changed the seafloor.

C In oregon, the undersea eruption itself changed the seafloor.

D In Oregon, the undersea eruption itself changed the seafloor.

Lesson 8
Punctuating Parenthetical Elements

CCLS

L.6.2.a: Use punctuation (commas, parentheses, dashes) to set off nonrestrictive/parenthetical elements.

Introduction When you want to include a **parenthetical element**, or a piece of extra information that is interesting but not absolutely necessary, you use punctuation marks to set it off from the rest of a sentence. You can use **commas**, **parentheses**, or **dashes**.

Type of Punctuation	When to Use	Example
Commas	to set off information that is not essential to understanding the rest of the sentence	Rachel Carson, **born on a small farm in Pennsylvania,** devoted her life to protecting the environment. She was always interested in nature, **even as a young girl.**
Parentheses	to set off nonessential information or to remind readers of something they may already know	Rachel Carson **(1907–1964)** did important research on the effects of chemicals on our water supply.
Dashes	to add emphasis, set off a new thought, or show a sudden change in thinking	Carson—**always passionate about nature**—was a powerful and persuasive writer. She began her writing by exploring life in the sea—**a world unknown to most readers**.

Guided Practice Add the punctuation shown in *italics* to set off the parenthetical information in each sentence.

Hint

When a parenthetical element is in the middle of a sentence, be sure to set it off with the same type of punctuation before *and* after.

Example:
Isabelle, also known as Izzie, is shy.
NOT
Isabelle—also known as Izzie, is shy.

1 Elizabeth Blackwell 1821–1910 grew up in a time when women were not welcome in many professions.
parentheses

2 She thought women would want to see a female doctor rather than a male about their health concerns.
commas

3 Blackwell was accepted into Geneva Medical School after being rejected by twenty other medical schools.
dash

4 Blackwell a determined person became the first woman to graduate from medical school in the United States.
commas

5 She later established a medical school just for women.
dash

For numbers 1–5, choose the answer that best punctuates the underlined part of each sentence.

1   Dr. Jonas Salk 1914–1995 discovered a cure for polio.

   A   Salk 1914–1995, discovered

   B   Salk, (1914–1995), discovered

   C   Salk (1914–1995) discovered

   D   Salk—1914–1995—discovered

2   Polio a disease that struck fear in parents was a terrible illness that could cripple children.

   A   Polio, a disease that struck fear in parents, was

   B   Polio, a disease that struck fear in parents—was

   C   Polio (a disease that struck fear in parents), was

   D   Polio—a disease that struck fear in parents, was

3   Jonas Salk's parents immigrants with little formal education themselves were determined that their children would succeed.

   A   parents—(immigrants with little formal education themselves) were

   B   parents immigrants with little formal education themselves, were

   C   parents immigrants with little formal education themselves— were

   D   parents (immigrants with little formal education themselves) were

4   At medical school, Salk began researching influenza the virus that causes the flu.

   A   influenza the virus, that causes the flu.

   B   influenza—the virus—that causes the flu.

   C   influenza (the virus) that causes the flu.

   D   influenza, the virus that causes the flu.

5   Salk's discovery of a polio vaccine for which he refused to accept money won him the admiration of all Americans.

   A   vaccine, for which he refused to accept money—won

   B   vaccine—for which he refused to accept money—won

   C   vaccine—(for which he refused to accept money) won

   D   vaccine for which he refused to accept money, won

Lesson 9
Varying Sentence Patterns

CCLS
L.6.3.a: Vary sentence patterns for meaning, reader/listener interest, and style.

Introduction Good writers use a variety of sentence types. They mix short and long sentences, and they find different ways to start sentences. Here are ways to improve your writing:

- Use different sentence types: statements, questions, imperatives, and exclamations.
- Use different sentence structures: simple, compound, complex, and compound-complex.
- Sometimes begin a sentence with a prepositional phrase or a dependent clause.

Draft

We went on an impressive field trip. We went to the science museum. The building was huge. It had many exhibits. I especially liked the laser exhibit. You should make sure to visit the museum.

Revision

Our field trip to the science museum really impressed me. The building itself was huge, and it was filled with exhibits. Do you dream of seeing actual lasers? At some point, then, be sure to visit the museum. You won't be sorry!

Guided Practice **Follow the directions to rewrite each sentence or pair of sentences.**

Hint

When a sentence begins with a dependent clause, use a comma to separate it from the main clause. When a sentence begins with a prepositional phrase, usually use a comma after the phrase.

1 Change this sentence to a question: It is fun to learn about insect colonies.

Is it fun to learn about insect colonies

2 Use the word *when* to combine these sentences: I looked at the museum map. I noticed a new insect exhibit.

I looked at the museum map when
I noticed a new insect exhibit.

3 Combine these sentences so that the new sentence begins with a prepositional phrase: It was near the entrance to the exhibit. The first thing I saw was a giant grasshopper.

_____

_____

Read the paragraphs for numbers 1–4. Then answer the questions that follow in each column.

> (1) Many of the insects were robots. (2) I almost thought they were real. (3) They moved like real insects. (4) They were much larger than real insects.

1 Which is the best way to revise sentence 1?

A For me, the insects were robots.

B When looking, many of the insects were robots.

C To my surprise, many of the insects were robots.

D Surprised, many of the insects were robots.

2 Which best combines sentences 3 and 4?

A They moved like real insects, or they were much larger.

B They moved like real insects, so they were much larger.

C They moved like real insects, but they were much larger.

D They moved like real insects, because they were much larger.

> (5) The tour guide told us that the robots show insect behavior. (6) A wolf spider seemed to rush toward me. (7) I was scared. (8) I remembered it was a robot spider.

3 Which is the best way to revise sentence 6?

A After a long time, a wolf spider seemed to rush toward me.

B At that moment, a wolf spider seemed to rush toward me.

C After the trip, a wolf spider seemed to rush toward me.

D Along with others, a wolf spider seemed to rush toward me.

4 Which is the best way to combine sentences 7 and 8?

A Remembering it was a robot spider, I was scared.

B I looked scared, but the robot looked like a spider.

C I was scared until I remembered it was a robot spider.

D I was scared when I remembered it was a robot spider.

Lesson 10
Consistency in Style and Tone

CCLS
L.6.3.b: Maintain consistency in style and tone.

Introduction

When you write, choose a style and tone that suit your purpose and audience. You might choose a formal style and serious tone for a report. For a personal e-mail, you might choose an informal style and humorous tone. Once you've decided on a style and tone, you need to be consistent.

- The words you choose and your sentence patterns form your **style**.

Formal	During meteorological events, animals tend to scatter.
Informal	It's raining. Look at that mouse run for cover. It's fast!

- Your tone shows your attitude toward your subject and/or readers. For example, a tone may be serious, playful, humorous, angry, calm, joyful, or sad.

Serious	Some animals seek shelter in and under trees or bushes.
Playful	Can a lizard use a tree as an umbrella? It sure can!

Guided Practice

Read the passage. Then rewrite the underlined sentences to match the style and tone of the rest of the passage.

Hint

The style and tone of the story are informal and casual. The underlined sentences contain language that is either too poetic or too technical. Replace them with language that matches the story's style and tone.

"Our camping trip is off to a great start," said Dad. We had just begun to unpack. Then crack, sizzle! Lightning flashed through the sky. Thunder made the mountains tremble in fear.

"Run to the car!" yelled Dad. "We'll wait it out there." After an hour, the rain stopped. When we exited the vehicle, we found that our belongings had absorbed a vast amount of moisture!

1 _____

_____

2 _____

_____

Read the paragraph below. Then answer the questions that follow for numbers 1–4.

Answer Form

1 Ⓐ Ⓑ Ⓒ Ⓓ
2 Ⓐ Ⓑ Ⓒ Ⓓ
3 Ⓐ Ⓑ Ⓒ Ⓓ   **Number**   ⧄4
4 Ⓐ Ⓑ Ⓒ Ⓓ   **Correct**

---

(1) Saving our local campground is of great importance. (2) First, it gives kids a bunch of outside stuff to do, like running around by the river. (3) There is also nothing quite like the thrill of snoozing under the stars, outside of the city. (4) I know that building new houses matters, but keeping a space for people to enjoy nature is necessary, too. (5) Can you imagine if this option were taken away? (6) No way, I say!

---

1 What revision of sentence 2 best matches the style and tone of sentence 1?

A First, it offers children outdoor exercise, such as hiking.

B First, it allows kids to finally get a chance to run around.

C First, it lets children do stuff, like run around outside.

D First, kids get to run around the river and do other outside stuff.

2 Which sentence should be deleted because it introduces a tone that is inconsistent with most of the paragraph?

A sentence 1

B sentence 4

C sentence 5

D sentence 6

3 Which best replaces the word snoozing in sentence 3 to add a formal style and serious tone to the paragraph?

A catching some z's

B falling asleep

C nodding off

D getting some shut-eye

4 Which sentence could be added to the paragraph without changing its style or tone?

A Nobody gets it!

B We need to stop those pesky builders from taking over!

C They've really got to leave our campground alone.

D We must preserve our local campground!

Lesson 11
Using Context Clues

CCLS

L.6.4.a: Use context (e.g., the overall meaning of a sentence or paragraph; a word's position or function in a sentence) as a clue to the meaning of a word or phrase.

Introduction When you come across a word you do not know in your reading, look for clues. **Context clues** are words and phrases in the text that give hints to a word's meaning.

Context Clue	Signal Words	Example
Definition	*are, is, means, or*	Larger animals often treat smaller animals as prey, **or something to be killed and eaten.**
Example	*like, such as, for example*	Predators, **such as** hawks, wolves, and coyotes, hunt rabbits.
Cause and Effect	*as a result of, because, and thanks to*	**Because** many animals eat rabbits, the number of wild rabbits has decreased.
Comparison and Contrast	*like, too, similarly, but, unlike, although*	**Although** wolves eat both plants and animals, hawks are completely carnivorous.

A word's position and function in the sentence can also be a clue to its meaning. For example, read the sentence below:

Brown bears are solitary animals and are often found alone.

You can tell that *solitary* is an adjective in this sentence. The adjective describes the bears. Then the word *solitary* is defined in the sentence. Since the bears *are often found alone,* this gives a good clue to what the word *solitary* means.

Guided Practice **Read the paragraph below. Circle context clues to help you figure out the meaning of the underlined words. Then tell a partner the meaning of the underlined words.**

Hint

Think about the different types of context clues. Look for words that signal examples, cause and effect, and contrasts. Then use the clues to help you figure out the meanings of the underlined words.

Marsupials are mammals that carry their young in pouches. The American opossum is a marsupial. Thanks to its defense mechanisms, the opossum keeps itself safe from predators. When threatened, it hisses, growls, and bites. If this doesn't work, the opossum reacts in an unusual way. Although many animals move quickly to escape danger, the opossum collapses and pretends to be dead. This is an unconscious response to stress that is similar to jerking your hand away from a hot object before thinking.

Read the paragraph. Then answer the questions that follow for numbers 1–4.

Pangolins have a physical <u>resemblance</u>, or likeness, to an armadillo, with claws and armored bodies. When attacked, pangolins <u>thwart combat</u> by rolling into a hard ball and hiding. Like bats and other animals that sleep all day, pangolins are <u>nocturnal</u>. Because they lack teeth, eating tiny stones with their food is <u>critical</u> for digestion.

1 Which phrase from the paragraph best helps you understand the meaning of the word <u>resemblance</u>?

A have a physical

B or likeness

C with claws

D armored bodies

2 What does the phrase <u>thwart combat</u> mean in the paragraph?

A get attacked

B attack others

C avoid a fight

D start a fight

3 What does the word <u>nocturnal</u> suggest about the pangolins?

A They roll into hard balls.

B They are awake at night.

C They are like all other animals.

D They lack teeth.

4 What does the word <u>critical</u> mean in the paragraph?

A safe

B possible

C necessary

D imaginable

Greek and Latin Word Parts

CCLS
L.6.4.b: Use common, grade-appropriate Greek or Latin affixes and roots as clues to the meaning of a word (e.g., *audience, auditory, audible*).

Introduction

Many English words have Greek and Latin roots and affixes. By becoming familiar with them, you will be able to unlock the meaning of many words.

- **Roots** are word parts that have meanings but usually cannot stand alone. Sometimes roots combine with other roots to form words, such as *audiovisual*.

Root	Meaning	Root	Meaning
aud	"hear"	*mot, mov*	"move"
cycle	"circle, wheel"	*vis, vid*	"see"
therm	"heat"	*meter*	"measure"

- **Affixes**, such as prefixes and suffixes, can also be added to roots to form words, such as *interject*.

Prefix	Meaning	Suffix	Meaning
uni-	"one"	*-ance, -ence*	"state of"
bi-	"two"	*-ion, -al*	"action, process"
tri-	"three"	*-or*	"state" or "quality of"

Guided Practice

Circle the roots in the underlined words. Write the meaning of each root. Then tell a partner the meaning of the underlined words.

Hint

A suffix adds meaning to a root or word. Suffixes often give clues that indicate part of speech (noun, adjective, etc.). The suffix *-ence* usually signals a noun; the suffix *-al* usually signals an adjective.

1 Inez sat in the <u>audience</u> at a cooking show.

_____

2 The <u>motor</u> of the cake mixer broke. The chef needed help.

_____

3 He made a hand <u>motion</u> for Inez to come up on stage.

_____

4 As he worked, she kept an eye on the oven <u>thermometer</u>.

_____

5 Because she had great <u>vision</u>, this was an easy task.

_____

For items 1–4, read each sentence. Then answer the question.

1 "Watch how I extend the dough with my hands," said the chef.

The prefix *ex-* means "out," and the root *tend* means "stretch." What does the word <u>extend</u> mean in the sentence?

A pull it in different directions

B form it into small balls

C loosen it with water

D cut it into small pieces

2 "Next, I add the equivalent of a teaspoon of spice," explained the chef.

The prefix *equi-* means "equal," and the root *vale* means "worth." What does the word <u>equivalent</u> mean in the sentence?

A half portion

B cost

C same measure

D double the amount

3 "Are my directions audible?" asked the chef.

The root *aud* means "hear," and the suffix *-ible* means "able." What does the word <u>audible</u> mean in the sentence?

A necessary

B too complicated

C realistic

D loud enough

4 Inez told the chef she was grateful for the cooking lesson.

The root *grat* means "pleasing," and the suffix *-ful* means "having or giving." What does the word <u>grateful</u> mean in the sentence?

A eager

B thankful

C greatly impatient

D responsible

Lesson 13
Using a Dictionary or Glossary

CCLS

L.6.4.c: Consult reference materials (e.g., dictionaries, glossaries . . .) . . . to find the pronunciation of a word or determine or clarify its precise meaning or its part of speech.

Introduction Many words have more than one definition and can serve as more than one part of speech. When you are reading or writing, use a dictionary to check the precise meaning of a word or phrase.

- Words in a **dictionary** appear in alphabetical order. Each entry provides the pronunciation, the part of speech, and the meanings of the word. Sample sentences are often included to clarify meaning.

> **account** (ə kount') *n.* **1.** a record of events or time period **2.** money in a bank **3.** worth, importance
> **account for** *v.* **1.** to be the main reason for: *Heavy rain accounted for the flooding.* **2.** to explain: *I can't account for the dog's barking.*

When there is more than one meaning, each definition is numbered.

The abbreviations show the part of speech: *n.* stands for *noun* and *v.* stands for *verb*.

> **extract** (ĭk străkt') *v.* **1.** to pull out **2.** to obtain or get meaning, pleasure, or information from something **extract** (ĕk' străkt) *n.* **3.** an excerpt or part of a text **4.** a flavoring

The pronunciation of the word is in parentheses. For some words, the pronunciation depends on the part of speech.

- A **glossary** is similar to a dictionary. It is an alphabetical list of special words that are used in a book. Each entry defines the word as it is used in that book.

Guided Practice Read the paragraph. Use the entries above to find the meanings of the underlined words and phrases. Write the number of the correct meaning above each word or phrase.

Hint

Identify how a word is used in a sentence before you use the dictionary. If the word is used as a noun, then you should read the definitions given for a noun.

Our museum has an exhibit on Chinese art. The catalog includes <u>extracts</u> from books about the landscape paintings. Many people <u>extract</u> pleasure from viewing these paintings. However, various <u>accounts</u> suggest that these paintings were also used to teach life lessons. If the paintings were used to teach morals, then scholars could <u>account for</u> the wide use of symbols that stand for character traits.

For numbers 1–4, use the dictionary entries to answer the questions.

> **express** (ĭk sprĕs') *v.* **1.** to say or state **2.** to communicate ideas or feelings **3.** to squeeze or press something out   *n.* **4.** type of transportation that moves with few or no stops   *adj.* **5.** specific: *I bought these apples for the express purpose of baking a pie.* **6.** stated **7.** moving with few or no stops

> **reflect** (rĭ flĕkt') *v.* **1.** to bend back light **2.** to show an image, to mirror **3.** to show clearly or reveal: *The novel reflects the writer's unhappiness.* **4.** to consider seriously: *You need to reflect on your actions.* **5.** to bring negative attention to: *The team's rowdiness reflected on the school.*

1 What part of speech is <u>express</u> as used in this sentence?

My mother and I took the express train to the museum.

A noun

B adjective

C verb

D adverb

2 Which definition of <u>express</u> best fits this sentence?

One artist painted a gloomy landscape to express the theme of grief and loss.

A Definition 2

B Definition 3

C Definition 5

D Definition 6

3 Which definition best fits <u>reflect</u> as used in this sentence?

Many landscape paintings reflected the artist's mood.

A Definition 1

B Definition 3

C Definition 4

D Definition 5

4 Which definition best fits the way <u>reflect</u> is used in this sentence?

When you view a Chinese landscape painting, reflect on the artist's message.

A Definition 2

B Definition 3

C Definition 4

D Definition 5

Lesson 14
Using a Thesaurus

CCLS
L.6.4.c: Consult reference materials (e.g., . . . thesauruses) . . . to find the . . . word or determine or clarify its precise meaning. . . .

Introduction

You can use a thesaurus to make your writing more precise or interesting. A **thesaurus** provides synonyms and antonyms for particular words.

- A thesaurus lists words in alphabetical order. Each entry gives the part of speech, the definition, and a list of synonyms. Antonyms, if any, are also included.

> **bitter** *adj.* **1.** a strong, unpleasant taste: *The white part of a lemon rind is bitter.* **acrid, unpleasant** *Antonyms: sugary, sweet* **2.** harsh and cold: *Winter has been bitter this year.* **rough, severe** *Antonyms: mild, pleasant* **3.** having or showing resentment: *Al felt bitter when he lost his job.* **angry, resentful, sullen** *Antonym: friendly*

> **claim** *v.* **1.** to need: *This issue claims our attention.* **deserve, demand, require 2.** to say that something is true: *Nola claims that bees sleep at night.* **state, declare, insist** *Antonym: deny* *n.* **3.** a statement that something is true: *The ad makes the claim that Brand X is the best flour.* **assertion, allegation, declaration** *Antonym: denial*

> When there is more than one meaning, each definition is numbered.

> Sometimes there is a sample sentence.

> Some words can serve as more than one part of speech.

Guided Practice

Read the paragraph. Use the thesaurus entries above to answer the questions about the underlined words.

Hint

Remember: A *synonym* is similar in meaning to another word. An *antonym* has the opposite meaning of the word.

Nearly 2,600 years ago, people in Mexico and Central America drank a <u>bitter</u> chocolate drink, which they made from cocoa beans. Some scholars <u>claim</u> that people drank chocolate even longer ago.

1 Which words are synonyms of *claim* as used in the paragraph?

_____

2 Which word is an antonym of *claim*? _____

3 Which words are synonyms of *bitter* as used in the paragraph?

_____

4 Which words are antonyms of *bitter*? _____

For numbers 1–4, read the sentence. Then use the thesaurus entry to answer the question.

Answer Form

1 Ⓐ Ⓑ Ⓒ Ⓓ
2 Ⓐ Ⓑ Ⓒ Ⓓ
3 Ⓐ Ⓑ Ⓒ Ⓓ   **Number**
4 Ⓐ Ⓑ Ⓒ Ⓓ   **Correct** /4

---

significant *adj.* **1.** expressing a meaning: *Dad gave Lee and Arlo a significant glance when they started to argue.* **meaningful, informative** *Antonym: meaningless* **2.** having influence: *Thu has a significant job with the Government.* **important** *Antonyms: insignificant, unimportant*

---

1 As the food of rulers, gods, and everyday people, chocolate was significant for the Maya.

Which is a synonym for <u>significant</u> as it is used above?

A meaningful

B unimportant

C insignificant

D meaningless

---

permit *v.* **1.** to allow to do something: *I'll permit you to pick plums.* **allow, authorize** *Antonyms: forbid, prohibit* **2.** to be favorable: *We'll have a picnic if the weather permits.* **accommodate, oblige** *n.* **3.** written permission: *The contractor got a permit to build a home.* **license, permission**

---

2 The Aztecs, however, would permit only certain people to drink it.

Which is an antonym for <u>permit</u> as it is used above?

A license

B allow

C forbid

D oblige

---

powerful *adj.* **1.** physically strong: *The oxen are powerful.* **strong, mighty** *Antonyms: weak, frail* **2.** able to influence: *Leaders are powerful people.* **high-ranking, influential** *Antonym: low-ranking*

---

3 Only the powerful members of Aztec society drank the sacred beverage.

Which is a synonym for <u>powerful</u> as it is used above?

A high-ranking

B powerless

C weak

D frail

---

valuable *adj.* **1.** having monetary worth: *Gold is valuable.* **precious** *Antonym: cheap* **2.** having use or importance: *A job teaches you valuable skills.* **useful, worthwhile** *Antonym: worthless*

---

4 Cocoa beans were so valuable that the Aztecs used the beans as money.

Which is an antonym for <u>valuable</u> as it is used above?

A useful

B worthwhile

C precious

D cheap

Lesson 15
Figures of Speech

CCLS

L.6.5.a: Interpret figures of speech (e.g., personification) in context.

Introduction One way that writers make their writing lively and vivid is by using **figures of speech**. A figure of speech is an imaginative, or nonliteral, way of using language. It might describe something in an unexpected way, or it might even stretch the truth.

- **Personification** is a figure of speech that gives human-like qualities and actions to something that is not human. Writers use personification to create a picture in the mind of the reader or to convey a mood.

> The steep trail **dared Mia** to take another step.
>
> **Sneaky** tree roots were **hiding** under leaves and twigs, **ready to trip her**.

Nonliving things, such as tree roots, can't dare someone, be sneaky, or hide with the intention of tripping someone. The figures of speech help the reader picture the trail and sense the lurking dangers.

- **Hyperbole** is a figure of speech that uses exaggeration for emphasis or effect.

> **It took forever** to reach the top of the mountain.

It doesn't really take "forever" to climb a mountain. The figure of speech emphasizes the length and difficulty of the climb and conveys Mia's frustration.

Guided Practice **Read the passage. Underline each figure of speech, and identify it by writing *P* for personification or *H* for hyperbole. Then discuss the meaning of the figure of speech with a partner.**

Hint

As you read, ask yourself:

"Do any verbs show a nonliving thing doing something a person can do?"

"Do any adjectives give human-like qualities to nonliving things?"

"Do any sentences exaggerate the truth?"

By the time Mia's parents set up the tent, it was raining. Mia would never forgive them for this trip! Her legs were still complaining from the climb, and the mean rain was punishing her family for camping in October.

The next morning, though, Mia woke up refreshed. She thought, "I must have slept for days!" Outside the tent, the sun smiled through the leafy trees.

For numbers 1–5, what does the underlined figure of speech mean in each sentence?

1 A <u>bold wind grabbed Mia's cap</u> as she and her parents hiked down the trail.

A The wind was bold and pushy.

B The wind blew Mia's cap off her head.

C Mia took her cap off her head because of the wind.

D Someone took Mia's cap.

2 When they reached the pond, Mia exclaimed, "<u>There must be a million ducks here!</u>"

A "There are one million ducks at the pond."

B "I've never seen ducks before."

C "There are a lot of ducks here."

D "I can guess the number of ducks."

3 Suddenly, <u>clouds gathered and chased the sun out of the sky.</u>

A The clouds were faster than the sun.

B The clouds pushed the sun out of the sky forever.

C The clouds had an important meeting.

D The sun disappeared quickly when clouds filled the sky.

4 The <u>rain ignored Mia and her family's plans</u> to go out on a rowboat.

A The rain did not affect the plans Mia and her family had.

B Mia and her family enjoyed their time out in the rowboat.

C Other people enjoyed rowboats, but not Mia's family.

D Mia's family had made plans, but now it was raining.

5 Mia thought, "<u>I'd better get back to the tent before I drown!</u>"

A "I don't know how to swim so I better get back."

B "I must swim incredibly fast in order to survive."

C "I better get back to the tent fast, or I'll get really wet."

D "I'll really drown if I don't get to the tent fast."

CCLS

L.6.5.b: Use the relationship between particular words (e.g., cause/effect, part/whole, item/category) to better understand each of the words.

Introduction

An **analogy** shows the relationship between two pairs of words.

Here's an example:

> *fast* is to *slow* as *up* is to *down*

- To understand this analogy, think about the relationship between *fast* and *slow*. *Up* and *down* are related in the same way. The words in each pair are **antonyms**.

- There are different types of analogies. As you study the chart below, think about the relationship between the pairs of words.

Type of Analogy	Example
Synonyms	*small* is to *miniature* as *fast* is to *speedy*
Antonyms	*young* is to *old* as *smooth* is to *rough*
Cause/Effect	*tired* is to *sleep* as *hungry* is to *eat*
Part/Whole	*finger* is to *hand* as *petal* is to *daisy*
Item/Category	*carrot* is to *vegetable* as *cherry* is to *fruit*

Guided Practice

Write a word to complete each analogy. Then write the type of analogy on the line below.

Hint

To identify the relationship between the words in the first pair, ask yourself: Are the words synonyms or antonyms? Is the first word the cause and the second word the effect? Is the first word a part and the second word a whole? Is the first word an item and the second word the category?

1 *scale* is to *fish* as *fur* is to _____

_____

2 *ice* is to *freeze* as *fire* is to _____

_____

3 *lighten* is to *darken* as *tighten* is to as _____

_____

4 *prevent* is to *stop* as *rescue* is to _____

_____

5 *hurricane* is to *storm* as *tulip* is to _____

_____

For numbers 1–5, choose the correct word to complete each analogy.

1 *trip* is to *fall* as *drop* is to _____

A water

B clumsy

C spring

D break

2 *page* is to *book* as *leaf* is to _____

A autumn

B green

C grass

D tree

3 *hurry* is to *rush* as *find* is to _____

A lose

B locate

C search

D hunt

4 *clumsy* is to *graceful* as *friendly* is to _____

A kind

B skillful

C hostile

D thoughtful

5 *hammer* is to *tool* as *sofa* is to _____

A soft

B relax

C room

D furniture

Lesson 17
Denotation and Connotation

CCLS

L.6.5.c: Distinguish among the connotations (associations) of words with similar denotations (definitions) (e.g., *stingy, scrimping, economical, unwasteful, thrifty*).

Introduction   A word can have two kinds of meanings. A word's **denotation** is its dictionary definition. A word's **connotation** is the feeling that people associate with the word.

Compare these examples:

Positive Connotation	Negative Connotation
My older cousin Cal is **clever**.	My older cousin Cal is **sly**.
He asks questions because he is **curious**.	He asks questions because he is **nosy**.

The dictionary definition of the word *clever* means almost the same as the dictionary definition of *sly*. The words have similar denotations. The words *curious* and *nosy* also have similar denotations. However, they have very different connotations. The words we use carry feelings. The reader uses these feelings to form opinions.

When you write, think about the connotations of the words you choose. Ask yourself: "What effect will my words have on my readers?"

Guided Practice   **Read the sentences. Write *P* if the underlined word has a positive connotation. Write *N* if the underlined word has a negative connotation.**

Hint

Read each underlined word. Ask yourself: What feelings do I connect to the word? If the feelings are good, the word has a positive connotation. If the feelings are bad, the word has a negative connotation.

1 Cal is a very <u>thrifty</u> person. _____

   Cal is a very <u>stingy</u> person. _____

2 He wears <u>classic</u> styles. _____

   He wears <u>old-fashioned</u> styles. _____

3 Every morning he <u>trudges</u> to work. _____

   Every morning he <u>sprints</u> to work. _____

4 Cal drives an <u>antique</u> car. _____

   Cal drives an <u>ancient</u> car. _____

5 His wife <u>insists</u> that he fix the car himself. _____

   His wife <u>encourages</u> him to fix the car himself. _____

6 One day, Cal's son <u>requested</u> a room of his own. _____

   One day, Cal's son <u>demanded</u> a room of his own. _____

For numbers 1–3, read the sentence. The answer choices have similar denotations. Which answer choice has the most <u>positive</u> connotation?

Answer Form
1 Ⓐ Ⓑ Ⓒ Ⓓ
2 Ⓐ Ⓑ Ⓒ Ⓓ
3 Ⓐ Ⓑ Ⓒ Ⓓ
4 Ⓐ Ⓑ Ⓒ Ⓓ   **Number**
5 Ⓐ Ⓑ Ⓒ Ⓓ   **Correct** ╱5

1 Cal and his wife had a <u>debate</u> about moving to a new home.

A quarrel

B dispute

C discussion

D disagreement

2 Cal said, "We can turn the office into an <u>acceptable</u> bedroom."

A pleasing

B usable

C functional

D workable

3 Cal's wife wanted to move, and she was <u>stubborn</u> about it.

A pushy

B defiant

C obstinate

D determined

For numbers 4 and 5, read the sentence. The answer choices have similar denotations. Which answer choice has the most <u>negative</u> connotation?

4 On moving day they <u>transported</u> all their belongings to their new home.

A sent

B lugged

C moved

D carried

5 Cal really likes the <u>unusual</u> architecture of the house.

A odd

B rare

C unique

D uncommon

Photo Credits

Page 4, a9photo/Shutterstock

Page 8, Stephen B. Goodwin/Shutterstock

Page 24, Ralf Juergen Kraft/Shutterstock

Page 35, Brown/Shutterstock

Page 75, Can Balcioglu/Shutterstock

Page 108, Steven Frame/Shutterstock

Page 117, mumbojumbo/Shutterstock

Page 119, Dawn Hudson/Shutterstock

Page 146, rook76/Shutterstock

Page 219, KVASAY/Shutterstock

Illustration Credits

Illustrations by Six Red Marbles